DECISION on PALESTINE

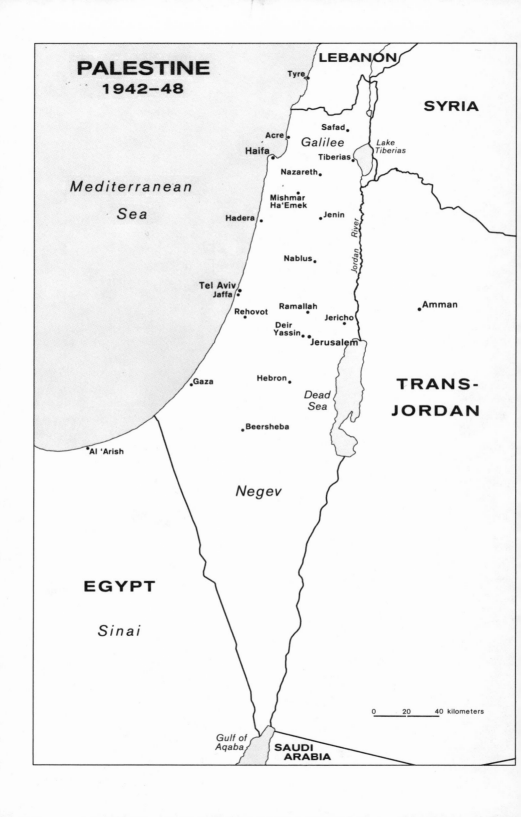

PALESTINE
1942–48

LEBANON

SYRIA

Tyre

Safad

Acre
Haifa

Galilee

Lake Tiberias

Tiberias

Mediterranean Sea

Nazareth

Mishmar Ha'Emek

Jenin

Hadera

Jordan River

Nablus

Tel Aviv
Jaffa

Rehovot

Ramallah

Jericho

Amman

Deir Yassin

Jerusalem

Hebron

Dead Sea

TRANS-
JORDAN

Gaza

Beersheba

Al 'Arish

Negev

EGYPT

Sinai

0   20   40 kilometers

Gulf of Aqaba

SAUDI
ARABIA

DECISION on PALESTINE

How the U.S. Came to
Recognize Israel

EVAN M. WILSON

HOOVER INSTITUTION PRESS
Stanford University, Stanford, California

*The Hoover Institution on War, Revolution and Peace, founded at
Stanford University in 1919 by the late President Herbert Hoover,
is an interdisciplinary research center for advanced study on
domestic and international affairs in the twentieth century. The views
expressed in its publications are entirely those of the authors
and do not necessarily reflect the views of the staff, officers,
or Board of Overseers of the Hoover Institution.*

Hoover Institution Publication 218

*To Ambassador Richard B. Parker, who inspired
me to undertake this project; and to all of my
colleagues in the old Near East Division of the State
Department, who encouraged me to complete it—*

Contents

Illustrations

Following page 159

The Old State Department Building

President Roosevelt and King Ibn Saud aboard the cruiser *Quincy*, February 14, 1945

Chaim Weizmann testifying before the Anglo-American Committee of Inquiry in Jerusalem, March 1946

A session of the UN Special Committee on Palestine in Jerusalem, June 1947

Syrian irregulars of the Arab Liberation Army on guard in northern Palestine, April 1948

Haganah recruits drilling openly near Tel Aviv before the end of the British Mandate

Damage caused at the headquarters of the Jewish Agency, March 1948

David Ben-Gurion reading the proclamation of Israel's independence at the Tel Aviv Art Museum, May 14, 1948

The Union Jack is lowered for the last time in Palestine

President Truman with Clark Clifford, William Hassett, Matthew Connelly, and Charles G. Ross

Original draft of the White House statement for the press announcing recognition of Israel

Secretary Marshall's letter to Eliahu Epstein announcing U.S. recognition of the new state of Israel

MAPS

Palestine, 1942–48 (*frontispiece*)

Palestine, UN plan of partition, 1947 (*p. 114*)

Preface

It was in May 1942 that the leaders of the world Zionist movement met in a hotel in wartime New York City and set as their goal the establishment of a Jewish state in Palestine.

It was in May 1948, only six years later, that a group of embattled leaders of the Jewish community in Palestine met in a museum in Tel Aviv and proclaimed the establishment of the State of Israel: a remarkable achievement indeed. And the proclamation of Israel's independence came fifty years after the founder of the Zionist movement, Theodor Herzl, had predicted that the Jewish state of his dreams would come into being in fifty years' time. The story of these six short years (1942–48) is the story of this book.

My aim is not so much to tell how these events came about as to explain what the role of the United States was, and why. Thus, after reviewing all the significant data for the period, I shall attempt to evaluate the conflicting pressures on the U.S. government with a view to advancing a definitive interpretation of our Palestine policy, as well as some thoughts for the future. Many of the sources employed have only recently become available. They include the U.S. diplomatic archives and the published *Foreign Relations of the United States;* material in the Roosevelt and Truman libraries, the British Public Record Office, and the Zionist archives in New York and Jerusalem and the many books and articles on the period; interviews with key personalities of the period; and my own recollections while serving as Palestine desk officer in the Department of State for most of these six years.

Responsibility for Palestine affairs in those days came under the Division of Near Eastern Affairs, which was identified in the Department by the symbol NE. My immediate supervisor was Gordon P. Merriam, and first Wallace S. Murray and then Loy W. Henderson was our chief.* We reported to Secretary of State Cordell Hull (who was to be succeeded by Edward R.

---

*In a 1944 reorganization of the Department, our Division became an Office of Near Eastern and African Affairs (known as NEA), one of whose component units was a Division of Near Eastern Affairs (NE), which continued to deal with Palestine and of which I became Assistant Chief in 1946. NEA was the forerunner of today's Bureau of Near Eastern and South Asian

Stettinius, Jr., James F. Byrnes, and General George C. Marshall) and to the Under Secretary of State, first Sumner Welles, then Stettinius, Dean Acheson, and Robert A. Lovett. Because of the special way in which the Palestine question was handled by the U.S. government, we were also frequently in touch with the White House of Presidents Franklin D. Roosevelt and Harry S. Truman.

The Near East Division in the early 1940s was something of a backwater. It was concerned with a part of the world that was relatively unknown and that accounted for only a minor part of our foreign relations. The thirteen or fourteen officers attached to the Division at the time, nearly all of whom had seen previous service in the Near East, had pretty much a free hand in dealing with such matters as came before them.

When I entered the Division as its most junior member, I had seen something of the Near East as a result of three years' service in Egypt. I had asked to be assigned to that area because I was thinking of applying for training as an Arabic specialist. Although I later decided against this, it did turn out that almost all of my thirty-odd years of service was connected with the region.

From Egypt I had visited Palestine several times and had had my first exposure to the controversial Arab-Jewish problem. My wife and I went to Palestine on leave and traveled fairly extensively around the country, after reading a few books on the subject. I can recall that, feeling we were getting pretty well acquainted with the Arab point of view, we asked someone to recommend something to read on the Jewish side. It thus was early on in my association with the Palestine problem that I became aware that there were two sides to the question and that one had to make allowance both for the desire of the Jews to build up the National Home and for the desire of the Arab population for self-government.

I think I can honestly say that in taking up my duties on the Palestine desk I was conscious of no prejudice or bias one way or the other. My general approach to the problem was one of trying to find an accommodation, a reconciliation, between the conflicting interests of the parties to the dispute. This attitude was consistent with my background and training as a member of the generation of the 1930s. At Haverford College I had acquired what the Quakers call a "concern" for international conciliation and world peace—it is no coincidence that Haverford should have contributed for many years a larger proportion, per capita, of graduates to our Foreign Service than any other college or university in the country.

Affairs. The Department customarily employed, and still employs, the term "Near East" to denote the area frequently referred to as the "Middle East." I shall use these two terms interchangeably. For the sake of brevity, I shall also refer to our organization as a whole as "NE" or as the "Near East Divison," even though after 1944 this designation, strictly speaking, was confined to the NE component in NEA.

At Oxford, and later at Geneva, I had studied international relations with the late Sir Alfred Zimmern and had acquired a deeper interest in world affairs. I had observed the workings of the League of Nations at first hand and had seen that it was of primary importance that the United States should participate in any future world organization. I had spent the summer of 1933 in Germany, just after Hitler came to power. I had read *Mein Kampf* and attended Nazi rallies. I had witnessed the terrifying grip of the Nazi movement on the German people and had felt the rumbling of the fear that lay in store for the future.

Our generation was a generation of idealists. We read books like Clarence Streit's *Union Now* and Salvador de Madariaga's *Disarmament* and we were impressed by such writers as Walter Lippmann and Vera Michaelis Dean. In Washington, we followed the hearings of the Nye Committee and learned about the arms manufacturers—the "merchants of death" as they were called. This was the period of the Oxford Union's vote against fighting "for King and Country," of the White Feather Society of Oxford, which, complete with appropriate tie, called for a policy of pacifism. These were the days when Winston Churchill was branded a warmonger for proposing that Great Britain should rearm against the menace of Nazi Germany, and when the Cliveden Set was advocating appeasement.

Many of us rejected both the pacifism and the isolationism that were so prevalent in the 1930s. What we sought was a better world order than the one that had followed the First World War. We wanted to avoid the mistakes of the preceding generation, mistakes which with the Treaty of Versailles and the imposition of reparations had sown the seeds of another war.

On the Palestine desk, and in later years of involvement in the Arab-Israel problem, I always considered that I was able to avoid being biased toward one side or the other in the conflict. My approach was based on the premise that both Arabs and Jews had rights in Palestine, that the problem arose from a conflict between two rights.

In NE we very much had it in mind that Palestine was only one of more than a score of countries with which the Division had to deal. Our task, under Departmental directives, was to carry out United States policies toward the countries of the Near East and to proffer advice regarding the promotion and protection of U.S. interests. We in NE and NEA could take cold comfort from the fact that our failure to come down flatly on one side or the other in the Palestine dispute caused us to be regarded as pro-Jewish by the Arabs and pro-Arab by the Jews.

As my thinking on the substance of the Palestine question evolved, especially following a visit that I paid to Palestine in 1946 (as will be recounted in Chapter 6), I came to the conclusion that for our government to advocate the establishment of a Jewish state in Palestine against the will of the majority of the inhabitants of that country (the Arabs) would be a mistake that would have an adverse effect upon world peace and upon U.S. interests.

In taking this position, which was shared by most of my colleagues in NE and NEA and abroad at the time, I realized that I was bound to be considered as anti-Zionist by the Zionist Jews, that is, those who sought the establishment of a Jewish state in Palestine. However, during the early and mid-1940s Jewish opinion, both in this country and elsewhere, was divided into Zionist, non-Zionist, and anti-Zionist factions. The closing of the ranks behind the Zionist position did not occur until the Palestine question was before the United Nations in mid-1947, after I had left the Department for the field. In handling the Palestine question I always was conscious of the fact that there was an important Jewish interest in Palestine and I made it a point to cultivate Jewish as well as Arab contacts.

To understand the Palestine problem as we encountered it in 1942–48, or indeed to understand the Arab-Israel conflict today, it is essential to have some knowledge of the historical background. In fact, it is particularly important in the case of Palestine, since, as the Peel Commission put it in 1937, "No other problem of our time is so deeply rooted in the past." Anyone who attempts to summarize the history of the Palestine problem must approach the task with trepidation, however. The pitfalls inherent in such an effort have never been more cogently described than by the late George Antonius in his classic account of the Arab national movement, *The Arab Awakening,* as follows:

> For the historian, the study of the Palestine problem is beset with particular difficulties. In the first place, the material is enormous and widely scattered. In the second place, it is to an unusual degree conflicting and inconsistent. Thirdly, a large proportion of it which on inspection appears relevant and promising turns out, when sifted, to rest upon false assumptions and questionable data. Lastly, the passions aroused by Palestine have done so much to obscure the truth that the facts have become enveloped in a mist of sentiment, legend, and propaganda, which acts as a smokescreen of almost impenetrable density. (p. 386)

Until the First World War, there was no Palestine problem. Palestine was a part of the Ottoman Empire and the population was overwhelmingly (about 90 percent) Arab. It was the introduction, under the Balfour Declaration and the Mandate, of Jewish immigrants in such numbers as to lead the Arabs of Palestine to believe themselves threatened that caused the conflict, a conflict that has not been resolved to this day. The problem in the twenties was complicated by the rise of Arab nationalism and by the contradictory nature of the promises respecting Palestine made by the British in the course of wartime negotiations with the Arabs, the Jews, and the Allies.

To the Arabs, in order to gain their support in the war against Turkey, the British promised independence in an area which, though not precisely defined, had always been considered by the Arabs to include Palestine.

To the Jews, whose connection with Palestine had never been broken since antiquity and whose interest in the land had been enhanced by the rise of Zionism (the movement which promoted the return of the Jews to Palestine and was eventually to seek the establishment of a Jewish state there), the British promised in the Balfour Declaration to work for the establishment in Palestine of "a national home for the Jewish people" (likewise not defined), with the important provisos that nothing be done to prejudice the rights of what were called the "existing non-Jewish communities in Palestine" (that is, the Arabs), or the rights of Jews elsewhere in the world. The pledge was given to the Jews largely for the purpose of enlisting Jewish support in the war and of forestalling a similar promise by the Central Powers. At the time, according to the best information available, Jews cannot have accounted for more than 9 percent of the population of Palestine.

During secret negotiations with the French, the Imperial Russians, and the Italians concerning the disposition of Ottoman territories after the war, the British promised that Palestine would be placed under international administration. However, at the San Remo Conference in April 1920, attended by Great Britain, France, and Italy, with the United States as observer, it was decided that Great Britain should be given the Mandate for Palestine. The text of the Mandate repeated the entire text of the Balfour Declaration and placed the British under obligation to "facilitate Jewish immigration" and encourage "close settlement by Jews on the land." Unlike the other mandates covering former Turkish territories, there was no provision for termination of the Mandate and only a vague reference to self-determination.

The early years of the Mandate were relatively quiet. Few Jews came to Palestine and in fact in the 1920s there was a net emigration of Jews. Almost immediately, however, a gulf began to develop between the Arab and Jewish communities. Arab resentment was voiced and as early as 1920 there were Arab riots.

Immigration increased markedly with the rise of Hitler in Germany and indeed it can be said that had it not been for Adolf Hitler there would be no Jewish state today. By 1939 Jews numbered 450,000, or 30 percent, of a total total population of 1,500,000 and Jewish-owned land had increased from 148,500 acres after the First World War to 383,250 acres.

As tension grew between the communities, the British sent out a series of commissions to study the problem, but none of them was able to resolve the basic contradiction between the Arab claim to self-government and the development of the Jewish National Home.

In 1939, just before the outbreak of the Second World War, at a time when the Axis powers were cultivating the Arabs assiduously, the British issued a White Paper setting a quota of 75,000 for Jewish immigration over the next five years, at the end of which the consent of the Arabs of Palestine would be required for any further immigration. By this time it was clear that the basic issue in Palestine was the continuance of Jewish immigration, since this would determine the nature of the future Palestine state.

In the chapters that follow, I shall examine the story of our growing involvement in Palestine between 1942 and 1948 in the light of what I conceive to be three main themes which run through the narrative. I present these themes here as questions. In the Epilogue I shall reexamine them and try to make some assessment of our Palestine policy during the period under review. The contributions of the two Presidents, Roosevelt and Truman, to that policy will be assessed as we go along.

The first question is whether the steady trend of United States policy in the direction of the Zionist position in these years, ending in our outright endorsement of the concept of a Jewish state, was inevitable or whether it could have been prevented. In other words, could the dilemma in our Palestine policy stemming from the conflict between the Jewish interest and the Arab interest have been resolved in any other way except by our coming out, as we eventually did, on the Jewish side of the dispute, with all the consequences that this implied for our relations with the Arab world?

Second, given a "tilt" in our policy toward the Jews, did this mean that we would adopt a wholly pro-Jewish attitude or would we seek to achieve the greatest possible degree of accommodation between the two conflicting points of view?

A third question is that of the extent to which the career men in the State Department, of whom I was a junior member, were able to influence the decisions which Presidents Roosevelt and Truman had to take respecting Palestine, in the context of a variety of considerations, domestic political, global, economic, and humanitarian, that confronted them. Also, just how aware were the two Presidents of the probable consequences of their decisions so far as the situation in the Middle East was concerned?

After an Introduction, which will provide the setting for the events to be related, I launch into the narrative portion of the book, starting with the year 1942.

Acknowledgments

Obviously, in the preparation of a book that has required some five and a half years of research and study, it is impossible for me to mention all those persons, in the United States and abroad, who have been of assistance to me.

To begin with, however, I want to express my warm thanks to several of my colleagues from the old State Department who read my manuscript and made many helpful suggestions: Loy W. Henderson, Gordon P. Merriam, Fraser Wilkins, and (before his untimely death) Robert M. McClintock. The resulting book is really a joint effort on the part of all of us.

The Historian of the Department of State, Dr. David Trask, and his predecessor, Dr. William M. Franklin, have given me encouragement throughout, and the assistance of Dr. Paul Claussen of the Office of the Historian has been invaluable on many occasions.

At the National Archives, I received full cooperation from Mr. Milton O. Gustafson, chief of the Diplomatic Branch, and his staff. My thanks also go to the Acting Director of the Franklin D. Roosevelt Library at Hyde Park, Mr. William J. Stewart, and to the Chief Archivist and the Director of the Harry S. Truman Library at Independence, respectively Dr. Philip D. Lagerquist and Dr. Benedict K. Zobrist, and their assistants.

During the course of my research I paid several visits to the Zionist Archives and Library in New York City, where the Director and Librarian, Mrs. Sylvia Landress, was uniformly helpful.

In England, I received very great assistance from two British colleagues, Sir Harold Beeley, my Foreign Office opposite number in the years covered by this book, and Sir John Martin, who dealt with the Palestine question in the Colonial Office for so many years. I should also like to express my appreciation to Mr. Derek Hopwood of the Middle East Center, St. Antony's College, Oxford, and to the staff of the Public Record Office, London.

In Israel, I received considerable assistance from Dr. Michael Heymann, director of the Central Zionist Archives, Jerusalem; Dr. A. Alsberg, director, Israeli State Archives; and Mr. Ari Rath, senior editor of the *Jerusalem Post*, who arranged for me to peruse the archives of that newspaper. I am also indebted more than I can say to an Israeli colleague of long standing, H. E. Eliahu Elath, who was the recipient of the official notification in 1948 of President Truman's recognition of Israel (reproduced here with his kind permission), and to an Israeli scholar, Dr. Amitzur Ilan, who gave me many helpful suggestions.

Scholars in this country from whom I have received particular assistance are Dr. J. C. Hurewitz, director of the Middle East Institute at Columbia University; Dr. George Rentz, formerly of the Hoover Institution and now with the Johns Hopkins University; Professor George Lenczowski of the University of California; and Professor Bernard Reich of George Washington University. I am particularly grateful to Dr. Hurewitz for allowing me to use several of the documents from his two-volume collection as appendixes to this volume. I should also like to thank Mrs. William A. Eddy for the photograph of her husband with Roosevelt and Ibn Saud. Here and there, in the notes to the text, I have identified a number of other individuals who gave me their assistance in particular matters.

Finally, I should like to thank Mrs. Shirley Taylor and Mr. Russell Bourne for their editorial assistance; Mr. R. David Wert for preparing the maps; Mrs. Silfa Meredith for typing the manuscript; and my wife, for her patience and constant encouragement.

EVAN M. WILSON

Washington, D.C.
November 10, 1978

Introduction: The Setting and the Cast of Characters

THE OLD STATE DEPARTMENT

Dean Acheson remarks in his book *Present at the Creation* that the State Department of the early 1940s was closer to the State Department of the nineteenth century than to the department that he was to head shortly after the Second World War. It therefore seems logical to begin with a few words of description of the setting in which the officers of the Department carried out their duties. The ornate building at the corner of Pennsylvania Avenue and 17th Street, dating from the 1870s, with its high ceilings, white-painted swinging doors, and long corridors paved with alternating black and white marble squares, was reminiscent of some exclusive club.[1] The total personnel was so small that everyone knew everyone else. A good deal of attention was paid to tradition and to doing things in the Department's customary style.

Critics of the Department sometimes said that its policies and way of life were as Victorian as the building itself. In 1947 the Department moved into a new building that had been designed for the War Department and that now forms the nucleus of the State Department complex in Foggy Bottom. It was hoped that this move might result in a streamlining of Departmental procedures, but whether this has come about is debatable.

At the head of the Department we knew was Cordell Hull, a veteran of the Spanish-American War and a distinguished-looking man who had had a distinguished record in Congress before becoming Secretary of State in 1933. Hull approached every problem with deliberation and caution, whether in his office or on the croquet lawn where he found his favorite relaxation. It was commonly known in Washington that he and the Under Secretary, Sumner Welles, were not on good terms and that Hull resented Welles's inside track to the White House. Hull, in fact, was never one of President Roosevelt's intimates: for example, the President never even showed the minutes of the 1943 Tehran Conference to his Secretary of State.[2]

Welles was a patrician who had had a long diplomatic career in Latin America. He had been a schoolmate of Roosevelt's at Groton. In the extensive correspondence between the two men preserved at the Roosevelt Library in Hyde Park, he addresses the President as "Franklin." Also at the library are copies of letters addressed to Hitler, Mussolini, and a number of other leaders at the time of Welles's 1940 mission to Europe, in which Roosevelt refers to him as a "boyhood friend."

Welles had pronounced Zionist sympathies, more so perhaps than we realized at the time. This emerges from the many references to him in the literature of the period and especially in the correspondence of the Zionist leadership to be found at the Zionist archives in New York and Jerusalem. Many of Welles's own statements, as recorded in the published *Foreign Relations of the United States* (Near Eastern series) and in his own writings in later years, provide further confirmation of this. Indeed, he was the principal high-level contact of the Zionist leaders, and in early 1943, for example, it was he who took Dr. Chaim Weizmann, president of the World Zionist Organization and of the Jewish Agency for Palestine, to call on Roosevelt.

In the summer of 1943, matters came to a head and Hull asked the President to remove Welles. As Under Secretary, Roosevelt selected Edward R. Stettinius, Jr., then serving as Administrator of Lend-Lease. Stettinius, a former steel executive, had the reputation of being a capable administrator, but Roosevelt clearly expected that in matters of policy Stettinius would follow his lead.

The next year (1944) Hull, in failing health, submitted his resignation, and Stettinius moved up to the Secretaryship. Joseph C. Grew, a veteran career diplomat who had been Ambassador to Japan at the time of Pearl Harbor, became Under Secretary.

Stettinius's administrative good sense resulted in a far-reaching and much needed reform of the Department's organization, but with Roosevelt in charge he made relatively little impact on foreign policy. In 1945 he presided over the San Francisco Conference, at which the United Nations Organization was set up, and thereafter devoted much time and attention to the world body.

Shortly after assuming office in April 1945 on the death of Roosevelt, President Truman replaced Stettinius with James F. Byrnes. In doing so he yielded to widespread criticism that Stettinius, who under the law then in effect would succeed to the presidency, lacked wide governmental experience and indeed had never held elective office. Byrnes was a prominent member of the Democratic party who had served as Senator, as Justice of the Supreme Court, and in the Executive Office of the President. Simultaneously, Dean Acheson, formerly Assistant Secretary of State, was appointed Under Secretary.

Not long after Byrnes took over the Department, I attended a meeting in his office to discuss the Palestine question. Byrnes, who had the courtly manner of an old-fashioned Southern politician, sat at his desk, rocking back and forth in his big chair, his feet in their high-button shoes barely touching the floor. From time to time, as the meeting progressed, he took shorthand notes—he had been trained as a court reporter and the accounts of several conversations he had with the British Ambassador regarding Palestine appear in the *Foreign Relations* in the form of dialogue, just as he recorded them.

Byrnes's time was largely taken up with attendance at interminable meetings of the Council of Foreign Ministers and he devoted little attention to Palestine. In fact, he rather pointedly washed his hands of the problem and repeatedly stated that he was leaving it to the President to handle. Thus it was Acheson with whom we usually dealt on such matters as required top-level consideration in the Department. In taking on this assignment Acheson managed to overcome a certain reluctance which he felt at becoming involved in Palestine affairs because of his close friendship with Justice Felix Frankfurter, who was a prominent Zionist supporter (their daily walk downtown from their Georgetown homes was a familiar sight to the celebrity-watchers of the period).

Acheson, who had an outstanding legal career and who later was to serve as Truman's fourth Secretary of State, was an impressive figure who looked the perfect diplomat. He had a keen mind and an incisive wit and our frequent contacts with him were always enjoyable as well as educational. With his very considerable skill in drafting he imposed on us the same high standards that he set for himself.

Truman tells us in his *Memoirs* that he soon became dissatisfied with Byrnes and his free-wheeling tactics. In January 1947 he availed himself of Byrnes's resignation, which had been in the President's desk drawer in the Oval Office for a year, and appointed General George C. Marshall as Secretary. Marshall, the wartime Army Chief of Staff and one of the most respected figures in the country, had recently been serving in China on a special mission for the President.

Like his predecessor, Marshall resisted getting involved in Palestine, preferring to focus on the problems of European recovery and East-West relations. In mid-1947, Robert A. Lovett, a New York lawyer and member of the Wall Street firm of Brown Brothers, Harriman, succeeded Acheson as Under Secretary. This was of importance to the Department's work on Palestine, as Marshall delegated almost all of it to his Under Secretary.

The Division of Near Eastern Affairs, under which Palestine came, was headed in the early 1940s by the redoubtable Wallace S. Murray, whose previous Near Eastern experience had been in Iran. He had been with the Division since 1925 and Chief since 1929. To be precise, Murray had the title

"Adviser on Political Relations," while his deputy, Paul H. Alling, was the nominal chief of the Division, but since the two of them worked very closely together as a team, the titles made no real difference. Immediate supervision over the work relating to Palestine came under Gordon P. Merriam, assistant chief of the Division and one of the earliest crop of Arabist Foreign Service officers.

In 1944, as a result of the Stettinius reorganization, an Office of Near Eastern and African Affairs was created with Murray as Director and Alling as Deputy Director. This office was the forerunner of the Bureau of Near Eastern and South Asian Affairs of today. The Division of Near Eastern Affairs, with Merriam as chief, then became one of the component elements of the Office. In early 1945, Murray was appointed Ambassador to Iran while Alling went to Morocco as Diplomatic Agent and Consul General. Murray's successor was Loy W. Henderson, then serving in Baghdad. First George V. Allen, then Henry S. Villard, and later Joseph C. Satterthwaite held the position of Deputy Director; all three were career Foreign Officers with area experience. These changes took place as the State Department and the Foreign Service were beginning to expand to meet our nation's postwar global responsibilities. Additional staff was taken on, and many of our legations were raised to embassy status.

THE OLD NEAR EAST DIVISION: ITS CHARACTER AND ITS PERSONALITIES

A 1937 article on the Department made the comment that the Near East Division "is not often marked with excitement . . . our relations with these peoples are not important."[3] A similar attitude of condescension prevailed in other offices of the Department, to the extent that when I was assigned to Cairo in 1938, a friend in the European Division commiserated with me by saying: "The Near East! Nothing ever happens there."

That the problems of the Near East were indeed not of primary importance in the Department of prewar days is revealed in a passage from Hull's *Memoirs* in which he lists the pressing matters which were on his desk when he became Secretary of State. Although he mentions over a dozen problems, not one of them relates to the Near East.

The Division was still rather quiet when I entered it in 1943. The entire Division numbered only fourteen officers: by way of comparison, today's Bureau has a staff of over 150. As an indication of the workload, Palestine was handled by a desk officer along with Egypt and Iraq. The Palestine work, however, was soon to register a dramatic increase, as is shown by the number of pages devoted to it in the *Foreign Relations* volumes: 1942, 21 pages; 1943, 82; 1944, 97; 1945, 166; 1946, 167; 1947, 330; and 1948, one entire volume.

We were housed in a few offices along the west side of the third floor of the old Department. Two other desk officers (dealing with Turkey and Saudi Arabia), a secretary, and I were crowded into a room (No. 345) which had accommodated a single officer up to the outbreak of the war. Merriam was squeezed into an adjoining cubbyhole. Working conditions were chaotic most of the time. In the long Washington summers the heat became almost unbearable as the afternoon sun beat down. There was of course no air conditioning and though it was customary in those days to dismiss the government employees when the thermometer touched the mid-90s, the urgent nature of our work and the small size of our staff did not generally make it possible for us to leave early. With the aid of the salt tablets which we kept handy we managed to put in a full six-day week, rarely leaving before six or seven in the evening.

Even under normal conditions our room would have been full enough, and we often were crowded beyond capacity when officers arriving from the field or awaiting transportation to a post abroad—and there were always delays under the aircraft priority system—made the Division their headquarters. As soon as the doors of the Department opened in the morning these individuals would rush to preempt the chairs standing by our desks. We called them the "kibbitzers." This invasion caused problems when any of us had visitors, as frequently happened.

The visitors to the office gave us plenty of problems in any event. Once, when the Saudi desk officer and the Turkish desk officer both had a number of callers grouped around their desks, the Saudi desk officer asked a question and one of the Turkish visitors replied. Fortunately there were not too many instances of this sort, but things could get rather touchy when the Saudi desk officer, for example, was receiving an Arab visitor and I was receiving a Jewish one. Simultaneously the Turkish desk officer, who had a wide acquaintance among the members of the press covering the Department, was apt to be entertaining some correspondent who might not be above taking advantage of the opportunity to overhear what the rest of us were saying.

On top of this general *va et vient,* the phones kept ringing incessantly and our lone secretary kept pounding away at her typewriter: incidentally she was the only person in the room who was allowed to have one, as all typewriters had been taken away from the officers when the war began. It was this same secretary, Marilyn Woods, who unwittingly provided me with an anecdote which I often used afterward in my work, when she remarked one day in bewilderment: "Mr. Wilson, I don't understand why you let yourself get so bothered about Palestine when everyone knows it says in the Bible that the Jews are going back there some day!" Miss Woods, in the end, literally got herself to a nunnery, and gave up the Department in favor of a convent.

In the field, the Division had supervision over some thirty-nine Foreign

Service posts, including one embassy (Turkey), ten legations, and twenty-eight consular or other offices. Beginning in 1944 there was also an officer attached to the Embassy in London (Raymond A. Hare) who followed Near Eastern developments from that vantage point and reported to the Division. Hare subsequently had a distinguished career, and held a number of high-level positions in the Department, as well as serving as ambassador to several Near Eastern countries.

Within the Department, the officers concerned with Palestine had frequent contact with two scholars who had been brought in from academic life to work on postwar planning in the Division of Territorial Studies—Dr. Philip W. Ireland and Professor William Yale, who with several members of our Division made up the so-called Interdivisional Area Committee on Arab Countries. One of their colleagues was Ralph Bunche, who although not working directly on Palestine at this time was to be intimately associated with the problem later on as the second United Nations Mediator for Palestine and for many years thereafter as Under Secretary-General of the UN. In the early 1940s, Bunche was one of the few blacks holding positions at the officer level in the Department. Washington was a very different place in those days. I recall that when any of us wanted to go out to lunch with him there were only two places where we could go—Union Station and the YWCA.

Then there was Lieutenant Colonel Harold B. Hoskins, who had been born in Beirut and was sent out to the Near East on special missions in 1942 and 1943. Though not a member of the Division, Hoskins participated in many of the important discussions of the Palestine question and his name appears frequently in the official documents for the period. Because of his background and his contacts in the White House and the Pentagon, Hoskins sometimes played a key role, as for example in the case of the resolutions introduced into Congress in early 1944 respecting Palestine. Although the published documents do not reveal it, he was largely responsible for the shelving of the resolutions at that time. He was a cousin of Colonel William A. Eddy, also born in Beirut and Arabic-speaking, who interpreted for FDR and Ibn Saud.

The Foreign Service posts under the supervision of the Near East Division, like the Division itself, were staffed largely by officers who had had experience in the area. This was natural enough from the administrative standpoint, but there was also a sound reason why it should be so. As one authority on the Department and the Foreign Service pointed out at the time, the Near East Division, like its counterpart the old Far Eastern Division, dealt with "questions that often have little or no resemblance to the problems of Western nations."[4] Not only were there profound cultural differences between the peoples of the Near East and ourselves, but the work of the Division was set apart by special problems stemming from capitulary rights (still in force in certain countries as late as the mid-1940s) and the presence in the area of important American educational, medical, missionary, and archaeological institutions. In other words, the Division handled many problems outside the range of ordinary diplomatic and consular work. It had thus become a *sine qua non* that its personnel should have experience in the area. Indeed, it should be noted that shortly after the Near East Division was established in the year 1909, it was made a Departmental requirement that the Division be staffed by officers who had served in the Near East. This policy was still being generally followed when I joined the Division in 1943.[5]

There was nothing sinister in this, but it gave rise to accusations that the officers dealing with the Palestine problem tended to side with the Arabs against the Jews. This led to repeated requests by the Zionists that jurisdiction over Palestine be taken out of the Division and placed in a special office dealing with Jewish affairs. It also led to allegations that some of the officers in question were anti-Semitic, a charge repeated, I am sorry to say, by Truman in his *Memoirs*.

In point of fact, we in the Near East Division and in our posts overseas were simply trying to further United States interests. A corollary of this happened to be that most of us considered that the establishment of a Jewish state in Palestine would be detrimental to our other interests in the Near East. The published diplomatic correspondence for these years contains many warnings to this effect, but this is not the same as promoting the Arab point of view in the dispute. Some of these officials may have been slow to recognize the significance of the American Jewish interest in Palestine, but the accusation of anti-Semitism (in the loose sense of anti-Jewish) is wholly unwarranted. We could take little comfort from the fact that we were often thought by the Arabs to be pro-Zionist because our work brought us into contact with Jews. This was just another consequence of the dilemma inherent in our Palestine policy.

The personality of Wallace Murray dominated the old Near East Division. Murray had a quick mind, a formidable knowledge of Near Eastern affairs, and a lively appreciation of the importance of the area to the United States. At the same time, he did not suffer fools gladly and he tended to show a proprietary attitude toward everything that he considered to be within his bailiwick. At this period the division chiefs were constantly feuding with one another and Murray was a past master at defending his prerogatives. Toward the Palestine question, he held very firm views, based on long exposure to that vexing problem. His manner toward the Zionists sometimes implied that he regarded them as intruders on an otherwise placid, or comparatively placid, Near Eastern scene. As a consequence, his meetings with the Zionist leadership, which were infrequent, were marked by a certain coolness on both sides and he was often a target of criticism on the part of the Zionists and their supporters in Congress. Dr. Weizmann, for example, states categorically in his memoirs (*Trial and Error*, II, 425) that Murray was "an avowed anti-Zionist and an outspoken pro-Arab."

Certainly, the record contains a number of instances in which Murray expressed opinions that could not be regarded as sympathetic to the Zionist point of view. Among other things, as the *Foreign Relations* papers show, he warned President Roosevelt against the harmful effects of Zionist agitation on the war effort, and he recommended against approaching the British to keep Palestine open to Jewish immigration. Small wonder that when word spread in 1945 that he was to go out to the field, the Zionist leaders called on Acting Secretary of State Grew and urged Murray's replacement by someone who, as they put it, "understood the whole broad problem of the Jews and Palestine."[6]

In all fairness to Wallace Murray it should be pointed out that though he frequently gave voice to his deep-seated suspicion of Zionist motivations, and though he was never one to remain silent when the occasion called for forthrightness, he was a devoted public servant whose overriding concern was to do what he thought was right for the American interest. His reports to his superiors were notable for the prescience which they displayed and for accurately forecasting, at this comparatively early date, the effect that the adoption of a pro-Zionist policy would have on the standing of the United States in the Near Eastern region.

So formidable was Murray's reputation that our opposite numbers in the British Foreign Office regarded him with some trepidation. The British record of his 1944 visit to London, in the Foreign Office Palestine files at the Public Record Office, London, contains a number of comments expressing surprise that he turned out to be, unexpectedly, quite affable in his dealings with British officials.

Murray's deputy, Alling, had likewise served in the area and had been in the Division for many years, but he was the antithesis of Murray in personality. He had a genial, kindly manner and was universally popular. He succeeded in calming down many a visitor who found Murray's acerbic approach a bit hard to take. Like his chief, he had a wide-ranging knowledge of Near Eastern matters, particularly those pertaining to Syria and Lebanon, where he had seen service.

Merriam, too, was experienced and knowledgeable. His approach to the explosive Palestine issue was marked by a calm, businesslike manner. His drafting ability was a tremendous asset in dealing with the subtleties and nuances of the problem.

Henderson, Murray's successor, was a very different type. His Foreign Service background, prior to going to Iraq, had been in Eastern European affairs and his approach to the problems of the Near East showed a broader perspective than that of many who had concentrated on that one area. He was objective and fair in his attitude toward the Palestine question, and sincerely interested in finding a solution. In view of this it is ironic, though perhaps inevitable, that he should later have been so fiercely attacked by the Zionists. Henderson encouraged those of us who were concerned with Palestine to have Jewish as well as Arab contacts, and Departmental meetings with the Zionists became less stiff and formal than in the past. A revealing comment on the contrasting styles of Murray and Henderson is to be found in Lord Trevelyan's little book on diplomacy. Trevelyan, who served in Washington during the war as a representative of the government of India, writes: "We had first to deal with Mr. Wallace Murray, whom we found difficult and openly hostile to the British in India. He left and was succeeded by Mr. Loy Henderson. The whole situation was transformed by his friendly and helpful approach."[7] Even so consistent a critic of the Department and its Palestine policy as the chairman of the Political Committee of the extremist United Zionists-Revisionists of America, Dr. Joseph B. Schechtman, found Henderson to be sincere, not an anti-Semite, and seeking what he conceived (mistakenly, Schechtman thought) to be the American interest.[8]

THE OLD NEAR EAST DIVISION: RESPONSIBILITIES AND OPERATIONS

In considering the way in which the Palestine question was handled by the Near East Division, it must be borne in mind that the Division was responsible for our relations with over a score of countries, of which Palestine was only one. Essentially our task was to carry out United States policy toward the countries of the area and to protect and promote U.S. interests. Sometimes the latter were in conflict, as in the case of Palestine. In such an event, we did not consider that it was incumbent on us to pursue any single interest at the expense of another, but rather to attempt to reconcile the conflicts to the extent that seemed to be possible within the context of overall policy objectives. It follows that the criticism sometimes made by Zionists to the effect that we were remiss in not promoting the Jewish National Home more assiduously was wide of the mark. Not only was this not our principal task, but also (and this is the essential point) we never received instructions from the Secretary of State or the President that it should be so. Conversely (and this is equally important), we never were instructed to favor the Arab side in the dispute. It goes without saying that to carry out our duties in the light of the dilemma imposed by our conflicting commitments required a high degree of detachment and objectivity.

The responsibilities of NE, as listed in the 1946 *Register* of the Department of State, are reproduced in Appendix B. It will be noted that we were specifically charged with making recommendations to the Secretary with regard to the area of our jurisdiction, including Palestine. There thus can be no basis for alleging, as has sometimes been done in Zionist circles, that NE was interfering in our government's Palestine policy: this was our duty.

With two exceptions noted below, the day-to-day operations of the Near East Division were generally similar to those of the other geographical or political divisions of the Department. Divisional papers, whether calling for action or simply transmitting information, customarily originated at the lowest level, that is, the desk officer, and proceeded up through channels to higher authority, with the most important papers, those intended for the President, receiving approval of the Secretary or Acting Secretary. A given paper, by the time it reached the top level, might have been redrafted one or more times to incorporate the suggestions of officers along the way. Through the system of clearances, though this was not so burdensome as it became later on, the papers were made to reflect the views of all officers having an interest in the matter in hand, in other divisions, at higher levels of the Department, or even in other agencies. This process naturally involved a certain amount of give and take, but it could be said that by the time it had been completed a consensus of U.S. policy on the subject had been reached.

Because of problems peculiar to the Palestine issue, there were two important respects in which the work of the Near East Division differed from that of the other divisions. In the first place, a very considerable portion of the paperwork relating to the Palestine problem had to receive the personal attention of the President—which brought the desk officer into much closer touch with the White House than was the case elsewhere in the Department. Secondly, the special way in which matters pertaining to Palestine were handled by the U.S. government gave rise to a whole range of problems that were unique as well as frustrating in the extreme. Frequently we were kept in the dark about important developments that took place at higher levels. We were dependent on the press for learning which Zionist leaders had been received at the White House, and what the President had said to them, or, in some cases, allowed them to make public in his name. Perhaps the worst example of this occurred in August 1945, when as will be recounted in Chapter 5, President Truman wrote Prime Minister Clement Attlee of Great Britain urging the immediate entry into Palestine of 100,000 displaced Jews. A month later, the Division was still seeking confirmation of press reports that Truman had approached Attlee on the subject.

There were many other examples of this sort of thing, especially when the Palestine question was before the United Nations in 1947 and 1948. Indeed, an examination of the material available today in the Roosevelt and Truman libraries, as well as in the Zionist archives, has provided me with a number of surprises in the way of things of which I had not been aware during the time I was on the Palestine desk.

A fact of life to which we had to resign ourselves was that we were generally unable to find out what U.S. policy toward Palestine was. As early as 1942, Murray proposed that President Roosevelt should be asked to define our policy, but no answer was forthcoming. Later on, in spite of many attempts, the Department never obtained from President Truman any clear set of instructions as to the line to take. Thus we were forced to operate more or less in a vacuum.

One thing, however, was certain: whenever a Presidential statement favorable to the Jewish side gave rise to Arab protests, as was frequently the case, it was the Near East Division that was called on to smooth things over and prepare a reply. After we had exercised our ingenuity in an effort to provide some plausible explanation, a grateful President would initial our draft and the reply would go out. We became quite accustomed to this syndrome: Presidential statement, Arab protest, reply prepared by NE, Presidential approval.

It is not surprising that with these frustrations some of us developed ulcers and that at times we despaired of ever being able to carry out the duties assigned to us. In retrospect the wonder is that a handful of officers, working mostly under difficult wartime conditions, should have been able to achieve so large an output of important policy papers as appears in the annual *Foreign Relations* volumes, and still to have kept up with our other daily tasks.

THE WHITE HOUSE AND PALESTINE

Palestine was an issue both in our foreign relations and in our domestic politics. Thus it tended to be handled in two separate ways, and the State Department often did not know what the White House was doing. Roosevelt had an assistant—David K. Niles—who dealt with minority groups, including the Jewish community, and thus served as the Jews' point of contact at the White House and was often consulted by the President regarding Palestine. Ironically, Niles was housed in the old State Department building, directly below Murray and Henderson, but we never saw him and had no idea of his activities.

Under Truman, Niles continued to be one of the most influential Presidential advisers on Palestine. Another was Judge Samuel I. Rosenman, who was Special Counsel to the President from 1943 to mid-1946, when he was succeeded by Clark M. Clifford, who was to play a key role at the time of Truman's recognition of Israel.

The advice regarding the domestic aspect of the Palestine problem which the President received from members of the White House staff, from Congress, or from the Democratic National Committee, was something that was never passed to us in NE. Forrestal's *Diaries* first made public the intervention in the Palestine question of Chairman Hannegan of the Democratic National Committee. Considerably more information on this general subject is now available in the Roosevelt and Truman libraries.

The papers in the two Presidential libraries, as well as in the Niles collection and in the Zionist archives, provide ample evidence of the involvement of the White House in the Palestine question. As will be brought out in this book, at times the intervention of the White House staff was decisive, notably in 1947–48 but on certain earlier occasions as well. The consequences in terms of our Middle Eastern policy as a whole are evident to this day.

THE JEWISH COMMUNITY IN PALESTINE
AT THE TIME OF PEARL HARBOR

"We shall fight the war as if there were no White Paper, and we shall fight the White Paper as if there were no war." This characteristic assertion by David Ben Gurion, the fiery chairman of the Jewish Agency Executive in Jerusalem, conveys very expressively the mood of the Jewish community in Palestine during the early years of the Second World War. With the outbreak of war in September 1939, Palestine had become relatively quiet as the focus of world attention shifted elsewhere, to the Western Desert and to Europe. This was in marked contrast to the years immediately preceding, when the country had been in constant turmoil.

Initially, the Jewish community offered its full cooperation to the British in the war against Germany. There was of course no question as to where the Jews stood as far as Hitler was concerned, and many of them hoped that their cooperation might lead to a relaxation of the White Paper restrictions on Jewish immigration and land settlement. Some 18,000 Palestine Jews enlisted in the British forces, and the community did a great deal to help the British war effort, particularly in connection with military orders placed with Jewish industry. Jewish terrorist activity, which had sprung up immediately after the release of the White Paper, now declined.

However, as the months passed, with no sign that the British had any intention of modifying the White Paper policy, Jewish resentment grew. The Jews of Palestine began to seek ways of bringing in as many refugee Jews as possible from occupied Europe, legally or illegally, and to agitate for a separate Jewish fighting force.

The Jewish community, the *Yishuv*, was highly organized. Its most important body was the Jewish Agency, which was created specifically by the Mandate and which represented in Palestine the interests of the World Zionist Organization. The Agency had the responsibility of promoting the development of the Jewish National Home. At this time, Dr. Chaim

Weizmann was serving as president both of the World Zionist Organization and of the Jewish Agency. The chairman of the Agency's Executive, as already noted, was Ben Gurion; the head of the Political Department was Moshe Shertok (later Sharett); and the treasurer was Eliezer Kaplan. A prominent figure in Zionist circles in Palestine was Goldie Myerson (later Golda Meir) who at the time was a member of the *Vaad Hapoel,* the Executive of the *Histadrut,* the influential General Federation of Jewish Labor, which had connections with every segment of Jewish life in the country.

The Jewish community had already developed into something of a state within a state, with its own executive (the Jewish Agency), legislature (the *Vaad Leumi* or National Council), trade union system (the Histadrut), and even its own military organization, the underground *Haganah* (meaning "defense"). So well organized, in fact, was the Yishuv that all of us who followed the Palestine scene knew, long before the Jewish state came into being, that if the Jews were to secure their state Weizmann would be the president, Ben Gurion the prime minister, Shertok the foreign minister, Kaplan the finance minister, and so on; and this is what came to pass. Eventually I got to know all of the persons named and can testify that, individually and collectively, for sheer ability they were superior to the members of most European cabinets of the day.

The Yishuv was divided into a complex of political parties, with the Labor party, known as *Mapai,* which provided most of the leadership, generally having the support of the majority. To the right of the political spectrum were the religious parties and the so-called Revisionists, or New Zionists, a radical splinter group founded by the late Vladimir Jabotinsky which called for a Jewish state on both banks of the Jordan. The Revisionists had their own illegal army, the *Irgun Zvai Leumi* or National Military Organization, headed by Menachem Begin who was to attract considerable world attention in later years and who in May of 1977 became Prime Minister of Israel.

It should be added that in the left wing of the Yishuv there was a substantial minority of Jews who favored a binational state of both Jews and Arabs.

THE ARAB COMMUNITY IN PALESTINE

The Arab community could not have been more different from the Jewish. The Arabs were split into factions and had never been successful in organizing themselves as a political entity. First of all, they were divided along religious lines, with the Moslems in the majority but with substantial Christian and Druze elements. In addition, there had always been great rivalry between the big landholding families, of which the most prominent were the Husseinis, who were violently anti-British, and the Nashashibis, who tended to be more conciliatory toward the Mandatory power. The head of the Husseini clan, Haj Amin al-Husseini, the *Mufti,* or chief Moslem dignitary, of Jerusalem and president of the Supreme Moslem Council, had also headed an Arab Higher Committee formed in 1936 in an effort to unite all the different Arab factions during the revolt which the Arabs launched in that year in protest against continued Jewish immigration. Following the collapse of this rebellion in 1937, the Higher Committee was outlawed by the British authorities. The Mufti fled to Iraq, while his cousin and chief lieutenant, Jamal al-Husseini, escaped to Syria.

By the start of the Second World War, the Palestine Arab community was in complete disarray, with no effective leadership. Although the White Paper had been designed chiefly as a bid for Arab support, it was not welcomed by most of the Arabs in the country, who agreed with the exiled Mufti in opposing any further Jewish immigration.

During the critical early years of the war, there were no disturbances on the part of the Palestine Arabs, but they showed next to no enthusiasm for the war effort. Arab enlistments in the British forces never came to more than 9,000— another contrast with the Jews.

THE SITUATION IN THE ARAB EAST

By early 1942, the status of the various portions of the Arab world was as follows. Trans-Jordan was officially a part of the Palestine Mandate but had been exempted from the application of the Jewish National Home as early as 1922 and had its own regime under the Emir Abdullah, a member of the Hashemite dynasty.[9] The Levant States (Syria and Lebanon) were a French mandate. Iraq, which had been a British mandate until 1932, was an independent kingdom ruled by another Hashemite, the young King Feisal. Since 1936 Egypt had been nominally independent, also with a young king, Farouk, who was beginning to show marked Italian sympathies. The British were permitted by treaty to maintain sizable bases in Egypt and to station troops there (as they also were in Iraq). After war broke out, Egypt became virtually an armed camp and was the principal base for British military operations in the Western Desert.

In the Arabian Peninsula, Saudi Arabia had been united and independent under the strong leadership of King Abdul Aziz Ibn Saud, one of the giants of the Arab world. Yemen was the only other independent state in the Peninsula, as the various sheikhdoms along the Persian Gulf were under one form of British protection or another.

Thus at the time of the Second World War substantial portions of the Arab world were still under various types of Western tutelage, with the British in the paramount position nearly everywhere. The situation in the Arab countries was characterized, then as now, by acute rivalries, notably that between the Hashemites and the House of Saud. An Arab national movement had been in existence since before the First World War but had not yet proved to be an effective instrument of cooperation between the Arabs, even over the issue of Palestine. Indeed, when I went out to Egypt in 1938, there was some doubt on the part of many of us—and of many Egyptians—as to whether Egypt should be considered an Arab state. In briefing me for my assignment, the desk officer in the Department did not even mention the Palestine problem as a factor in U.S.-Egyptian relations. He confined himself to telling me that there was only one subject at issue between the United States and Egypt: our quota on long-staple cotton (which incidentally remains an issue to this day).

It is safe to say that up until the time of the British victory at Alamein in the Western Desert in the fall of 1942, the prevailing opinion among the Arabs was that the Allies were going to lose the war. In view of the gains made by the Axis in the Balkans and North Africa, this is not surprising. In the years preceding the war, moreover, the Arabs had been subjected to an intensive propaganda campaign on the part of the Germans and Italians. This was now stepped up. The Mufti, from his base in Iraq, engaged actively in anti-British intrigues throughout the Arab countries. In April 1941, he was instrumental in bringing about a coup in Iraq which installed a pro-Axis regime there under Rashid Ali al-Gailani. The British invoked their treaty and intervened militarily, overthrowing the Rashid Ali government in a short time. The Mufti again escaped, and by the end of the year had made his way to Germany. He was to spend the rest of the war in Berlin, directing Axis propaganda activities aimed at the Arabs and raising a Moslem force to fight against the Allies.

THE WORLD ZIONIST ORGANIZATION

The Zionist Organization, founded in 1897 by Theodor Herzl, the father of the Zionist movement, was an international body which by the late 1930s had branches in approximately fifty countries and a membership of just under one million Jews. The president of the Zionist Organization always served also as president of the Jewish Agency. Since 1920, with the exception of a short interval in the 1930s, these two positions had been held by Dr. Chaim Weizmann, who was of Russian birth but had been a British subject for many years. He was to become the first president of Israel.

The highest Zionist organ was the biennial Congress, which had last met in August 1939 in Geneva, on the eve of the war. Sensing that a world crisis was fast approaching, the members of the Congress had delegated the supreme policy-making authority to the Inner General Zionist Council, which was based in Palestine.

The outbreak of war and the swift Nazi occupation of so large a part of Europe of course rendered Zionist activity impossible in many parts of the continent, as Jews were rounded up and sent to concentration camps. The result was that in the first two years of the war the chief centers of Zionist activity were Jerusalem and London, where Dr. Weizmann continued to reside (he did not go to Palestine between 1939 and 1944).

Weizmann, although in his late sixties when war came and in failing health, remained a powerful figure in the movement. A chemist by profession, he had been of great service to the British government in the First World War, because of his discovery of a new process for making acetone, used in the manufacture of smokeless powder (it was said that schoolchildren all over England were put to gathering horse chestnuts, which formed the basis for Dr. Weizmann's formula). Through his connections with members of the British War Cabinet, he was largely responsible for getting the British government to issue the Balfour Declaration in 1917.

In subsequent years Weizmann had served as chief spokesman for the Zionists with the Mandatory government. He was a skillful negotiator and a believer in the policy of "gradualism," that is, of working with the British to fulfill Zionist goals within the framework of the Mandate. This policy, however, had been severely shaken by the White Paper. The Zionists in fact were beginning to realize that the White Paper was going to be responsible for a fundamental change in their relations with the British, since it meant that they could no longer count on the Mandatory to assure the continuation of Jewish immigration, which they hoped would lead to an eventual Jewish majority in Palestine. If the White Paper were to remain in force, the British would become the chief hindrance, rather than the chief help, to the achievement of their aims. These considerations raised the possibility that in the future the movement would pass into the hands of activists who, unlike Weizmann, were prepared to mount a direct challenge to the British government.

Dr. Weizmann, however, still had immense prestige among Zionists and he was to dominate the movement for some time to come. I recall vividly the impression he was to make on the Anglo-American Committee of Inquiry in 1946 (see Chapter 6), with his powerful personality, his thoughtful presentation, and his close physical resemblance to Lenin (we were told that during the First World War, when both men were living in Switzerland, they were often mistaken for each other).

THE AMERICAN JEWISH COMMUNITY

By 1942 the Jewish community in the United States numbered between four and five million. In 1939 it had accounted for only 29 percent of world

Jewry, but this percentage was to rise substantially with the wartime extermination of European Jews by the Nazis. By the end of the war, roughly half of the Jews in the world would be located in the United States.

American Jews enjoyed an influence in politics out of proportion to their numbers because they were concentrated in a small number of key cities and states. They were highly organized and were active participants in a variety of causes but traditionally had not shown much enthusiasm for Zionism. Membership in American Zionist organizations, which stood at 150,000 in 1918, had declined to 50,000 by 1938. As a result, however, of such developments in the middle and late 1930s as the rise of anti-Semitism in the United States, the Arab revolt in Palestine, and the White Paper, Zionist membership had climbed back to the 150,000 figure by 1942. (By way of comparison, total membership in all U.S. Zionist groups reached just under 1,000,000 by 1948, the year of Israel's independence.)

Leading American Zionists at the time of our country's entry into the war, each of whom at one time or another served as president of the Zionist Organization of America (ZOA), were such figures as Louis Lipsky, Emmanuel Neumann, Rabbi Israel Goldstein, and of course Rabbi Stephen S. Wise and Rabbi Abba Hillel Silver.

Wise and Silver, who will appear frequently in this narrative, were very different in personality and approach. (Observers often compared Wise with Weizmann and Silver with Ben Gurion.) Both were Reform rabbis. Wise, the senior of the two, had served as president of the ZOA in the 1930s. From 1925 to 1949 he was president of the American Jewish Congress, a Zionist body which was virtually indistinguishable from the ZOA. Rabbi Wise was a Democrat and a great admirer of President Roosevelt, with whom he carried on an extensive correspondence for many years: it was said that Roosevelt took his well-known expression "the forgotten man" from one of Wise's sermons. [10] Wise believed in working through the Administration in Washington and following more conventional methods. Silver, a Republican, distrusted Roosevelt and government officials in general. His motto, which he took from the Old Testament (Psalm 146:3) and frequently cited when criticizing the Administration, was "Put not your trust in princes." He believed in techniques of mass persuasion and was eminently successful in applying them.

Any account of the Jewish community in our country should also mention the influential American Jewish Committee, the leading non-Zionist body in the United States. This group did not come out for a Jewish state in Palestine until 1947, but it was in frequent touch with us in matters affecting the Jewish National Home (to which it gave general support) and the refugee question. Maurice Wertheim was president of the Committee in 1942; he was succeeded the next year by Justice Joseph M. Proskauer, who remained at the head of the group for many years. Another prominent figure on the Committee was Jacob Blaustein, who was chairman of the Executive.

Between the outbreak of war in 1939 and Pearl Harbor, the mood of American Jews was ostrichlike, characterized by isolationism and apathy. In the months immediately following our entry into the war, they showed a reluctance to agitate the Palestine question, fearing this might be harmful to the war effort. Their attitude had not yet been influenced by the Nazi extermination program, which did not become generally known until late in 1942.

U.S. INTERESTS

In December 1941 when the United States entered the war, our interests in the Middle East were not extensive. The isolationism that had dominated our foreign relations in the 1920s and 1930s had contributed to our playing a minor role in the area. It was true that every American president beginning with Woodrow Wilson had gone on record in favor of the Jewish National Home and that this was the purport of a resolution passed by the Congress in 1922. These declarations of policy, together with the support extended over the years by individual Americans of the Jewish faith to the development of the National Home, had undoubtedly created an American interest in the Jewish side of the Palestine dispute. On the other hand, such stake as we had in the Middle East at the time seemed to be more on the Arab side than on the Jewish. Our commercial interests, our missionaries and educators (going back to the mid-nineteenth century, the American University of Beirut, for example, having been founded in 1866)—all combined to start us off on a good footing with the Arab world in the years following the First World War. It was already evident that there was a latent conflict between our Jewish and our Arab interests in Palestine. This conflict was to become much more obvious in the next few years.

Since it has sometimes been alleged that, even by the time of Pearl Harbor, United States oil interests were so deeply involved in the Arab world as to affect our handling of the Palestine question, it might be worthwhile to put this matter in perspective. Up to 1942, American companies had invested in oil exploration and production in four Arab countries: Saudi Arabia, Bahrein, Iraq, and Kuwait. Only in the first two of these was there 100 percent American participation, and in all four of them production, which amounted to only a fraction of that attained in later years, was greatly curtailed after war broke out in 1939. In Saudi Arabia, oil had not been found in commercial quantities until 1938. In that year, output totaled just over 1,000 barrels per day, as compared with between 7,000,000 and 8,000,000 at the present time (1978). It was not until after the war was over that the United States started becoming involved in the development of Middle East oil on a massive scale.

BRITISH POLICY

The conflicting pledges respecting Palestine made during the First World War remained to plague the British administrators during the more than thirty years that they governed the country. They had in fact undertaken a virtually impossible task—as the Peel Commission itself recognized in 1937 when it pointed out that the Mandate was "unworkable." How, indeed, to establish a national home (whatever that meant) in Palestine for the Jewish people (however defined) without prejudicing the rights of the great majority of the population (the Arabs), was a problem which the British were never able to solve. It is hardly surprising that they often seemed to vacillate between the rival claims of the two parties.

As the situation in the Middle East evolved in the prewar period and as the Axis powers intensified their bid for Arab support, the British found themselves more and more in the position of making decisions that ran counter to Jewish aspirations, culminating in the White Paper of 1939. By this time, the British were really making decisions about Palestine for reasons that had little to do with Palestine, that is, for reasons related to the situation in the Arab world and its implications for British strategic interests.

After war broke out, the major British concern, as far as the Middle East was concerned, was to maintain the lifeline to India and to prevent the Germans and Italians from taking over the area. The decision taken in August 1940, shortly after the fall of France and just before the Battle of Britain, to reinforce the British Eighth Army in Egypt at the expense, if need be, of the defense of the British Isles, shows better than anything else the vital importance that British strategists attached to the region. Further evidence of this was provided in June 1941 with the creation in Cairo of the post of Minister of State Resident in the Middle East, with cabinet rank—a position held successively by Oliver Littleton (later Lord Chandos), Richard G. Casey, and Lord Moyne.

Although a majority of Winston Churchill's war cabinet, which held office from May 1940 to July 1945, were in sympathy with the Zionist cause (notably the Prime Minister himself), the issue was not of immediate urgency, certainly not in comparison with the problems of the war, and thus it only came to the forefront after the war was over.

An important aspect of British rule in Palestine, and one which was bitterly resented by the Jewish community, who considered that with their generally European background they were superior to the native Arabs, was that Palestine for administrative purposes came under the Colonial Office. It thus frequently happened that an official would find a tour of duty in Jerusalem, Nablus, or Haifa sandwiched between service in Kenya, Malaya, Nigeria, or other outposts of the Empire.

In the Churchill government the Colonial Secretary was Colonel Oliver

Stanley. The ranking permanent official of the Colonial Office was Sir George Gater. He was regarded as hostile by the Zionists, although I have not been able to unearth any evidence to bear out this allegation. A key official of the Colonial Office who had already had considerable connection with the Palestine question, having served as secretary of the Peel Commission in 1936–37, was John M. Martin (now Sir John Martin). During the war years he was a member of Churchill's personal staff, but he kept up his connection with Palestine, partly by lunching regularly with Dr. Weizmann, who was living at the Dorchester Hotel in London. This provided liaison between the Prime Minister and the head of the Zionist Organization. After the war, Martin returned to the Colonial Office and as Assistant Under Secretary supervising the Mediterranean Department (which quaintly enough dealt with Palestine, Cyprus, Malta, and Gibraltar) and later Deputy Under Secretary, was intimately concerned with the Palestine question right up to the events of 1947–48. He was always one of the most cooperative of our British colleagues, and he has helped me with the preparation of this book. During the war years the British High Commissioners in Palestine were first Sir Harold MacMichael, then Lord Gort, and finally Lt. General Sir Alan Cunningham. Cunningham stayed until 1948 and thus was the last to hold this post.

The Colonial Office handled only the day-to-day administration of Palestine affairs. Foreign policy matters relating to Palestine were of course handled by the Foreign Office, specifically by its Eastern Department which throughout these years was headed by C. W. Baxter, a career official who later became Minister to Iceland. Baxter reported to the Superintending Under-secretary of State, Sir Maurice Peterson, another career man who was later Ambassador to Turkey. Baxter's position corresponded more or less to that of Gordon Merriam in the U.S. State Department and Peterson's to that of Wallace Murray or, later, Loy Henderson. The Foreign Office Palestine desk during these years was held by a succession of officers, notably H. A. Caccia (now Lord Caccia), later Ambassador to Washington, H. M. Eyres, R. M. Hankey (later Lord Hankey), and finally Harold Beeley (now Sir Harold), who was not then a career Foreign Service officer but who came to the Foreign Office in 1945 from the Royal Institute of International Affairs (Chatham House).

Beeley quickly showed himself to be a master of the intricacies of the Palestine problem. He continued to be associated with it during the consideration of the question at the United Nations in 1947 and 1948. As will be explained in Chapter 6, he and I worked closely together in 1945–46 as secretaries of the Anglo-American Committee of Inquiry. We have been associated together since, and he has been unfailingly helpful to me.

When the Churchill government was turned out of office by the British electorate in the summer of 1945, Ernest Bevin became Foreign Secretary in the new Labour government, replacing Anthony Eden. For a short time George Hall was the Labour Colonial Secretary but he was soon succeeded by Arthur Creech-Jones, a former trades union official who was almost entirely subservient to Bevin, under whom he had worked for many years in the labor movement. From then on, it was often said that Bevin and Harold Beeley determined British Palestine policy.

To summarize the attitudes of the Foreign Office and the Colonial Office toward the Palestine question, I should say that the Foreign Office tended to see matters from the Arab point of view throughout this period, while the Colonial Office never gave up the hope of bringing about an accommodation between the parties.

We now turn to the unfolding of United States Palestine policy during the critical years 1942–48.

1
✿ ✿ ✿ ✿ ✿ ✿ ✿ ✿

The Biltmore Program
Calls for a Jewish State

In the months that followed the commencement of hostilities in 1939 events came with great swiftness: the collapse of Poland, the "phony war," the ill-fated British venture in Norway, the German attack on the Low Countries, the accession to power of Winston Churchill, the entry of Italy into the war, the fall of France, the battle of Britain, the German thrust through the Balkans and invasion of Russia, and the growing crisis in the Far East. During these months, I was serving in Egypt, where the war was brought home to us when Italy came in and fighting began in the Western Desert. We evacuated our families to a place of safety (ironically, Jerusalem) and began to cope with blackouts and air-raid precautions. In early 1941, the collapse of Mussolini's Ethiopian empire for a time lessened the pressure on the British forces in the Middle East and opened the Red Sea to American shipping.

Then came Pearl Harbor and the entry of the United States into the war—a United States which up to that time had maintained a curiously detached attitude toward the conflict, epitomized, in the fall of 1941, by the bare passage, with only one vote to spare, of the renewal of the Selective Service Act of 1940 by the House of Representatives. Roosevelt's sympathies were of course with the Allies and we had started to aid the British through the destroyers-for-bases deal and Lend-Lease. In the summer of 1941 Roosevelt had had his first meeting with Churchill and they had agreed on the program of common goals known as the Atlantic Charter. But the American public was still essentially isolationist, relying on the 1937 Neutrality Act, prohibiting the shipment of arms and ammunition to belligerent powers, to keep the war at a distance.

Many of us greeted the news of Pearl Harbor with a sense of relief that we were at last in the battle against Hitler, but as the country plunged into war the prevailing mood was one of uncertainty. Roosevelt, as usual, struck the right note, in his State of the Union message in January 1942: "We have already tasted defeat. We may suffer further setbacks. We must face the fact of a hard war, a long war, a bloody war, a costly war."[1]

Against this background, in the spring of 1942, the American Emergency Committee for Zionist Affairs, which (like the Inner General Zionist Council in Jerusalem) had been set up as an interim body at the last prewar Zionist Congress in 1939, convened an "extraordinary political conference" to be held in New York City with the idea of formulating a new Zionist program in the light of wartime developments. The immediate causes for the conference were, first, an article in *Foreign Affairs* for January 1942 by Dr. Chaim Weizmann, president of the World Zionist Organization, which revived the idea of a Jewish state;[2] and second, the sinking in February 1942 of the refugee ship *Struma* off Istanbul with the loss of 763 Jewish refugees.[3] The stated purpose of the conference was to discuss the future of Palestine, the possibilities for cooperation with non-Zionist bodies, and ways of obtaining a "united representation of Jewry" at the peace conference that would follow victory over the Axis.

More than 600 delegates, representing the four principal American Zionist bodies—the Zionist Organization of America, Hadassah, Mizrachi, and Poale Zion—met at the Biltmore Hotel in New York from May 9 to 11.[4] Besides the Americans, there were representatives from Zionist organizations in Europe and Palestine, including Weizmann and Ben Gurion. Thus the meeting in many ways took the place of a World Zionist Congress, which could not be assembled because of the war. But it was particularly significant that for the first time a meeting of the entire Zionist movement had been convened by American Zionists, and in the city of New York, for this indicated an important shift in world Jewish focus from Europe to the United States.

The meeting at the Biltmore was addressed by, among others, Weizmann and Ben Gurion, and by Rabbi Silver, who now moved to a position of leadership among American Zionists. Weizmann, always the apostle of moderation, urged that nothing be done to interfere with the British war effort. Ben Gurion and Silver, however, took a more forthright line. Ben Gurion wanted the conference to reaffirm the original purpose of the Balfour Declaration and the Mandate, which he described as the establishment of a Jewish Commonwealth in Palestine; Silver asked for the adoption of a militant program.

This was the stand the conference wanted, and in response the delegates overwhelmingly adopted an eight-point platform, drafted by Weizmann's associate Meyer W. Weisgal, which called for the abrogation of the White Paper, for the opening of the doors of Palestine to Jewish immigration under the control of the Jewish Agency, for the creation of a Jewish army, and finally for the establishment of Palestine "as a Jewish Commonwealth integrated into the structure of the new democratic world"—that is, as a Jewish state.

Ben Gurion returned to Palestine and later in the year obtained the acceptance of the Biltmore Program (as it came to be called) by the Inner General Zionist Council, the top policy-making body of the Zionist Organization. This was not accomplished without considerable effort, since many of the Jews in Palestine preferred either a binational state or partition into separate Jewish and Arab states, rather than a Jewish state in the whole of Palestine. By that time, however, more and more details of the Nazi extermination policy were coming out of occupied Europe and this helped Ben Gurion obtain approval for the program.

The real importance of the Biltmore Program was that here for the first time the Zionist movement came out officially for a Jewish state in Palestine. This was a radical new departure attributable chiefly to the influence of the American Zionists, a majority of whom had been in favor of a state since the late 1930s. From now on it would be the American wing of the movement that would spearhead the drive for a state. In other words, the American Jews assumed the role of leader in the campaign for statehood, a campaign that was to prove victorious in only six years' time.

It must be repeated that the Biltmore provisions were a good deal more advanced than any that had so far been voiced by the official Zionist movement. Indeed, the program was reminiscent of the position of the Revisionists. This very point was made by the British Embassy in Washington in an *aide-mémoire* to the Department of State. The Embassy commented that "official Zionist policy had now been shown publicly to be maximalist" and that this could have severe repercussions in Palestine and elsewhere.[5]

The Biltmore Program, like Weizmann's *Foreign Affairs* article, was based on the assumption that after the war there would be at least two million Jews wanting to go to Palestine. The decimation of European Jewry at the hands of the Nazis undermined this assumption, and as we shall see, the movement eventually came around to the idea of partition, that is, of a Jewish state in a part of Palestine. For the next few years, however, the Biltmore Program determined Zionist policy. The Weizmann policy of "gradualism" was now virtually abandoned, and Weizmann began to lose influence to a more militant group who looked to the Ben Gurions and the Silvers for guidance. These latter saw the Biltmore resolutions as a mandate for immediate action, whereas Weizmann tended to think of them as a statement of maximum demands.[6]

Meanwhile, the course of the war had been going against us and our allies. The Japanese had taken Hong Kong, Malaya, Singapore, the Netherlands East Indies, and the Philippines, and had advanced into Burma. In the Western Desert, German and Italian forces under the leadership of Field Marshal Rommel had begun their all-out attack on Egypt. In Russia, the Germans registered their farthest advance and soon were at the gates of Stalingrad. With these stirring events taking place in so many theaters of war it is not surprising that the news of the Biltmore Conference should have been buried on page 37 of the *New York Times*.

Much Zionist activity during the year 1942 centered about the proposal for a separate Jewish fighting force. The Zionists promoted this project because it gave concrete expression to the principle of Jewish nationalism and because the force could be the nucleus of a future Jewish army in a Jewish state. They also hoped that the establishment of such a detachment could gain them a seat at an eventual peace conference, corresponding to the forces of the various members of the United Nations.

A full-scale campaign was launched by a New York organization calling itself the "Committee for a Jewish Army of Stateless and Palestinian Jews," a number of whose sponsors had Revisionist sympathies. When Churchill visited Washington in June, hundreds of letters were addressed to him on the subject. The Zionist leadership joined in the appeal for a Jewish army, and Weizmann, who happened to be in Washington at the same time, was active in pursuing the project with British and American officials. Neither the British government nor the American government, however, was willing to endorse the proposal, because of its nationalistic overtones. Eventually, in 1944, the British yielded to repeated Zionist appeals and permitted the formation of a separate Jewish Brigade Group, which participated in the fighting in North Africa and Italy on a fairly limited scale.[7]

It is now known that the decision to exterminate the Jewish population was taken by the Nazi leadership at a meeting at Wansee on January 20, 1942.[8] Several times during 1942, as word of the extermination program began to filter out of occupied Europe, Jewish leaders approached the U.S. Administration, either to seek confirmation of these reports or to ask for a statement of sympathy with the plight of the persecuted Jews. Often these approaches were made to Roosevelt or Welles by Rabbi Wise. In May and again in July, Roosevelt, at Wise's urging, sent messages to Jewish rallies in Chicago and at Madison Square Garden in New York City. It was Wise's practice to send to the President a draft of what he would like the President to say on such occasions, but often these drafts were toned down by the White House, since the President, while sympathetic, did not wish to commit himself completely to the Zionists.

In September the Jewish Affairs Institute of the American Jewish Congress, a Zionist body of which Wise was the head, published what was stated to be the first documented account of the Nazi extermination policy. The existence of this policy was not confirmed by the State Department until late in November, when Welles informed Wise of a message received from the American Minister in Switzerland giving details of the Nazi program. Wise then took a delegation of Jewish leaders to call on Roosevelt. They urged the President to issue a statement denouncing the Nazi policy, which he did on December 17, pledging that those responsible for these atrocities would be punished. Prime Minister Winston Churchill made a similar statement.

However, although Roosevelt and Churchill were prepared to condemn the

Nazi leaders for their persecution of the Jews, they were unwilling to raise the matter with the German government, either directly or indirectly, because of the "unconditional surrender" policy. In retrospect, there is a real question as to what could have been done, in wartime, to save the Jewish population of occupied Europe. Even if these unfortunate victims of Hitler's hatred could somehow have been removed from Nazi control, public opinion in the United States, including a majority of Jewish opinion, was firmly opposed to changing our immigration laws to permit any substantial number to come to this country, and the prospects for finding havens elsewhere in the world were decidedly limited. In any event, in spite of the disturbing reports that now began to come more and more to world attention, no one, not even the Zionist leadership, really believed that there would be a wholesale extermination that would eventually result in the loss of some six million Jewish lives.

The Zionists reacted sharply to the formation, in November, of an anti-Zionist body, called the American Council for Judaism, which had as its main premise the assertion that the Jews were a religious group, not a nation. The name of the group was chosen by Rabbi Morris S. Lazaron of Baltimore, one of the organizers. Others prominent in the Council were Lessing J. Rosenwald, the former chairman of Sears, Roebuck & Company, who became its president; Rabbi Elmer Berger, its executive director; Arthur Hays Sulzberger, publisher of the *New York Times*; and Sidney Wallach of the American Jewish Committee. Although the Council for Judaism never attained a membership of more than 15,000, its leaders were highly articulate and their activities soon began to annoy the Zionists, who wanted the American Jewish community to present a united front on the question of Palestine. In response, the Zionists set up a special organization called the Committee on Unity for Palestine with the express purpose of combating the Council for Judaism.

Meanwhile, in Palestine, another American Reform rabbi, Dr. Judah Magnes, president of the Hebrew University, had started an organization called *Ihud* (Union) which called for a binational state—and was for that reason also opposed by the official Zionist leadership.

On the twenty-fifth anniversary of the Balfour Declaration (November 2) the Zionists obtained a statement from 63 Senators and 192 members of the House of Representatives reaffirming support for the Jewish National Home and urging that "now more than ever" there was need for a Jewish homeland so that the survivors of Nazi persecution could find new lives in Palestine. In response to a request by a group of rabbis on the same occasion for an indication of our government's views, Secretary Hull issued a statement praising the contribution of American citizens in building up the Jewish National Home in Palestine, deploring the Nazi persecution of the Jews, and reaffirming our support for the Atlantic Charter. This anodyne declaration, with its sweeping generalizations, was the only government statement during all of 1942 that even mentioned Palestine. It can certainly not be called a statement of our policy regarding Palestine.

Balfour Day, incidentally, coincided with Montgomery's breakthrough at Alamein in the Western Desert. This success, followed a few days later by the Allied landings in North Africa, was a turning point in the war in Africa. It provoked one of Winston Churchill's most remembered comments, when he said "Now this is not the end. It is not even the beginning of the end. But it is perhaps the end of the beginning."[9] In the Pacific, meanwhile, the U.S. fleet had begun to take the initiative following the battles of the Coral Sea and Midway earlier in the year.

The record of the Near East Division's involvement in the Palestine question during 1942 is not extensive. In June and again in July, Wallace Murray urged that the United States should issue a statement condemning Zionist agitation as counter to the war effort, but Roosevelt took the attitude that in the existing situation in the Middle East, the less said by everyone the better. On several other occasions during the year Murray submitted memoranda to his superiors that were critical of Zionist aims and warned of the consequences of following a pro-Zionist policy.

Meanwhile Under Secretary Welles was saying (to a British official) that the Palestine problem could be solved only by the creation of a Jewish state and (to the Zionists) that "not the slightest commitment" would be made to the Arabs without consulting them (the Zionists) and securing their agreement.[10] Neither of these statements appears in the *Foreign Relations* volume or in the Department archives, however.

The United States
Finds a Policy

The year 1943 opened with some encouraging developments for the Allies. In the Pacific we finally wrested control of Guadalcanal from the Japanese, while on the Russian front the Germans were forced to surrender at Stalingrad. In January, Roosevelt and Churchill met at Casablanca to discuss the North African campaign and to issue their "unconditional surrender" declaration.

In terms of U.S. Palestine policy, 1943 was a crucial year in that our government for the first time, under pressure of circumstances, adopted a definite line of policy. Since this was also the year that I joined the Near East Division (after an interval of nearly two years following my departure from Cairo in late 1941, during which I did economic warfare work in Mexico City and Washington), I had an opportunity to become familiar with this policy in the early stages of its development.

Up to this time, the United States had not had to have more than a vague attitude toward the Palestine problem. Most Americans, if asked, would probably have said that the Jewish people should be allowed to return to their ancient homeland as the Bible said, but there was very little if any real knowledge or understanding of the Middle East among the public at large. During the 1920s and early 1930s, American Jews had not brought much pressure to bear on the U.S. government to follow a particular line of policy with respect to Palestine, and since we had only a limited involvement in the Near East, the basic conflict of interest—Jewish versus Arab in Palestine—was of no great or immediate concern to us. Of course the dilemma was there, as our policy makers well knew, and it was thus all the more understandable that they should have preferred to have us stand on the sidelines and leave this particular headache to the British.

Secretary of State Hull very definitely took the attitude that Palestine was a British responsibility. He directed that this, and no more, should be said in reply to inquiries received by the Department. In 1936, 1937, 1938, and 1939, in response to the urging of American Jews and their supporters in Congress that we intervene with the British government respecting some particular aspect of the Palestine question, Hull had authorized the American Embassy at London to make an approach to the British, but mainly this had been in the form of informal, oral inquiries.

After Pearl Harbor and the entry of the United States into the war, the Palestine problem began to come more actively to the notice of officials in Washington. By 1943, it was evident that our government could no longer confine itself to generalized statements based on United Nations principles, or on the Atlantic Charter. This was because of the interaction of two factors: the growing Zionist agitation in this country and the reaction to this in the Arab world.

Zionist activity, which began building up after the Biltmore Conference in May 1942, was steadily increasing. In January 1943, representatives of thirty-two national Jewish membership organizations met in Pittsburgh with the purpose of organizing a representative body to develop a common program of action respecting "the postwar status of Jews and the upbuilding of a Jewish Palestine." This led to the American Jewish Conference, numbering 501 delegates, which met at the Waldorf Astoria Hotel in New York City later in the year. Of the delegates, 379 were elected by local and regional Jewish groups and 122 were appointed by the national organizations. The Zionists worked hard to secure the selection of a preponderant Zionist majority among the delegates, with the result that approximately four-fifths of the total number were regarded as having Zionist sympathies.

The Conference passed a number of resolutions, of which the most important endorsed in its entirety the Biltmore Program. This resolution was adopted as the result of an impassioned speech by Rabbi Silver, who repeated his remarkable oratorical performance of the previous year at the Biltmore Conference. Asserting that the Balfour Declaration had not been intended to be merely "an immigrant aid scheme," Silver argued that the establishment of a Jewish Commonwealth in Palestine was "essential for the salvation of a people fighting for its very life" and that rescue of European Jews, free immigration into Palestine, and statehood were "inseparable links" in a single chain.

Silver's speech met with an emotional response on the part of the assembled delegates, many of whom were moved to tears. "Hatikva," the Zionist anthem, was sung over and over and Silver was roundly cheered. From then on, it was clear that the Conference would come out for the full Biltmore program, even though some delegates, notably those representing the non-Zionist American Jewish Committee, questioned the wisdom of this. When the final vote was taken, there were only four delegates who dissented.[1]

This vote was particularly significant because it came from a convention of delegates representing the whole spectrum of the Jewish community, not just Zionists, as had been true of the Biltmore Conference. This point was stressed by a delegation of the Conference leadership that called on Secretary Hull to present him with a set of its resolutions, which were described as "the expression of the will and opinion of the overwhelming majority of the American Jewish community." The subsequent withdrawal of the American Jewish Committee from the Conference (which was a continuing body) did not minimize its importance, for it was now clear that the vast majority of American Jewish opinion supported the Biltmore appeal for a Jewish state.

The Interim Committee of the Conference immediately launched an intensive propaganda campaign with the goal of bringing American public opinion to sympathize with Zionist aims and of eliciting pledges of support from public officials at all levels. The ultimate purpose was to win the United States government over to the concept of a Jewish state in Palestine. The campaign was designed to appeal first to those who were impressed by the humanitarian argument and by the need to rescue the victims of Hitler's persecution; second, to those who believed that the return of the Jewish people to Zion was a fulfillment of biblical prophecy; and third, to those who saw the Zionist Jews in Palestine as a liberal, progressive, and democratic element in the Middle East. The link between the plight of the Jewish refugees and the necessity for a Jewish state was always stressed. The line taken was often strongly anti-British.

The American Emergency Committee for Zionist Affairs was reorganized as the American Zionist Emergency Council, which took over the direction of the campaign with an annual budget of $500,000. Rabbi Silver and Rabbi Wise were named co-chairmen. The Emergency Council, generally known as AZEC, with headquarters in Washington, operated through a network of local committees, of which there were 200 by 1944 and 380 the following year. A series of AZEC circulars, in the Zionist archives in Jerusalem, reveals the scope of the operation and the methods employed: members were to be prepared on short notice to organize a letter- or telegram-writing campaign and to conduct demonstrations; contact was to be maintained not only with Jewish groups but also with non-Jewish, especially Christian Protestant, groups; speakers' bureaus were to be set up and the publication of books and press articles was to be subsidized. One million leaflets were distributed every year.[2]

As a result of all this, the White House, Congress, and the State Department were buried under an avalanche of paper. Frequently the same individual would send identical telegrams, for which I recall being told the Zionists had obtained a cut rate, to the President, his two Senators, his

Congressman, and the Secretary of State. Eventually the telegraph company did not even separate these messages but would bind them in bundles and truck them over to the Department, where they were stacked in the basement. (In 1938, during an earlier campaign, stacks of telegrams had been brought into the Near East Division and piled on the Palestine desk. The press had carried photographs of the desk officer, a relatively short man, buried under the accumulation, leading to a tradition in the Division that holders of the desk had to be six feet tall or taller.) The campaign became world wide and reports were received by the Department from virtually every Foreign Service post, giving the text of petitions from local Zionist groups.

Only one member of Congress, Senator Josiah W. Bailey of North Carolina, refused to endorse the Zionist position and wrote to the President opposing it.[3] The main opposition to the AZEC and its activities, however, came not from supporters of the Arab side in the dispute, including the oil companies, but from other Jewish organizations, non-Zionist and anti-Zionist.

As Zionist activity grew in this country, the Arab world became anxious, and its leaders began to inquire as to the U.S. government's attitude. Their concerns were made known in three principal ways: (1) through representations by Arab diplomats in Washington, of whom there were only a handful in those days; (2) through messages from our posts in the field; and (3) most significantly, through reports from two envoys who visited the Near East during the year on special missions for the President, Lt. Colonel Harold B. Hoskins and Brig. General Patrick J. Hurley.

The Egyptian Minister, Mahmoud Hassan, called at the Department twice during the year to register protests against the activities of the Zionists. On the first occasion he saw Secretary Hull and on the second, Under Secretary Welles. Hassan made it clear that his government had every sympathy for the homeless Jews, but considered that the Zionist agitation for a Jewish state was having the most serious effects in the entire Arab and Moslem world. When Hull inquired what the Minister saw as a solution for the problem of the Jewish refugees, Hassan made the interesting suggestion that the members of the United Nations (then twenty-nine in number) should each "take their proportional share of Jews from all over the world." Later in the year, the Iraqi Minister, Ali Jawdat, called on Wallace Murray in NE to lodge a similar protest.

Our Minister in Cairo, Alexander Kirk, reported to the Department on a number of occasions during 1943 that the activities of the American Zionists were arousing some anxiety in Egypt and were threatening to undermine the "long-standing heritage of good will toward the United States in this area," as well as adversely affecting the war effort. Kirk, who was also accredited at the time to Saudi Arabia, reported in April after a visit to that country that King

Abdul Aziz Ibn Saud had asked him to convey to President Roosevelt his deep concern with respect to Palestine and the effect that Zionist activities were having on U.S.-Arab relations.

Later in the year we appointed a separate Minister Resident in Saudi Arabia, James S. Moose, Jr., who reported to Washington that during his first call on the Emir Feisal, Ibn Saud's son and Minister of Foreign Affairs (later king), Feisal at once brought up the question of Palestine and urged that it was only "elementary justice" that the Arabs should not be called upon to "suffer further" at the hands of the Jews.

Hoskins, who as implied in the Introduction held a reserve commission in the Army but was on detail to the State Department, spent three and a half months in the Near East in late 1942 and early 1943 on a mission for the President and the Joint Chiefs of Staff, which had the strong backing of Welles. He reported under date of January 23 from Cairo that if matters were allowed to drift further, "a very bloody conflict is in the making" which would "inflame not simply Palestine but in varying degrees all of the Moslem world from Casablanca to Calcutta."[4] He particularly noted the "ever-present Arab fear of American support for political Zionism" and asserted that the Arabs were "uncompromisingly against" the establishment of a Jewish state in Palestine, which in Hoskins's view could only be achieved by force.

Hurley, who had been Secretary of War under President Hoover and in 1942 had become the U.S. Minister to New Zealand, was designated by Roosevelt as his Personal Representative in the Middle East, to act as an observer and report directly to him on general conditions in Egypt, Syria and Lebanon, Iran, Iraq, Palestine, and Saudi Arabia. (The sending out of special envoys like Hoskins and Hurley was characteristic of Roosevelt's handling of our foreign affairs and was symptomatic of his underlying distrust of the career Foreign Service officers, for whom it caused innumerable headaches.) Hurley's report, dated May 5, 1943, was submitted direct to the White House and was later forwarded by the President to the Department for comment. Hurley, like Hoskins, took a gloomy view of the prospects for U.S. relations with the Arab world, unless something could be done to curb the Zionists. He told the President that he had found "deep-seated Arab hostility" to any attempt to promote Jewish immigration into Palestine with the aim of creating a Jewish majority, and eventually a Jewish state, in that country. He added that throughout the Arab countries he had encountered the conviction that the United States was intent on establishing a Jewish state in Palestine.[5]

Although Arab anxiety was mounting as a result of the activities of the American Zionists, the Arab propaganda effort was pitiful. An Arab Information Office was not opened in Washington until 1945, and, partly because our media were not as friendly to the Arabs as to the Jews, it never succeeded in getting its message across to the public. The Arab-Americans, furthermore, mostly Christians with no strong feelings about Palestine and numbering some 500,000 as compared with 5,000,000 American Jews, were never an effective force.[6]

The occasion for a more positive formulation of our attitude toward Palestine came in the spring of 1943, when King Ibn Saud wrote a letter to President Roosevelt expressing his grave concern and the concern of all Arabs about Zionist aspirations in Palestine. The President's reply, dated May 26, 1943, is important because it contains the first expression of the so-called "full consultation" formula. "It is the view of the Government of the United States," Roosevelt said, "that no decision altering the basic situation of Palestine should be reached without full consultation with both Arabs and Jews."[7] The letter thus marked the beginning of a formal U.S. policy toward Palestine, in great contrast to the vague generalities of public statements on the subject up to that time. None of my former colleagues in the Near East Division whom I have consulted can recall, nor do the archives reveal, who it was who was responsible for our first using the "full consultation" formula. It was, however, being employed by the British at this time and indeed had its origins in a statement made by Lord Cranborne, now Lord Salisbury, in the House of Lords in May 1942.

This formulation, with slight variations in wording, became the cornerstone of our Palestine policy and was used repeatedly by our government over the next few years. The pledge was loosely worded and subject to differing interpretations, but it proved invaluable to the Department (and to Presidents Roosevelt and Truman) when, as became increasingly the case, the Zionists elicited from the President some statement favorable to their cause. Inevitably such statements would lead to Arab protests, and messages would be prepared in the Near East Division, for the President's signature, assuring the Arabs that whatever might have been said did not denote any change in the "basic situation" and that it was still our policy that they (as well as the Jews) should be consulted.[8]

The recent publication of the U.S. diplomatic correspondence for the 1940s in the *Foreign Relations* series and also the opening up of the Department's archives have performed an important service in that they show that the text of every one of these messages was specifically approved by the President. Each of the messages in the *Foreign Relations* carries a notation to this effect, and the original copies of the messages, in the archives, bear the President's initials. There can thus no longer be any basis for alleging, as has been done, that these messages were sent out by the Department behind the President's back.[9] Admittedly the messages were not made public at the time, but this was at the instance of the White House, not the Department.

The "full consultation" formula did not mean, as has also been alleged, that the consent of the Arabs had to be obtained before there was any change in the "basic situation." Our commitment to the parties in the dispute was to consult them, and in 1946, as will be explained in Chapter 6, we carried out consultations with Arabs and Jews and thereafter maintained that in so doing we had discharged our commitment.

Like so many aspects of our Palestine policy, our formula was not acceptable to either Jews or Arabs. When it was eventually made public in late 1945, AZEC protested on the grounds that the Arabs did not have any standing in the dispute. The Arabs for their part always maintained that they had never been adequately consulted, especially on the crucial issue of Jewish immigration into Palestine. They saw our actions as supporting the Zionists, whatever our words might say. Indeed, it has always seemed to me that the attempt to carry water on both shoulders was an all but impossible task which for the most part convinced only ourselves in the Near East Division that we were being objective.

While Ibn Saud and Roosevelt were exchanging letters, important events were taking place on several war fronts. The British were winning the battle of the Atlantic against the German submarines, and by mid-May the Axis powers had been driven out of North Africa. During the summer came the Allied capture of Sicily, the resignation of Mussolini, the invasion of the Italian mainland, and the surrender of the Italian government, although fighting was to continue in the north of the country for another year and a half.

In May of 1943 Dr. Weizmann announced that the Jewish Agency was opening an office in Washington, to be headed by Dr. Nahum Goldmann, a member of the Jewish Agency Executive and president of the World Jewish Congress, a Zionist body affiliated with the American Jewish Congress. Goldmann was one of the most distinguished of the Zionist leaders. This was another indication of the importance which the leadership was now attaching to the role of the U.S. government in the Palestine question. Wallace Murray reacted to this news in characteristic fashion. He sent a memorandum to the Secretary, pointing out that the Mandate for Palestine, which had created the Jewish Agency, had stipulated that the Agency should operate at all times "subject to the control" of the British authorities. Murray recommended not only that no official recognition be accorded to the Washington office of the Jewish Agency, but also that if any communication be received from that office it be returned with the request that it be submitted to the Department through the British Embassy (which of course was hardly to the liking of the Zionists in view of their strained relations with the British government). I doubt that this procedure was actually followed, but later on Murray did go so far as to instruct us that if for any reason we should find it necessary to communicate with Dr. Goldmann we should address him at his street address without mentioning the Jewish Agency. After Loy Henderson took over from

Murray as our chief in 1945, this policy was relaxed. The representatives of the Agency were welcomed to NE and I readily obtained Henderson's concurrence in our using its full name in our letters from then on.

A matter that was the subject of considerable discussion on several occasions during 1943 was the question of issuing a joint Anglo-American statement on Palestine. This project, which was strongly advocated by Hoskins and Murray and opposed by the Zionists, would have taken the position that any decision on Palestine should be postponed until after the war. The statement would have included the "full consultation" formula. In Murray's words, the purpose would have been to "put an end to the current agitation for a Jewish state." Welles, incidentally, opposed the plan. The British and American governments several times reached agreement to issue a statement, and Roosevelt twice approved a text (see Appendix G). However, when Judge Samuel I. Rosenman, who was serving as Special Counsel to the President, leaked the proposed text to the Zionist leadership in July 1943, there was immediate protest. Hull then decided to seek the backing of the War Department, but when Secretary of War Henry L. Stimson informed him that the military situation in the Middle East did not justify issuing such a statement, the matter was dropped, to the consternation of the British.[10] The subject arose again later in the year and early in 1944, but no action was ever taken. The question may well be asked whether a statement of this sort would have achieved its stated objective of warding off pressures on both governments. Indeed, in an interview in June 1974, the late Colonel Hoskins agreed with me that in retrospect it was unlikely that the statement would have had the effect desired at the time.

One of the more bizarre episodes of the year resulted from a decision taken by Roosevelt, Welles, and Weizmann, on their own without consulting the Near East Division, to send Hoskins to see King Ibn Saud and try to arrange a meeting between him and Weizmann so that they could work out a settlement of the Palestine question. The idea had been broached to Weizmann some years earlier by the British Arabist H. St. John Philby, a confidant of Ibn Saud's, who thought that the Arabs might be persuaded to let the Jews have Palestine in exchange for a payment to Ibn Saud of some twenty million pounds, and Weizmann had, it appears, brought it up with both Churchill and Roosevelt on several occasions. We in NE were very skeptical of the whole idea when we heard of it, for it seemed highly unlikely that Ibn Saud would ever agree to any such proposal, and certainly not at that time, when the Arabs were so suspicious of the Zionists because of the increased agitation over Palestine and when, furthermore, Ibn Saud was no longer in urgent need of revenue.[11]

We were right. Ibn Saud refused to see Weizmann or to have anything to do with the scheme. The only concrete result of the incident was that when

Hoskins saw Roosevelt in September to report on his mission, Roosevelt made a number of interesting comments regarding the Palestine question. In the course of a long conversation Roosevelt said that he thought that after the war most of the European Jews would not want to go to Palestine but would want to return to their homes (this view was shared by many officials at the time, although opinions were to change later on). On the future of Palestine, he told Hoskins that he was thinking of a trusteeship with a Jew, a Christian, and a Moslem as trustees.

This idea of the President's formed the basis of a paper prepared in the Near East Division in late 1943, which was the first attempt in the Department to put together some thoughts on the future of Palestine. As we soon came to realize, this early trusteeship plan was hardly realistic. Essentially, what was proposed was a body comprising three Christians, two Moslems, and a Jew which was to advise the trustee (Great Britain) regarding the desires and complaints of the different religious groups having an interest in the Holy Land. Details of the plan were not elaborated, but it is hard to see how anyone could have expected such a simplistic scheme, based on religious considerations alone, to have coped with the complex political issues inherent in the Palestine problem.

It was not long before we saw the shortcomings of any proposal along these lines. A paper that we prepared for the 1944 talks with the British, as will be noted in Chapter 3, states flatly that "a trusteeship exercised by the three religious groups would be a failure." It was again recommended that Palestine be constituted as an international territory with Great Britain as the trustee, but it was now provided that the Arab and Jewish communities should form "autonomous political entities with wide powers of local self-government." There was to be a board of overseers representing the three world religions, but its role would be a minor one and the emphasis was to be on the development of self-governing institutions. [12]

With some refinements, the thinking of the Near East Division concerning a future solution for Palestine continued to run in this direction right up to the adoption of the partition plan by the General Assembly of the United Nations in late 1947. Such a solution was reasonable, but it did not, of course, take sufficiently into account the domestic political imperatives that were to come more and more to the forefront of the U.S. government's handling of the Palestine question during these years. Nor did it take sufficiently into account, as we were later to realize, the driving force of nationalism among both Arabs and Jews—which more than thirty years later is still the dominant feature of the conflict.

In November 1943, Roosevelt, Churchill, and Stalin held their first meeting at Tehran. The meeting resulted in some far-reaching decisions regarding the conduct of the war, but there was very little discussion of

Middle Eastern questions, and none at all of Palestine; it was an indication of the relative priorities in the thinking of the wartime leaders.

March 1944 was the expiration date of the five-year period during which Jewish immigration into Palestine was to be allowed to continue under the terms of the 1939 White Paper. In anticipation of this date, Jews in this country had been exerting constant pressure on our government to intervene with the British to extend the date and expand the immigration. On December 13, 1943, Hull sent for the British Ambassador, Lord Halifax, and told him that he and the President were in favor of the extension of the immigration quota after the March deadline.[13] The Ambassador replied that the British government was already planning to take action along these lines, as not all the certificates available had been used. This in fact was done, and the intention had been already announced in the House of Commons on November 10 (though Hull in his *Memoirs* claims credit for the action).[14] But the Jews were eager for the American government, too, to take some positive steps. At the Anglo-American refugee conference held in Bermuda in April 1943 the British had refused to have Palestine placed on the agenda, but as more and more stories of Nazi atrocities were reported, the Zionists kept up their campaign for Palestine.

In December, Roosevelt, who had had several ideas of havens in various parts of the world for Jewish refugees, sent a well-known attorney and personal friend, Morris L. Ernst, to London to explore the possibilities with British officials.[15] But Ernst soon found that any suggestions for an alternative to Palestine would never get anywhere either with the Zionists or with politicians generally in the United States. Reluctantly, he abandoned the project.

For a number of reasons U.S. immigration quotas during these years were substantially unfilled—the difficulties of travel were an obstacle in themselves, and also, for reasons of national security, visa applications were being scrutinized with extra care to prevent enemy agents from entering the country. There were a good many complaints alleging red tape and obstructionism on the part of the State Department's personnel dealing with the refugee problem and with visa matters, but there is no basis for claiming, as has been done, that these officials were responsible for the loss of European Jewry. I think it is safe to say in this connection that all of my colleagues who were dealing with the refugee question in those years were distressed by the frustrations and disappointments which their work entailed. The security issue was an especially thorny one: how was the overworked, conscientious consular officer to be sure that the visa applicant with the concentration camp number plainly tattooed on his forearm was indeed one of Hitler's victims and not a Nazi spy? As the visa regulations became more and more voluminous, the entire process became more and more cumbersome, and visa officers quite naturally grew cautious in the extreme. But that is not the same as deliberately delaying the process, or being anti-Semitic, as some critics have charged.[16]

As the year 1943 drew to a close, the following was the situation in the Near East Division as far as Palestine policy was concerned. We had evolved some language (the "full consultation" formula) which we hoped might serve as a statement of U.S. government policy but which might have the drawback of meaning all things to all men. We had advanced a tentative plan for the future of Palestine but were becoming aware that the plan needed modification. And we had been unsuccessful in getting agreement at the highest level to issuing a public statement of policy, which in any event might not have achieved the primary purpose that its sponsors had in mind. All the time, while we were turning in this not very impressive record of accomplishment, the flood of Zionist pressure mail was rising higher and higher in anticipation of the coming election year.

Palestine Becomes a Political Issue

As the year 1944 got under way, the Palestine question began taking on more and more importance as part of American domestic politics. The Zionist propaganda campaign launched in 1943 was intensified in an all-out effort to get the American government firmly committed to the creation of a Jewish state in Palestine.

On the war fronts, the Allies went on the offensive during the early part of the year. The Red Army drove the Germans out of the Ukraine, crossed into Poland, and entered Romania, then started toward Odessa and the Crimea. In the Pacific, American forces landed in the Marshall Islands and attacked the Japanese at Truk. In Europe, the beachhead at Anzio was established in mid-January, and in March the long siege of Monte Cassino began. Round-the-clock aerial bombings of Germany also started.

In late January, the American Zionist Emergency Council succeeded in obtaining the introduction into both Houses of Congress of identical resolutions calling for unrestricted Jewish immigration into Palestine and for the "reconstitution" of that country as a "free and democratic Jewish Commonwealth" (see Appendix H).[1] These resolutions, which had bipartisan backing, were a pet project of the Council's co-chairman, Rabbi Silver. Their language was very similar to that of the Biltmore Program, except for the substitution of the word "reconstitute" for "be established," which clearly implied that the new Zion was the fulfillment of biblical prophecy. Few people saw any inconsistency in "a free and democratic Jewish Commonwealth" that was two-thirds Arab.

Official Washington was flooded with petitions urging approval of the resolutions, but almost immediately Arab protests also began coming in. These were on a much smaller scale, but they were serious enough to cause anxiety in the Executive branch. Murray submitted a memorandum to his superiors drawing attention to the consequences to our position in the Near East if the resolutions should pass, and the Department sent out instructions to our Foreign Service posts telling them to take the line, in discussing the matter, that "passage of the resolutions by either or both Houses would be only an expression of the individual members of that House and would not be binding on the Executive branch or an expression of the foreign policy of the United States."[2]

Chairman Sol Bloom of the Committee on Foreign Affairs of the House of Representatives wanted the Department to testify at public hearings which he was holding, but Secretary Hull was reluctant to become involved and sought to pin responsibility for opposing the resolutions on the War Department. Secretary of War Stimson, with the President's approval, wrote a letter to the chairmen of the Senate and House committees stating that the resolutions were prejudicial to the war effort. The ever cautious Hull then wrote a letter to these same chairmen saying that "in view of the military considerations advanced in this regard by the Secretary of War, it is believed that, without reference to its merits, no further action on this resolution would be advisable at this time." These letters were not made public.[3]

The House Foreign Affairs Committee conducted several days of hearings, at which the testimony was overwhelmingly in favor of the resolutions. All the major Zionist organizations were heard. The only opposition came from the American Council for Judaism and from three witnesses (two of them Arab-Americans) who supported the Arab point of view.[4]

As Zionist pressure for passage of the resolutions continued, so did the reaction in the Arab world. The Egyptian and Iraqi ministers together called on Acting Secretary Stettinius, to express the concern of their governments. Later the Egyptian returned to the Department and handed Paul Alling of NE a note stating among other things that recent developments were giving rise to the impression among the Arabs that "America is supporting the Jews at the expense of the Arabs."

Our representatives in Baghdad, Damascus, Jidda, and Beirut telegraphed the Department to relay the anxiety and dismay expressed to them by local officials. Loy Henderson, then serving as Minister at Baghdad, reported a conversation with the prime minister of Iraq, Nuri Said, a prominent leader in the Arab world, during which Nuri pointed out that the German radio broadcasts in Arabic were making frequent use of the Congressional resolutions in an effort to "create a lack of confidence among the Arabs in the sincerity of purpose of the Allies." Henderson also reported that the chief officials of the Iraqi Senate and Chamber of Deputies were telegraphing their opposite numbers in our Senate and House expressing the hope that the resolutions would not pass. Our Chargé d'Affaires in Damascus told the Department that similar representations were being made by officials of the Syrian Parliament.

An interesting byproduct of these Arab parliamentary protests was that they elicited a characteristic comment from President Roosevelt. When Speaker Sam Rayburn of the House forwarded to the President a telegram he had received from the Iraqi parliamentarians, Roosevelt replied somewhat cynically that this message "is merely one of a volume of protests which have come in from practically all the Arab and Moorish [sic] countries. It merely illustrates what happens if delicate international situations get into party politics."[5] In other words, the President was well aware of the Arab attitude and of the complications caused by moves in Congress such as this.

The President and Secretary Hull urged Secretary Stimson to make his letter to the committee chairmen public, but Stimson resisted this. Colonel Hoskins was then sent by the State Department to the Pentagon and it was agreed that General George C. Marshall, chief of staff of the War Department General Staff, would go up to Capitol Hill and testify against the resolutions in a private meeting, which he did. It was hoped that Marshall's immense prestige would convince the members of Congress.

On March 9, Rabbi Wise and Rabbi Silver, who were becoming apprehensive that the resolutions might not pass because of Executive branch opposition, called on the President. They handed him a draft statement, much along the lines of the resolutions, which they asked him to issue. Roosevelt, according to Silver's later account of the meeting, spent some ten minutes reworking the draft and told them that on leaving the White House they could issue it as their statement.[6]

Wise and Silver told the press that the President had authorized them to say that the American government had never given its approval to the White Paper, and that he was happy that the doors of Palestine remained open to Jewish refugees. They also said that the President had given them assurances that "when future decisions are reached, full justice will be done to those who seek a Jewish National Home."

It is pretty clear that the two rabbis had hoped for some forthright statement of sympathy with the Zionist aims, and that the President, fully aware of the delicate issues involved, watered down their draft. In other words, he deftly turned the tables on Wise and Silver, who had no alternative but to make the best of it.

Even in its modified form the statement led to an immediate Arab reaction. It was given extensive coverage by the news media in a number of Arab countries and we received inquiries from our posts as to how to treat the incident. Henderson reported that for days the activities of the Zionists in the U.S. had been the "chief topic of discussion" among politically conscious Iraqis. Both the Imam Yahya, king of Yemen, and the Emir Abdullah of Trans-Jordan sent messages of concern and apprehension to Washington.

To counter this adverse Arab reaction, the President approved a circular telegram to our posts which pointed out, with some subtlety, that although it was true that the American government had never given its approval to the White Paper, it was equally true that we had never taken any position with respect to it. (This was Gordon Merriam's idea, as I recall.) The message noted that the rabbis' statement had referred to a Jewish National Home, not a Jewish state, and added that our policy was still based on full consultation with both Arabs and Jews. Commenting in general on our attempts to put a gloss on Presidential statements, the pro-Zionist author, Frank Manuel, has some rather harsh words to say about what he calls the "clever double-dealing" of the members of the Near East Division. He says that we might think we were practicing astute diplomacy when our efforts were only a "clumsy imitation of the British."[7] I believe, on the other hand, that we did pretty well, here and elsewhere, in getting the President out of a tight situation.

The shelving of the Congressional resolutions was eventually accomplished on March 17, when Stimson addressed another letter to Chairman Bloom of the House committee, reiterating that the passage of the resolutions would be "prejudicial to the successful prosecution of the war." Bloom made this letter public and announced that his committee would take no further action.[8] A similar statement was made by the Senate committee.

The entire episode turned out to be a bureaucratic muddle, with the State and War departments each trying to dodge responsibility for going on record as opposing passage. Silver claimed he had shown a draft in early January to Hull, who had offered no objection, but there is no record of this in the Department's files. Bloom also declared he had been given to understand there was no objection on the part of the Executive branch, as did Senator Robert A. Taft, one of the sponsors of the resolution in the Senate.

Later in the year, the War Department withdrew its objections to the resolutions and they were reintroduced into Congress. This was done in spite of the fact that Stettinius had told the Zionist leadership on November 15 that he and the President considered this step to be unwise. On December 6, Stettinius (who had succeeded Hull as Secretary of State at the end of November) was called before the Senate Foreign Relations Committee on short notice and persuaded the committee to shelve the resolutions a second time. The committee insisted, however, that the Department issue a statement opposing passage "from the standpoint of the general international situation." This was done and the resolutions were again withdrawn.[9] The *New York Sun* commented on the Department's statement by running a cartoon showing the Palestine desk officer, in striped pants and cutaway, holding up his hand and saying "No" to a throng of homeless Jewish refugees. (I framed the *Sun*'s cartoon and had it on the wall of my office throughout the rest of my tour in the Division.) Roosevelt, who was at Warm Springs at the time, later concurred in Stettinius's action and complimented him on the "fine manner" in which the problem had been handled by the Department.[10] As will be explained later, this was one of the last occasions on which the Department could be said to have played the decisive role in our Palestine policy.

The failure of the resolutions to pass caused a split between Wise and Silver, so serious that Silver, who had really instigated the resolutions in the first place and had been their strongest supporter, was forced to resign in late December as co-chairman of the American Zionist Emergency Council. (He returned to this position six months later.) Other Zionist leaders, including Chaim Weizmann, Moshe Shertok, and Nahum Goldmann, joined Wise in opposing Silver's tactics.[11]

To complete the story of the Congressional resolutions, they were revived and passed by both Houses in December 1945, although in a somewhat modified form providing merely for a "democratic commonwealth" rather than a "free and democratic Jewish Commonwealth."[12] These resolutions were in the form of concurrent resolutions, which, unlike the original Congressional Resolution of 1922, did not require Presidential approval. By that time the war was over, attention had been diverted to other aspects of the problem, and there was very little reaction in the Arab world or elsewhere. One year earlier, the circumstances were such that passage of the resolution at that time would have had an unfortunate effect on the standing of the United States in the area.

One of the turning points of the war had come in June 1944, with the Anglo-American landings in Normandy that signaled the invasion of Nazi-occupied Europe. Rome had fallen earlier in the month. Later in the summer came such events as the unsuccessful assassination attempt against Hitler and the Allied landings in southern France. Paris was liberated on August 25, and Allied advances continued on the Russian front and in the Pacific. In October, General MacArthur returned to the Philippines, and later that same month, at the Battle of Leyte Gulf—the biggest naval action ever fought—the destruction of Japanese naval power was accomplished. With these favorable developments on the war fronts, there was more opportunity for Washington and London to be thinking about such issues as Palestine.

During the summer of 1944, both the Republican and Democratic conventions, for the first time ever in a Presidential campaign, adopted platform planks expressing support for the Zionist position.[13] On July 26, Hull, at our prompting, sent a memorandum to the President, calling attention to the adverse effect that these developments were having on Arab opinion and urging that the leaders of both parties refrain during the campaign from making further statements of this nature. The record does not show that there was any response from the President, and in any event, the Palestine question continued to be an issue in the campaign. In September, Presidential Counsel Rosenman urged Roosevelt to speak to Prime Minister

Churchill, who had come over for the second Quebec Conference, about immigration into Palestine. Rosenman pointed out that the Republican candidate, Governor Thomas E. Dewey, was "making quite a play" about Palestine. He thought it would help the Democrats if it were known that the President had approached the Prime Minister on the subject.[14] (There is no record that Roosevelt did so.)

Just before the election, Roosevelt, in a letter to Senator Robert F. Wagner, chairman of a pro-Zionist group called the American Palestine Committee, went so far as to endorse the idea of a Jewish state (see Appendix I). This was the first such endorsement by an American president, although the pledge was so worded that it might be interpreted as having been given as a personal rather than official assurance. The Samuel I. Rosenman papers at the Roosevelt Library show that although Roosevelt did promise support for a Jewish state, he watered down (as in the case of the Wise-Silver statement earlier in the year) the draft desired by the Zionists.[15] Dewey thereupon countered with a similar endorsement.[16]

Again, Arab reaction was immediate. Our legations in Damascus and Baghdad and elsewhere were handed messages conveying Arab concern and resentment. Henderson told the Department that Dewey's endorsement of Zionist aims in Palestine had "created a sensation" (as the President's appointee, Henderson tactfully refrained from criticizing the President's similar action, but the implication was clear). He added that a pro-Zionist statement issued by former Under Secretary Sumner Welles (who was now a private citizen) had attracted particular attention because Welles was "regarded here more as an authority on American foreign policy than a politician."[17]

The Iraqi Minister for Foreign Affairs, Arshad al-Umari, assured Henderson that if our government should actually take steps to implement these campaign pledges, "Arab friendship for and trust in the U.S." would change instantly, inflicting a "bitter defeat" on those forces that were trying to point the Arabs in the direction of cooperation with the West.[18]

We in NE reported to Under Secretary Stettinius on October 27 that these political promises could only be taken by the Arabs as showing a "lack of good faith" on the part of our government, since they ran counter to our assurances to the Arabs that they would be consulted, and that we were afraid our long-term interests in the area were being threatened. A later memorandum, also prepared in NE and forwarded by Stettinius to Roosevelt, said that the recent pro-Zionist statements in the United States had given rise to a "wave of shocked disillusionment and protest" in the Near East and that this trend, if continued, would seriously prejudice the government's ability to protect American interests, including the important oil interest in Saudi Arabia.[19]

Earlier in the year, our chief, Wallace Murray, had been one of a number of State Department officers who had accompanied Under Secretary Stettinius to London for talks with the British on a variety of topics. In that way Murray and Dr. Isaiah Bowman, president of Johns Hopkins University, who was serving as a consultant to the Secretary of State on postwar problems, had had an opportunity to discuss the Palestine question with members of the Foreign Office dealing with the Middle East.

Murray and Bowman took with them a memorandum which I had prepared, entitled "Palestine: Topics for Discussion with the British." This memorandum covered a number of points on which the Near East Division was interested in learning the views of the British, such as Jewish immigration into Palestine, recent conversations held by British officials with Zionist leaders, the possibility that the British government might be considering the partition of Palestine, postwar plans for that country, and the proposed issuance of a joint Anglo-American statement. With respect to the future, there was attached to my memorandum the paper mentioned in Chaper 2 above, calling for a British trusteeship over Palestine, with the Arab and Jewish communities exercising wide powers of local self-government (see Appendix J).

The British confirmed their decision (mentioned in he preceding chapter) to continue the White Paper quota for Jewish immigration at the rate of 1,500 per month until the end of the war. On the question of the future of Palestine, the two sides exchanged tentative impressions. Bowman said that the thinking in the Department was tending toward a trusteeship, and the senior British representative, Sir Maurice Peterson, remarked that the Foreign Office "would go all out for such a solution." On the basis of this conversation, the Stettinius group, on its return to Washington, reported to the President and to Secretary Hull that the views of the British on the future of Palestine were very similar to ours and, specifically, that they had in mind "no territorial divison" of the country.[20]

The British representatives, however, had chosen not to reveal to our side that since August 1943 a high-level supersecret Cabinet committee had been meeting to consider the postwar status of Palestine and that the majority of this group was in favor of partition. The Foreign Office archives, recently opened to the public, give the details of the British planning and show that partition was opposed by the Foreign Office on the grounds that it would arouse violent Arab hostility, and that because of this opposition it was decided to postpone any decision until after the war.[21]

Even though Peterson was no doubt perfectly sincere in suggesting to Bowman and Murray that the Foreign Office would support trusteeship (which would mean that partition was ruled out), there seems to be no question but that the British did not want us to know about their top-level planning for Palestine. The reason emerges very clearly from a memorandum from Prime Minister Churchill to Foreign Secretary Anthony Eden in the same series of British documents. Churchill told Eden that he would like to show the Cabinet plan to the President but hesitated to do so because Roosevelt "would leak it to the Jews."[22] No doubt Churchill was thinking of what had happened the previous year, when the Zionists were able to block the proposed joint statement on Palestine because it had been leaked to them.

The Foreign Office papers contain a number of similar comments by British officials at the time which reflect their feeling that our government was too closely tied in to the Zionists and too much under their influence to be trusted completely. In the light of Churchill's comments above, it is rather ironic that it was Churchill himself, in a meeting with Weizmann in late 1944, who revealed to the Zionist leader that a Cabinet committee had been considering partition. Churchill (who was known to have Zionist sympathies) added that the Zionists could count on his continuing support.[23]

Early in 1944, because of continuing dissatisfaction with the State Department's handling of the refugee problem, Secretary of the Treasury Henry Morgenthau, Jr., had persuaded Roosevelt to set up a War Refugee Board consisting of the Secretaries of State, War, and Treasury to take over refugee operations. The Board had broad powers. Its personnel were very active, particularly in Turkey, which by virtue of its location offered promising opportunities for the rescue of refugees from the Nazi-occupied Balkan countries.[24] The Board's representative in Turkey was Ira Hirschmann, a New York businessman and public-minded citizen who showed great dedication and drive in carrying out his duties. His account of his experiences in the two books he wrote makes fascinating reading, especially with respect to the various cloak-and-dagger episodes in which he was involved.[25] In the Near East Division we thought highly of him. Hirschmann worked with Jewish Agency representatives in Ankara in trying to get Jewish refugees out of the Balkans and into Palestine. They were, however, hampered by bureaucratic obstacles and by technical difficulties such as the shortage of shipping. The number of those refugees who eventually reached Palestine, both legally and illegally, was relatively small. In any event, for most of the Jewish population of occupied Europe it was too late.[26]

Roosevelt's Last Months

By the time the Palestine resolutions had again been shelved in Congress, President Roosevelt had begun to focus increasing attention on his forthcoming meeting with Churchill and Stalin. Though he was weary, after three years of war, the President had some reasons for cautious optimism as the year 1944 drew to a close. The invasion of the European continent, now in its sixth month, was progressing well. In spite of the jolt administered by the Battle of the Bulge in late December, it could be said that the end was in sight as far as the war against Germany was concerned. Roosevelt, moreover, had just won an unprecedented fourth victory at the polls. During the campaign he had shown evidence of his old spark, as in his Teamsters' speech ("my little dog Fala") and on the day when he campaigned through the rain-lashed streets of New York City in an open car—a feat which prompted Churchill to send him a cable full of solicitude.[1] So it was with a considerable measure of confidence that the President faced the task of preparing for the meeting of the Big Three—a meeting at which decisions of the greatest significance for the future of the world would clearly have to be taken.

Roosevelt's prevailing frame of mind at the time is illustrated by a conversation which the new Secretary of State, Edward Stettinius, had with him on December 22. The Secretary had with him a memorandum on Palestine, prepared by the Near East Division, but F.D.R., showing signs of impatience, indicated that he did not want to get into that subject just then. The Secretary, in reporting back to Wallace Murray about his conversation, suggested that our memorandum be "worked into our general preparation for what is ahead"—meaning, that is, Yalta.

This was done, but as things turned out the subject was not discussed at the Yalta Conference. The paper that I prepared for the Conference is of some interest, however, as showing the thinking of the Department on the Palestine issue at this time, particularly as related to the Soviet Union and three-power cooperation. It pointed out that the American and British governments were committed to consulting the Arabs and Jews, and recommended that the British should accordingly be asked to begin carrying out this commitment. The results of their consultations should then be made available to the Soviet and U.S. governments so that a plan for a Palestine settlement could be worked out with the concurrence of all three great powers.[2]

This recommendation was not carried out either at Yalta or at the San Francisco Conference later on, where the Department made the same proposal, but it is interesting to speculate on what might have happened if the Soviet Union had been brought into the matter at this stage. In connection with the fact that our paper for Yalta was never used, it is worth mentioning that Jim Bishop, in his account of Roosevelt's last year, suggests that the ailing President was too tired to look at any of the briefing papers that had been prepared for the conference.[3]

Before leaving for the Big Three meeting, the President decided that on his way home he would meet with King Ibn Saud for a discussion of the Palestine problem. He did not consult his Secretary of State regarding this idea, but he did ask the advice of James M. Landis, the outgoing director of the American Economic Mission in the Middle East. Landis warned the President that Ibn Saud felt so strongly on the Palestine issue that he did not think the President should bring it up with him—and added that in his opinion the establishment of a Jewish state in Palestine would be contrary to the Atlantic Charter.[4] Roosevelt also remarked to his wife, in telling her about his plans for Yalta, that he intended to "see some of the Arabs and try to find a peaceful solution for the Palestine situation."[5]

The Zionists and their supporters were also busy preparing for the Yalta conference. Both Senator Wagner and Representative Celler wrote to the President urging prompt action along the lines of his pre-election pledge to Wagner. Celler, who had accompanied Roosevelt on the electioneering ride through the streets of Brooklyn, wrote: "My constituents regard you as a modern Moses. When you went through in that torrential downpour, the Italian and Irish sections were deserted but in my district people stood five to six deep on the sidewalks." Now, Celler continued, they are looking for results. Roosevelt's reply was typically candid: "Give me a chance, dear Manny," he wrote, "to talk with Stalin and Churchill. There are all sorts of schemes, crackpot and otherwise, being advanced. Perhaps some solution will come out of this whole matter. I don't want to see war between the one or two million people in Palestine and the whole Moslem world in that area—70 million." He struck the same note in his letter to Wagner: "There are about one million Jews [in Palestine]. They are of all shades, good, bad, and indifferent . . . 70 million Moslems want to cut their throats." (Roosevelt about doubled the number of Jews in Palestine.)[6]

Rabbi Wise, who had earlier suggested to Stettinius that the President should take an "expert" with him to the Big Three meeting (a proposal which of course met with the disapproval of the Near East Division) saw Roosevelt on January 22. He left a memorandum with the President urging the early establishment of a Jewish Commonwealth in "an undiminished and undivided Palestine." As was so often the case, no record exists of their conversation, but the general tenor is revealed in a letter which Wise wrote to Roosevelt on January 26 as a follow-up on their talk. Wise told the President that he would comment as follows on the points that had been raised by F.D.R.: first, contrary to the view put forward in certain quarters, Palestine's potential for water development is considerable; second, Arab fears of Jewish expansion are groundless; and third, the Zionists have reason to believe that the U.S.S.R. is not opposed to the creation of a Jewish state—in fact, Stalin recently said as much to President Benes of Czechoslovakia, whom Wise characterized as "a convinced Zionist of long standing."[7]

The meeting at Yalta, in the Crimea, took place from February 4 to February 11, and as already indicated did not touch on the subject of Palestine.[8] At Malta en route to the conference, the President told Churchill of his intention to see King Ibn Saud on this way home. Harry Hopkins reported that Churchill was "flabbergasted" on receiving this intelligence.[9] At the final dinner of the Big Three at Yalta, Roosevelt again mentioned his plans to see Ibn Saud. Stalin remarked that the "Jewish question" was a very difficult one. Roosevelt said that he was a Zionist—was Stalin? The latter responded: "In principle, but I recognize the difficulty." In reply to a question from Stalin the President said that he intended to review "the entire Palestine question" with the King. This irritated Churchill, who regarded the subject as his responsibility and did not see what the President had to contribute.[10]

The story of the colorful meeting of the President and the King at the Great Bitter Lake, midway down the Suez Canal, has become familiar, beginning with the Kings's journey up the Red Sea on board the American destroyer *Murphy*, the flock of sheep carried on the ship's fantail to provide food for the King's party (which included the royal fortune teller, the royal food taster, the chief server of the ceremonial coffee, the royal purse bearer, and ten guards chosen from the principal tribes of Saudi Arabia), the confrontation between the two leaders on board the cruiser *Quincy*, the President's gift of a wheelchair to the ailing King, and the rest. The meeting was marked with great cordiality and the two hit it off at once. Their interpreter was Colonel William A. Eddy, then serving as Minister to Saudi Arabia, who cleared the text of his memorandum of the conversation with both the President and the King shortly afterward.[11]

We at the working level in Washington learned of the meeting only some time later. We were enjoined to hold Eddy's memorandum of conversation very closely, because its contents might be politically damaging to Roosevelt. It is indeed difficult to reconcile the President's assurance to the King (which he later put in writing, see Appendix K) that "he would do nothing to help the Jews against the Arabs" with his October 1944 letter to Wagner pledging support for a Jewish state. [12] That the President allowed himself to make such a far-reaching commitment to Ibn Saud is a measure of the degree to which he was impressed by his unyielding attitude on the Palestine issue. The record shows that each time the President (disregarding Landis's advice) brought up the subject he came up against a stone wall of opposition from the King.

Roosevelt came away from the meeting with a vivid impression of Ibn Saud and with a sense of complete failure. He said this on a number of occasions before his death. Just after the meeting he told Stettinius (who had not been present) that the talk had been a memorable one and that on returning to Washington they would have to review our entire Palestine policy. Otherwise, the President was convinced there would be bloodshed between Arabs and Jews and "some formula, not yet discovered, would have to be evolved to prevent this." [13] Unfortunately, this formula was never to be revealed; but the President's comment was prescient.

When the President got home he appeared before a joint session of Congress to report on the Yalta Conference. In speaking of his meeting with Ibn Saud he remarked in an aside that he had learned more in five minutes about the Jewish problem—he did not say the Palestine problem, but the Jewish problem—than he would have learned in a lengthy exchange of letters. [14] This remark, which was certainly injudicious, caused an uproar in Zionist circles. Rabbi Wise asked for an early interview with the President.

Meanwhile, on March 3, Colonel Hoskins had another talk with Roosevelt, who again outlined his ideas for a postwar trusteeship for Palestine. During this conversation, the President told Hoskins that he "fully agreed that a Jewish state in Palestine could be installed and maintained only by force."

At about this time, King Ibn Saud approached the leaders of the other Arab states, suggesting that they send the President a collective protest with respect to Zionist intentions toward Palestine. This led to the President's receiving seven such letters, from Ibn Saud, the Regent of Iraq (Emir Abdul Ilah), the Emir Abdullah of Trans-Jordan, President Shukry Kuwwatly of Syria, the Imam Yahya (King of Yemen), the Prime Minister of Lebanon (Abdul Hamid Karame), and the Prime Minister of Egypt (Mahmoud Fahmy Nokrashy). Although not necessarily identical, these messages were to be "similar" and "simultaneous," as explained by the Iraqi Foreign Minister in a conversation with Minister Loy W. Henderson.

Typical of these communications was the letter from the Iraqi Regent, who told the President that "the Jews want to have Palestine only as a means for their future domination of the whole Arab world," that Palestine occupied a key position in the heart of the Arab nation which would "obstruct Arab unity, should it be in the hands of non-Arabs," and that "the Arabs, individually and collectively, regard the future of Palestine as a matter of life and death."[15] These were strong words, but they were characteristic of the Arab attitude that was developing.

To Ibn Saud, in a letter which we drafted in NE and which he signed on April 5 (just one week before he died), Roosevelt reaffirmed the assurances which he had given the King during their meeting at the Great Bitter Lake (see Appendix K).[16]

Rabbi Wise saw Roosevelt on March 16 and emerged from the White House to tell the waiting newsmen that the President stood by his October 15 pledge to Wagner. This led to further Arab protests. From Baghdad, our Chargé, who had taken over the Legation on Henderson's departure to succeed Wallace Murray in the Department, reported that the Prime Minister of Iraq had asked him to convey to the U.S. government the "keen disappointment" of the Iraqi government. From Damascus, our Chargé reported that as a result of Rabbi Wise's statement, students in the city had gone on strike and many telegrams of protest had been received. One of these, for example, charged that "the Zionist movement is a movement of colonization, the object of which is to take Palestine by force from the Arabs"—an action which, it was alleged, would be "contradictory to the principles of the Atlantic Charter."[17]

NE was again called upon to devise a reply. After obtaining confirmation from Jonathan Daniels, Roosevelt's press secretary, that the President had in fact authorized Wise to quote him in the sense reported, we came up with an explanation, which Roosevelt approved, to the effect that in talking to Wise he was of course keeping in mind our assurances that there should be no change in the basic situation without full consultation with both Arabs and Jews. Moreover, the Rabbi's statement to the press had referred merely to "possible action at some future time."

In forwarding this formula to Acting Secretary Joseph C. Grew, for submission to the President, we underlined our anxieties about the direction that U.S. Palestine policy was taking. Our memorandum pointed out that a statement of the sort that the President had allowed Rabbi Wise to make would result in undoing to a considerable degree the good effect of the President's meeting with King Ibn Saud. We added that the President's continued support of Zionist objectives might have the most far-reaching consequences as far as our interests in the Arab world were concerned—specifically our immensely valuable oil concession in Saudi Arabia.

In early April, in a second memorandum we reviewed the course of our policy from 1942 on. We expressed the view that the present trend of events might have "disastrous" consequences and we urged that the United States, with the President's concurrence, should adopt a definite policy toward the Palestine problem and adhere strictly to that policy, so as to avoid future trouble. This recommendation, however, was overtaken by the President's death.[18]

Concurrently, the situation on the various war fronts was one of continuing Allied gains. In late February, our Marines had landed on Iwo Jima. The invasion of Okinawa began on April 1. In Europe, our forces crossed the Rhine at the Remagen bridgehead on March 7 and reached the Elbe April 11. Vienna was liberated April 9. By this time, Roosevelt and Churchill had become increasingly concerned at Soviet breaches of the Yalta agreement respecting Poland.

At the end of March, unknown to us, the President had gone to Warm Springs, Georgia. It is now known that his physical condition had deteriorated sharply, and indeed this is confirmed by his completely illegible signature on papers in the files. On the evening of April 11, Secretary of the Treasury Morgenthau, an old friend, visited him at Warm Springs and was shocked at his appearance; his hands shook and Morgenthau could not be certain that he was really focusing on the matter which was the occasion of Morgenthau's visit—the future of Germany.[19]

At noon the next day, April 12, Roosevelt was having his portrait painted by Mme. Elizabeth Shoumatoff while he was signing his mail. It happened that the mail pouch that day contained some of the replies which we had prepared in answer to the Arab representations mentioned above. One account of Roosevelt's last hours tells how the President picked up one of these letters and read it. Then his face brightened. "A typical State Department letter," he remarked, looking pleased, to his secretary William D. Hassett, "it says nothing at all." We are not told which of the letters this was, but his comment, in a superficial sense, could apply to any of our familiar drafts reaffirming the "full consultation" formula. In a deeper sense these letters performed a very valuable service for the President and he knew it very well.

It was while he was engaged in this task that the President paused and said to Mme. Shoumatoff: "I have a terrific headache." He had suffered his fatal attack and was dead within a couple of hours. A rather gruesome outcome of this episode was that the letters that Roosevelt had signed were returned to us for dispatch to their addressees, though we were asked by the White House to do over the remainder for the new President's signature.[20]

As a sidelight to this account, when our Minister to Syria and Lebanon,

George Wadsworth, handed Roosevelt's letter to the President of Syria, the latter observed that it must be the only paper the President had signed on the day of his death. He offered to give it back to the United States government as a document of great historical significance. Wadsworth gently apprised Kuwwatly of the facts regarding the volume of Presidential mail.

ROOSEVELT'S CONTRIBUTION TO OUR PALESTINE POLICY

Roosevelt had the same liberal and humanitarian outlook as did many Americans of the Jewish faith and it was therefore natural that he should tend to sympathize with their attitude on the Palestine question. He was also well aware that most American Jews voted for him.[21]

At the same time, he knew the situation in the Middle East very well and he realized the complications that could result from our following a pro-Zionist policy or from injecting the issue into American politics. I quoted in the preceding chapter from his 1944 letter to Congressman Sam Rayburn on this very point. He also realized that bloodshed would result from any attempt to set up a Jewish state in Palestine. This is evident from his comments to Celler, Wagner, and Hoskins, quoted above. He was likewise aware that not all Jews were Zionists. For example, among his papers on Palestine at the Roosevelt Library in Hyde Park is a pamphlet written by Rabbi Morris S. Lazaron, one of the founders of the anti-Zionist American Council for Judaism, which Roosevelt had read and initialed.

There seems little doubt that Roosevelt was convinced that after the war he would be able to bring about a settlement between the Arabs and Jews, just as he thought he would be able to handle the Russians.[22] He was supremely confident of the magic of his personality, of his ability to conciliate conflicting points of view. Shortly before his death he told Frances Perkins, his Secretary of Labor and a close friend, that "the reason the Near East is so explosive is because the people are poor. . . . When I get through being President and this damn war is over, I think Eleanor and I will go out to the Near East and see if we can put over an operation like the Tennessee Valley system that will really make something of that country."[23]

After Yalta, Roosevelt also told his wife: "You know, Eleanor, I've seen so much now of the Near East, when we get through here I believe I'd like to go there and live. I feel quite an expert. I believe I could help to straighten out the Near East."[24]

Several of Roosevelt's associates, including Hull, Welles, and Herbert Feis, have recorded their belief that Roosevelt intended to devote his attention after the war to finding a settlement of the Palestine dispute. On the specifics of the problem he was thinking (as previously explained) of a trusteeship in which the world's three great monotheistic religions would participate, under the auspices of the new United Nations. Details of his ideas are not known, and were probably never elaborated.[25]

Roosevelt had a tendency to discount the strength of the Arab attachment to Palestine. In the early 1940s he spoke of moving the Palestine Arabs elsewhere and hinted that all Arabs were amenable to bribery. His meeting with Ibn Saud, however, changed his mind on this score.

An element in Roosevelt's attitude toward Palestine is the extent to which Rabbi Wise, a friend of long standing and an active Democrat, influenced him. In their correspondence, which commenced in 1929, Wise refers to Roosevelt as "the Chief" or "the Boss." The correspondence contains not only the usual birthday messages and "get well" letters on the part of Wise, but also many expressions of political support. Employing a favorite Zionist technique, Wise would frequently send a message to the President through one of Roosevelt's secretaries with the request that it be put on the President's desk. In one instance he asked Missy LeHand, Roosevelt's long-time private secretary, to place his letter "under the Chief's stamp album" where he would be sure to see it. Sometimes he slipped up, as when in early 1945 we find him telegraphing frantically to one of the secretaries saying that a previous telegram had "by inadvertence" been addressed to the President direct and asking that it be retrieved and brought to Roosevelt's personal attention.

Wise of course made frequent use of this channel of communication to advocate the Zionist point of view. The file is full of requests for messages to be read at Zionist rallies, and briefing papers and background memoranda on Palestine. Sometimes the two met without anyone else's being present. In April 1944, Grace Tully, Roosevelt's private secretary at that time, complained that no one knew what had transpired when the Rabbi had come in a few days before to talk to the President about Palestine.

There were a few instances where Justice Felix Frankfurter, a dedicated Zionist, brought the Palestine question to the President's notice, but generally Frankfurter preferred to remain in the background as far as Palestine policy was concerned. For example, he never accompanied the Zionist leaders when they called on the President or the Secretary of State.[26]

In many ways President Roosevelt's handling of the Palestine question remains an enigma. He left no coherent policy for his successor and some of his statements and actions are difficult to understand. Most American Jews thought of him during his lifetime as a strong supporter of the Zionist cause and on his death he was eulogized by Zionist leaders like Rabbi Wise and Rabbi Israel Goldstein. In more recent years, however, others have voiced their doubts. Jacques Torczyner, president of the Zionist Organization of America, said flatly in 1968 that Roosevelt was "not a friend" of the movement, and another Zionist leader, Nahum Goldmann, described him in

1969 as "not actually pro-Zionist" (Goldmann was not even sure where Roosevelt had stood on the question of a Jewish state). The most revealing comment of all comes from David K. Niles, an influential adviser on Palestine to both Roosevelt and Truman, who in 1962 expressed doubts that Israel would have come into being if Roosevelt had lived.[27]

The fact is that Roosevelt, with his political acumen and his uncanny ability to maneuver, was able to follow a course of action which did not fully commit him to either side in the dispute. His immense prestige made it possible for him to maintain this position to the end.

Roosevelt's handling of the Palestine question has to be viewed against the background of the war years and the great decisions that he was called upon to make. In this context, the Middle East, important as it was steadily becoming to the United States, played a completely minor role. There is scarcely a reference to the area, much less to Palestine itself, in the voluminous wartime correspondence between Roosevelt and Churchill.

Another point that should be borne in mind is that the nature of the Palestine problem was different in those days. The issue had not assumed great dimensions, the crunch was not yet on; the massive pressures centering around the issue of the Jewish displaced persons, as well as the closing of the ranks of the American Jewish community behind the Zionists, all came later, under Truman. In any event it was generally agreed, both in Washington and in London, that a solution for the Palestine problem would have to await the end of the war. This being so, it made sense for us to say, as we did in March 1945, that the President's endorsement of a Jewish state referred to "possible action at some future time."

Would there have been a Jewish state in Palestine if Roosevelt had lived? Was Niles correct in the assessment cited above? The answer depends on a number of imponderables: whether Roosevelt would have been able indefinitely to avoid coming down on one side or the other, whether the postwar pressures would have been as irresistible for him as they proved to be for President Truman, and whether the climate of the postwar world would have been different. It is possible that Roosevelt and Churchill, with Stalin's acquiescence, might have been able to pull off a compromise Palestine settlement where Truman and Attlee failed, but this is doubtful at best. It would certainly have required considerable use of force. It seems more likely, for reasons which will emerge as this story continues, that as a result of the unremitting pressures that developed, as well as the international situation prevailing in the immediate postwar period, the Jewish state was bound to come.

President Truman and the 100,000 Jews

The death of President Roosevelt and the accession of Harry S. Truman to the Presidency brought to that office a man with a fresh approach to the handling of the Palestine problem. Truman was immensely moved by the plight of the Jewish displaced persons in Europe. As he put it in his *Memoirs*: "the fate of the Jewish victims of Hitlerism was a matter of deep personal concern to me."[1] He was impressed by the argument that the solution to the problem of the Jewish refugees lay in their being allowed to go to Palestine. He was also influenced by his background in the Bible—his daughter tells us in her book on Truman that he had read the Bible through twice by the time he was twelve years of age.

Truman drew many of his liberal and humanitarian ideals from Woodrow Wilson, whom he greatly admired. Referring to the Balfour Declaration in his *Memoirs*, he says that he had always considered the Declaration to be an extension of Wilson's principle of self-determination. The statement seems naïve, since the application of self-determination to Palestine would also have had to work to the benefit of the Arabs; and it also seems naïve of him to express surprise, as he does elsewhere in the *Memoirs*, that some of us in the State Department should have had the view that the Arabs were opposed to the carrying out of the Balfour Declaration. This latter remark, incidentally, is hardly consistent with Truman's earlier acknowledgment that he was "fully aware of the Arabs' hostility to Jewish settlement in Palestine."[2]

Truman explains in his *Memoirs* that he drew a distinction in this thinking between the short-range objective of refugee relief and the longer-range problem of the future of Palestine. From the start, he considered the Zionist goal of a Jewish state to be of secondary importance, and it was not until October 1947, or about two and a half years after becoming President, that he finally decided to commit the U.S. government to the creation of a Jewish state. Throughout, he was determined, as he said frequently, that the United States was not going to send American troops to enforce any particular solution in Palestine. He does not appear to have seen any inconsistency between such a position and the virtual certainty that a Jewish state in Palestine could only be achieved through the use of force.

Being a highly experienced politician, Truman was well aware of how much political influence the American Jews exerted. This explains, for example, his insistence, in 1945, on deferring until after the New York City elections the receiving of four of our chiefs of mission from the Near East, who had already been waiting some four weeks to see him.[3] We often told ourselves in NE that if it was not a Presidential year or a Congressional year, it was a mayoral election year in New York. The four representatives in question (S. Pinkney Tuck, George Wadsworth, William A. Eddy, and Lowell C. Pinkerton) finally saw the President on November 10. According to Colonel Eddy, Truman explained frankly: "I'm sorry, gentlemen, but I have to answer to hundreds of thousands who are anxious for the success of Zionism: I do not have hundreds of thousands of Arabs among my constituents."[4] This was certainly the plain speaking for which Truman was famous. Truman also kept on his desk for a whole year the *pro forma* resignations of these same envoys before deciding to continue them in office.

On balance, it has to be said that Truman's handling of the Palestine question was very considerably influenced by domestic political considerations. Indeed, Dr. Emmanuel Neumann, the Zionist leader, conceded frankly in a 1953 article that Truman would never have gone so far in the direction of supporting the Zionist position if it had not been for "the prospect of wholesale defections from the Democratic Party."[5]

Truman was influenced in his handling of the issue by three members of his White House staff: Samuel I. Rosenman, David K. Niles, and Clark Clifford. These men supported the Zionist point of view and played key roles in our policy on Palestine.[6] In addition, there was Eddie Jacobson, Truman's former haberdashery partner who was an intimate friend with ready access to the White House. Jacobson's role, however, requires some clarification. He declared at one point that he had never been a member of any Zionist organization and Truman likewise says in his *Memoirs* that Jacobson "had never been a Zionist." Indeed, Jacobson does not appear to have shown any particular interest in the Palestine problem until after Truman became President. Then the Zionists, because of his close connection with Truman, began using him as a go-between with the President. This naturally led to their attempting to win Jacobson over to their point of view. From time to time, Jacobson talked to the President about the Palestine question, often in the company of A. J. Granoff, a long-time Kansas City friend of Truman's and Jacobson's, who has described how, when he and Jacobson went to the White House, the President would pull out of his right-hand desk drawer a foot-thick file on Palestine which he kept there. Until the fall of 1947 it appears that Jacobson's intervention with the President was concerned mainly with getting the gates of Palestine opened to Jewish refugees. By that time, the Palestine question had come before the United Nations General Assembly, and he was certainly one of those who urged the President to support partition. In the spring of 1948 he was evidently in favor of prompt recognition of the new Jewish state. The period of his greatest influence, however, was after Israel came into being, when he frequently served as an intermediary between Truman and the Israeli government.[7]

In June 1945, soon after acceding to the Presidency, Truman replaced Stettinius, who had been Secretary only since November 1944, with James F. Byrnes. Joseph C. Grew, who had served as Stettinius's Under Secretary, was succeeded by Dean Acheson. During Secretary Byrnes's tenure, the role of the Department in Palestinian affairs changed considerably. Byrnes's attitude was one of washing his hands of the problem as much as possible and leaving it to the President and Acheson to handle.[8] The result was naturally to diminish the authority of the Department in decisions respecting Palestine and to enhance that of the White House.

Within the Department, there were other changes. Early in 1945 Wallace Murray became Ambassador to Iran, ending his long period of supervision of the Department's Near Eastern work. He was succeeded by Loy W. Henderson, then serving as Minister at Baghdad.

Truman's first weeks in office were marked by a series of dramatic events in the European war. Within ten days of Roosevelt's death, the Russians were at the gates of Berlin and soon had encircled the city. The historic meeting between American and Russian forces at the Elbe River took place on April 25. Hitler and Eva Braun committed suicide in their bunker on April 30 and Berlin fell to the Russians on May 2, the same day that the German forces in Italy surrendered (Mussolini had been shot by partisans on April 26). The remaining German forces surrendered May 7 and V-E Day was celebrated May 8.

When Truman took over the Presidency, he was almost totally in the dark as to Roosevelt's policies—he had seen Roosevelt only eight times since his nomination as Vice-President the previous July. His term as Vice-President had lasted 82 days, and during this time Roosevelt had been in Washington less than 30 days. Truman became President on the evening of April 12, and on the morning of April 13 we pointed out to Secretary Stettinius that the Zionists would attempt at once to extract some commitment from the new President and that he ought therefore to be briefed on our Palestine policy as soon as possible. A memorandum in which we urged caution in any contacts with the Zionists went to the President on April 18, and two days later Rabbi Wise came to see him. Our memorandum is the one which Truman later described as "a communication from the 'striped pants' boys warning me to watch my step, as I really didn't know what was going on there and ought to leave it to the experts." This seems hardly fair, especially when I recall that our paper had been reviewed by Assistant Secretary James Clement Dunn, a diplomat of wide experience, who was one of the ablest drafting officers in the Department.[9]

It is typical of Truman's approach that he was looking forward to his meeting with Wise because he had always been interested in Palestine on account of its biblical associations. He realized, of course, that Wise had not come to see him to talk about the Bible, and when the subject of Palestine came up he was careful to limit himself to a generalized assurance that he would continue Roosevelt's policy.

Under date of May 1, a more detailed memorandum prepared in NE, with the background of the "full consultation" formula and of Roosevelt's pledge to Ibn Saud, went over to the White House. The papers of Presidential Counsel Samuel Rosenman at the Harry S. Truman Library reveal that Truman referred this memorandum to Rosenman for advice, but there is no record of Rosenman's reply. In any event, in the first few weeks of his Presidency, Truman, acting on the Department's recommendation, signed several letters to Arab leaders reiterating the U.S. position on consultation. The early months of Truman's Presidency represented the last time that the Department exercised a dominant role in our Palestine policy.

The Zionists were active in connection with the Conference at San Francisco in April, May, and June which set up the postwar United Nations Organization. Both the American Jewish Conference (Zionist) and the American Jewish Committee (non-Zionist) were named as consultants to the United States delegation. The Zionists were particularly interested in the Conference because President Roosevelt, in his last talk with Rabbi Wise in March, had apparently hinted that the Palestine question would come up at the Conference. It was evident, in any event, that some arrangements were going to have to be made regarding the termination of the mandate system.

The Zionists were also interested in the Conference because a number of Arab states were to be represented and it could be anticipated that they would promote the Arab point of view, as in fact they did. In addition to the American Jewish organizations mentioned, the Jewish Agency was represented by an observer who submitted a memorandum to the Conference urging that nothing be done to prejudice the "special rights of the Jewish people under the Balfour Declaration and the Palestine Mandate." After some debate, during which the Arab delegates sought to water down the language of Article 80 of the new UN Charter, dealing with the trusteeship system, a text was adopted into which the Zionists succeeded in getting inserted some wording which they indicated would be acceptable and which spoke of the rights of "any states or any peoples."[10]

The Palestine issue as such, however, did not come up at the Conference. Our delegation had with it the same position paper that had been taken to Yalta and it was again not used. Furthermore, regardless of whatever Roosevelt may have said to Rabbi Wise (and I have found no official record of their conversation), the Zionists had been put on notice that the Palestine question was not going to be discussed at San Francisco. Churchill had so stated in the House of Commons on February 27. With the ending of the war in Europe, Weizmann wrote the Prime Minister urging immediate implementation of the full Biltmore Program. The reply, dated June 9, in characteristic Churchillian style, went: "There can, I fear, be no possibility of the question being effectively considered until the victorious Allies are definitively seated at the Peace Table."[11] The Charter was signed at San Francisco, June 26, 1945, and approved overwhelmingly by the United States Senate on July 28.

Following the end of the war in Europe, preparations were made for a conference at Potsdam between Truman, Churchill, and Stalin. Our briefing paper for the conference contains a recommendation that the President should not press the Zionist point of view, as he was being urged to do, but should confine himself to inquiring as to the British government's intentions respecting Palestine.[12] Although Truman initialed "OK" on this paper, he did not follow the Department's advice. Instead he wrote to Churchill during the meeting urging that the White Paper restrictions be lifted. Clement Attlee, who had unexpectedly replaced Churchill as Prime Minister, replied that the matter would require careful consideration.

Just after arriving at Potsdam, Truman received word that the first test explosion of an atomic bomb had been carried out successfully at Alamogordo, New Mexico, thus ushering in the atomic age. The bomb was dropped on Hiroshima August 6 and on Nagasaki August 9, leading to the Japanese surrender on August 14 and to the end of the war on V-J Day, August 15. The Russians, pursuant to a pledge given by Stalin to Roosevelt at Yalta, had declared war on Japan on August 8—after Hiroshima and before Nagasaki.

After returning from Potsdam, the President was asked at a press conference on August 16 whether Palestine had been discussed there. He replied that he had discussed it with both Churchill and Attlee and went on to say, "We want to let as many Jews into Palestine as possible," although the matter would of course have to be "worked out diplomatically" with the British and the Arabs as he had "no desire to send half a million American soldiers to keep the peace in Palestine."[13] Expecting that this would lead to inquiries from Arab leaders, we prepared a circular telegram which went out to our representatives in the field, instructing them not to comment on the President's remarks or interpret them in any way.[14] That this was as far as we felt we could go shows how the State Department was losing control over

Palestine policy to the White House, a process that began with Truman's approach to Churchill mentioned above.

The Arab reaction was not long in coming. The Egyptian and Syrian diplomatic representatives in Washington called at the Department to express concern and to ask for clarification of the President's remarks about letting as many Jews as possible into Palestine. They were told we could not comment. A similar response was made by our Chargé in Baghdad to Fadhil al-Jamali, the director general of the Iraqi Foreign Ministry, a graduate of the American University at Beirut who was generally regarded as friendly to the United States. Jamali asserted: "The Arabs will resist a Jewish state in Palestine by any means whatsoever." Our Minister to Syria and Lebanon (Wadsworth) reported that the government of Lebanon, while making strong efforts to prevent the launching of a new anti-Zionist and anti-American campaign in the press, was apprehensive as to U.S. intentions.[15]

An offshoot of Truman's press conference was that Henderson got the Secretary's approval to ask the War Department for an estimate of how large a force would be needed to maintain order in Palestine in the event of Arab disorders following the lowering of the bars to Jewish immigration. The War Department's reply, dated September 19, stated that a force of 400,000 men, of which the United States would need to provide 200,000 to 300,000, would be required. This would mean an "indefinite delay" in our demobilization (already under way) and would have repercussions on the occupation of Germany and Japan.[16]

The thinking in NE at the time as far as Palestine was concerned emerges from a rather bland paper prepared under date of July 30 for a Congressional party that was visiting the Near East. This paper characterizes our Palestine policy as being "of a general and tentative character," based on the principle of an equitable solution, "with full consultation with both Arabs and Jews." The paper continues: "at the same time, our Government is doing all it can to help the Jewish refugees." In conclusion, we predicted that "serious trouble may be anticipated in Palestine.[17]

Meanwhile the President had decided to send Earl G. Harrison, the U.S. representative on the Intergovernmental Committee on Refugees, to inquire into the situation in the displaced persons camps in Europe, with particular respect to the Jewish inmates of the camps. Harrison reported that these Jews wanted to go to Palestine, and he recommended that 100,000 immigration certificates should be made available for this purpose, as had been proposed to the British government by the Jewish Agency. The President on August 31 sent Harrison's report to Attlee with a letter that was to have far-reaching consequences. Truman endorsed Harrison's findings and urged the speedy evacuation of as many as possible of the displaced Jews to Palestine.[18]

Truman forwarded the Harrison report not only to Prime Minister Attlee but also to General Dwight D. Eisenhower, the American commander in chief in Europe, who reported to the President that many of Harrison's findings with respect to the conditions under which the displaced Jews were living in the camps in Europe were either out of date or exaggerated.[19]

It is illustrative of the way in which the Palestine problem was being handled by this time that nearly a month later the Near East Division was seeking confirmation of press reports that the President had written Attlee on the subject. When we sought permission from Acting Secretary Acheson to query the White House, he was reluctant to have us do so, even when we pointed out that, ironically enough, through a bureaucratic mixup the White House had sent us Attlee's reply for action! (Acheson evidently felt that the matter was such a delicate one that it should await the return of Secretary Byrnes, who was in London attending a meeting of the Council of Foreign Ministers.) We also urged, unsuccessfully, as it turned out, that every effort should be made to clarify U.S. policy on Palestine, in view of the explosive potentialities in the situation.

The disarray into which our policy had fallen by this time is further revealed by the fact that Acheson had to telegraph Byrnes in London to say that a delegation of prominent Zionists had called on him to ask about rumors they had heard to the effect that Truman had been in touch with Attlee about Palestine. Acheson had told the Jewish leaders that he knew nothing of the matter. Byrnes in reply suggested that if Acheson were again approached by the Zionists he could say that the President had indeed written the Prime Minister, but that he did not know any details and that "information on the subject of that correspondence could be obtained only from the President or Mr. Attlee."[20]

Truman's letter reached Attlee at a time when the British government was debating what to do about the Palestine question, as it was obvious that with the end of the war it was necessary to make some decisions. The Labour Party, prior to the election which brought it to power in the summer of 1945, had endorsed a strongly pro-Zionist program, including a proposal for moving the Palestine Arabs to other parts of the Middle East. On assuming the responsibilities of office, however, the Labour leaders realized that a more restrained course of action was indicated. The weight of expert opinion, inside and outside the government, was that British strategic interests in the Middle East were so important that Great Britain could not afford to alienate the Arab world. This meant that partition, which as we have seen had been under consideration since 1943, was out of the question. The White Paper quota, which had been extended through the war years, was about to be exhausted and it was decided to continue Jewish immigration for the time being at the existing rate of 1,500 per month, it was hoped with Arab consent, while considering what the long-range solution would be.[21] Presumably, in this process of coming to a decision, the United States would at some point have to be consulted.

Attlee, therefore, seized upon Truman's message to respond with a proposal that the two governments should set up a joint body to examine the position of the Jews in Europe and the situation in Palestine. This led to the appointment of the Anglo-American Committee of Inquiry, of which I was to become one of the secretaries. The new committee was announced November 13, at which time the President made public his letter to Attlee. On repeated urging from the President, the British finally agreed that the main focus of the inquiry would be on Palestine, rather than the European Jews, and that the committee would be required to submit its report within 120 days. It was also agreed that the committee would be composed of six British and six American members, with a rotating chairmanship. The members were to be individuals of standing who had had no previous connection with the Palestine problem. The British announced that pending the result of the inquiry, Jewish immigration would continue at the 1,500 monthly rate.[22]

When the British proposal for a joint inquiry was received, Rosenman advised Truman to reject it. He pointed out that the timing of the proposal, coming as it did just before the election in New York City, was unfortunate. He expressed his full agreement with Rabbi Wise and Rabbi Silver, who had telegraphed the President objecting to the proposal on the ground that it represented merely a delaying tactic.[23] The Arabs likewise were suspicious of the project, and of the decision to continue Jewish immigration.

In October, the President received an urgent request from King Ibn Saud that the King's correspondence with President Roosevelt be made public. Rosenman was against such action but the President finally agreed with Byrnes that the Department (though not the White House) should publish Roosevelt's April 5 letter (see Appendix K) with a brief statement reiterating the "full consultation" formula. Subsequently, Roosevelt's exchanges with some of the other Arab leaders were made public in the Arab world. This lifting of the veil of the "full consultation" formula led to a statement (as previously explained) on the part of the American Zionist Emergency Council that the Arabs had no standing in the matter, but on the whole the Zionist reaction was restrained.[24]

As confirmation spread of Truman's approach to Attlee regarding the 100,000 Jews, Arab protests started coming in. The Prime Minister of Iraq handed a note to our Chargé d'Affaires saying that if the reports of Truman's approach to Attlee were to be confirmed, this would be "contrary to all the promises and undertakings, oral and written, which have been given to the Arabs that the U.S. would take no action with regard to Palestine without consulting the Arabs." He added: "The strength and military power of the U.S. is more than sufficient to compel the Arabs to acquiesce in any policy which the U.S. may impose . . . If this is the case, why all these charters and pledges, to which America has bound itself, for safeguarding human rights and liberties? . . . We do not wish at all to believe that Zionist influence in America can reverse facts so as to make right wrong and wrong right."[25] A few days later, the Iraqi press carried an article by Jamali, in which he declared that President Truman's attitude was one of "frank hostility" toward the Arabs.

The Emir Abdullah of Trans-Jordan cabled the President on September 29 referring to assurances he had received from both Roosevelt and Truman regarding "full consultation" and urging that the admission of 100,000 more Jews into Palestine would be an important matter requiring consultation with the Arabs. The Legation at Damascus also forwarded to Washington an *aide-mémoire* from the Syrian Ministry for Foreign Affairs expressing sympathy with the homeless Jewish refugees and saying the Arabs were willing to share in "any humanitarian scheme which helps persecuted Jews to secure a peaceful life." The note declared, however, that "one injury cannot be removed by another even more harmful" and that "in this case we shall be face to face with the Zionist Nazism against the Arabs instead of a German Nazism against the Jews."[26] The four Arab diplomatic representatives in Washington called jointly twice on Under Secretary Acheson and once on Secretary Byrnes to protest the recent developments.

Under date of October 23 the Department sent out a circular to its representatives in the Near East explaining (in words which began to have a familiar ring) that in making his approach to Attlee the President was, of course, keeping in mind the well-known policy of the United States with regard to consultation. The message added that there had been no change in that position. Later in the year our envoys were told that they should take the position that "consultation" did not mean "agreement."

The issue of the 100,000 Jews remained a burning one for many months. Rosenman told the President that their admission to Palestine would not constitute a "basic change" in the situation, but the Department took a contrary view. This was spelled out in a memorandum dated October 2 which we prepared for the Acting Secretary to send to the President. It would certainly appear that our position was correct, since Jewish immigration into Palestine was still being regulated at the time by the White Paper, which had provided that a total of not more than 75,000 were to come in without Arab consent. At all events, as will emerge later in this account, the British never did authorize the 100,000 to go to Palestine.

With further respect to the 100,000 Jews, it can be seen that at the rate of 1,500 per month or 18,000 per year, it would have taken just under six years for this number to have been admitted to Palestine. Actually, by January 1, 1945, a total of 76,251 Jews had entered Palestine legally since January 1, 1939, or some 1,251 over the maximum of 75,000 fixed in the 1939 White Paper for those who were to be allowed to come in without Arab consent.

It follows that the *immediate* admission of 100,000 more displaced Jews (which is what Harrison and Truman were asking) would certainly have been a "basic change" in the situation, as our memorandum of October 2 pointed out. In the event, a further 73,282 were admitted from all sources between January 1, 1945, and May 14, 1948, when Israel became independent, so that by the end of the Mandate more than twice as many had been admitted as had been foreseen in the White Paper. Not all of these would have been displaced persons.[27]

During the year 1945, the State Department's professionals, joined by James Forrestal, Secretary of the Navy and later Secretary of Defense, submitted a number or warnings as to the consequences of our government's pursuing a pro-Zionist policy. With the handling of the Palestine question passing more and more to the White House, it is not surprising that the members of the Near East Division should have devoted increasing time to the preparation of comprehensive postwar plans and policy studies—ten in all during 1945.[28] Many of these papers were drafted by William Yale, who by then had moved from the Division of Territorial Studies to the Near East Division, although several of us, including Merriam and myself, also had a hand in preparing them. By coincidence, one of the most elaborate of these plans (dated August 24) went forward to the Secretary just as the President, unbeknownst to us, was writing Attlee about the 100,000.[29] This was essentially the proposal for trusteeship, with autonomy for the Jewish and Arab communities, mentioned in Chapters 2 and 3 above, and summarized in Appendix J. Henderson's covering memorandum to the Secretary urged that our government should attempt to reach agreement with Great Britain, the Soviet Union, and France, on a plan of this sort and should then consult the Jews and Arabs before it was put into effect. Otherwise, he foresaw "years of political instability in Palestine and the Near East." Commenting on this proposal in his memoirs, Acheson remarks: "There is no record that this advice ever reached the President or that it would have worked if attempted, but it was surely a shrewd sighting of troubles to come and worth careful thought."[30]

The effect of these papers on the actual development of U.S. Palestine policy is conjectural, but we could at least take some comfort from the knowledge that we had flagged the difficulties that lay ahead.

I have already noted in the Introduction that with the outbreak of war in 1939, Jewish terrorist activity in Palestine had declined to a low level, as had illegal immigration. By the end of the war, as the British government continued to give no sign of repealing the White Paper or indeed of proposing any solution for the basic problems of the country, terrorism and illegal immigration began to intensify. The causes were the White Paper itself, with its implied denial of a fundamental article of faith among Zionists that all Jews had the right to go to Palestine, and the Holocaust, the slaughter of the Jews in Europe, which together produced in many of the Jewish community in Palestine a feeling of disillusionment and despair, even of desperation, and the conviction grew that they would have to take matters into their own hands.

In September 1945, the Jewish Agency Executive authorized its clandestine military arm, the Haganah, to participate in sabotage and similar activites along with the other underground organizations, the Irgun and the Stern Gang. A Haganah telegram dealing with this subject was intercepted by the British authorities, leading to a stiffening of the official British attitude toward the Jewish Agency. The first combined operation took place on the night of October 31/November 1, when widespread bombing incidents occurred. The Palestine railway system was the main target. In November a special assembly of the Jewish community endorsed a decision by the Jewish Agency Executive to sponsor large-scale illegal immigration. Even Dr. Judah Magnes, the apostle of moderation, concurred.[31]

At about the same time as the appointment of the Anglo-American Committee of Inquiry was announced, a Roper poll of American Jews showed an overwhelming majority to be in favor of the Zionist goal of a Jewish state in Palestine. Of the nationwide cross-section of the Jewish community questioned, 80.1 percent said they would support a Jewish state, 10.5 percent were opposed, and only 9.4 percent—an unusually small proportion—had no opinion.[32]

In December, Truman issued a directive to a number of government agencies asking them to facilitate the admission of displaced persons into the United States. He pointed out that there were some 39,000 places immediately available under existing quotas which could be used by refugees from the camps in the U.S. zones in Austria and Germany. The President made it clear, however, that he was not seeking any change in our immigration quotas or proposing any new legislation. Such a development did not occur until two and a half years later, when a bill providing for the entry of up to 400,000 refugees from Europe was introduced into the Congress.

6
☆ ☆ ☆ ☆ ☆ ☆ ☆ ☆ ☆

The Abortive Attempt at Anglo–American Cooperation

The Anglo-American Committee of Inquiry was the seventeenth of the eighteen commissions sent out to examine the Palestine question during the period of the British mandate. Its appointment brought me a welcome opportunity to return to Palestine and to gain some firsthand knowledge of the current situation there. As a member of the staff of the committee I was for the next five months fully exposed to the Palestine problem in all its aspects—a fascinating if at times frustrating experience. Since three of the members of the committee have written books on the subject, I shall limit myself to giving some of my own impressions of the committee and to trying to put its mission into proper perspective in the development of our Palestine policy.

The committee began its mission at a time when, in various parts of the world, the newly achieved peace was being seriously threatened. The "Grand Alliance" of the Second World War was already a thing of the past, and the Soviet Union was putting pressure on Turkey with respect to the Turkish Straits (the Bosporus and the Dardanelles). Greece was in turmoil and was threatened by the Communist bloc all along its northern borders. Iran, too, where Soviet troops had been in occupation of the northern part of the country since 1941, was tense and uneasy and there had been numerous instances of Soviet interference in Iranian internal affairs. The Council of Foreign Ministers had agreed at its London meeting in September 1945 that all foreign troops would be withdrawn from Iran by the following March 2 (that is, six months after the Japanese surrender), but as the year drew to a close there was no sign that the Russians would comply. In China, relations between the Chinese Nationalists and Communists had deteriorated so alarmingly that President Truman had decided to send General George C. Marshall there with the mission of trying to unite the country by peaceful means.

As soon as it was known that the United States would participate with Great Britain in this joint inquiry, we in the Near East Division began to make our preparations. We compiled long lists of persons who might be suitable for appointment to the committee (only one of our choices was eventually accepted) and we started thinking about ways in which we might be of help to the members. I was taken off my regular desk work and put to working full time on these preparations. We knew that the two governments had agreed that the committee would be wholly independent and we were aware that our Division was regarded with suspicion in some circles in this country. Therefore it behooved us to approach the mission with considerable circumspection.

The American members assembled in Washington for the first time on December 14. They called on the President, were entertained at lunch by Acting Secretary Acheson, and then met with Henderson and myself. A great many decisions of an administrative as well as a policy nature had to be taken. Many of these points had been the subject of preliminary exchanges between the Department and the Foreign Office. For example, it had been agreed that the expenses of the inquiry would be divided equally between the two governments and that no member of the staff or of the committee should be of either Arab or Jewish extraction. One of the first things to which the American members turned their attention was the selection of staff. They readily concurred in our suggestion that their principal secretary should be chosen from outside the Department. (It turned out later that the British members had approached this question from exactly the same point of view.) A number of candidates for the position were interviewed and the choice fell on Leslie L. Rood, an attorney recently released from military service. I was asked to serve as the junior of the two American secretaries, with duties dealing primarily with research. When the full committee went into operation its total strength was thirty-eight. This included research staff, administrative and clerical personnel, and several court stenographers.

Though the British had wanted the inquiry to begin in London, they came round to our suggestion that the logical course would be to begin hearings in Washington and then proceed to London, to the Continent, and to the Middle East. Thus the British members came across to the United States right after the Christmas holidays.

The American members soon began to receive voluminous quantities of data from various interested parties, and obviously there was a need for them to be briefed about our policy. I selected the most important papers, classified and unclassified, and gave a set of most of these to each of the American members, though I retained the custody of one or two highly sensitive ones such as the record of the conversation between Roosevelt and King Ibn Saud.

The committee's documentation, including materials submitted by the parties and the verbatim transcripts of the hearings, grew steadily in volume as the hearings progressed. They were transported from place to place in a series of footlockers and are to be found today in a U.S. government depository at Suitland, Maryland, outside Washington.

An indication of the way in which we in NE tried to maintain a low profile vis-à-vis the committee, so as not to give rise to any charges that we were trying to influence it, can be seen in the fact that we did not at first submit to the American members any of our plans for the future of Palestine. However, when one of them inquired if we had not done any thinking on the subject, we came up with a set of papers (drafted by William Yale) outlining four alternative solutions (Jewish state, Arab state, partition, and trusteeship) of which we indicated a preference for the fourth (see previous chapter). I also gave the committee the July 30 memorandum regarding our policy toward Palestine, which characterized our policy as being general and tentative in nature, based on full consultation with both Arabs and Jews.

The personalities of the twelve members of the committee made it a highly interesting group of men. It had been agreed by the two governments that each side would have a judge as its chairman. These were Joseph C. Hutcheson of the U.S. Fifth Circuit Court and Sir John Singleton of the High Court of Justice. On the American side, the members included William Phillips, former Under Secretary of State and Ambassador to Italy, one of the most distinguished American diplomats of his generation, recently retired; Dr. Frank Aydelotte, secretary of the Rhodes Trust and former president of Swarthmore College; Frank Buxton, editor of the *Boston Herald*; Bartley C. Crum, a politically minded attorney from San Francisco, who had the reputation of being something of an opportunist; and James G. McDonald, former League of Nations High Commissioner for Refugees. The two last-named caused us some concern in the Near East Division as we were pretty certain that they were the personal choices of Presidential Adviser David K. Niles, and that their sympathies would be with the Zionists. It turned out, in fact, that McDonald (who later became the first American ambassador to Israel), had made a number of statements favorable to the Zionist cause. He and Crum were to give undisguised support to the Zionist position through-out the mission of the committee and afterward.

Outstanding among the British members were Richard Crossman, a brilliant Labour M.P. whom I had known at Oxford, and Sir Frederick Leggett, whose experience as a conciliator of labor disputes made him a particularly apt choice. The other British members were Wilfred Crick, economic adviser to Midland Bank; Major Reginald Manningham-Buller, (later Lord Dilhorne), a Conservative M.P.; and Lord Morrison, a recently created Labour peer. None of the twelve had been to Palestine and almost without exception they tended to be prima donnas in one way or another. [1]

The British team included my opposite number on the Foreign Office's Palestine desk, Harold (now Sir Harold) Beeley, whom I was anxious to meet. As I have explained in the Introduction, Beeley had already acquired an enviable reputation as an expert on the Middle East. As one of Ernest Bevin's most influential advisers he would become closely identified with British Palestine policy over the next few years. He later had a distinguished career in the British diplomatic service. I quickly developed a close working relationship with Beeley, who was encountering many of the same problems with his members as I was with mine.

Not only was it the case that the British and American members were suspicious of their respective foreign offices. Each side also was suspicious of the other at first. This was because the members reflected the attitudes of their governments toward the inquiry. The British saw it primarily as a means of getting the United States committed to a joint policy. They emphasized the Middle Eastern aspect, while the United States placed greater weight on the need for action concerning the homeless Jews of Europe. In the circumstances, it is remarkable that the committee should have functioned as well as it did and that a real sense of solidarity should have developed among these twelve highly divergent personalities. As one member put it, they worked as one committee, not two.

When the British members reached Washington early in the new year, hearings were held, beginning January 7, in the Indian Treaty Room of the old State Department. With some few exceptions, all the hearings throughout were open to the public and to the press. A verbatim record was taken down and distributed to the members during the evening after each session. (One member, Richard Crossman, estimated that by the end of the committee's travels the transcripts, evidence, and other data that he had accumulated weighed over two hundred pounds.) Judge Hutcheson and Justice Singleton presided on alternate days. The testimony unavoidably involved much repetition, which often made the members impatient and restive. [2]

The first witness in Washington, appropriately enough, was Earl Harrison, whose report calling for the admission of 100,000 Jews to Palestine had led to the formation of the committee. The American Zionists were represented by Rabbi Wise and Emmanuel Neumann, among others. They spoke along familiar lines. The non-Zionists were represented by Judge Joseph Proskauer, chairman of the American Jewish Committee, who made it clear that he was not advocating a Jewish state. He urged, however, that the displaced European Jews should be allowed to go to Palestine and that the country should be placed under United Nations trusteeship. Lessing Rosenwald, president of the American Council for Judaism, told the committee that the Jews were a religious group, not a nation. He opposed the concept of a Jewish state and was sharply questioned on this point by McDonald.

Proposals for the economic development of Palestine under Jewish auspices were put forward by the economists Robert Nathan and Oscar Gass, and by Walter C. Lowdermilk of the U.S. Soil Conservation Service, who spoke of a Jordan Valley Authority modeled on the Tennessee Valley Authority. The Arab case was presented—not as ably as the Jewish—by three persons of Arab extraction and several former missionaries, one of whom was Wilbert Smith of the YMCA, whom I had known in Cairo. Crossman remarks in his account that he was surprised that the Arab case was presented so inadequately in Washington. The chief argument of these witnesses was simply that Palestine had an Arab majority and ought to become an Arab state.

Of particular interest was the appearance of Albert Einstein (who was later to decline the offer of the presidency of Israel).[3] He told the committee that he was not in favor of a Jewish state. Another who appeared was Dr. Frank W. Notestein of the Office of Population Research at Princeton, who demonstrated that the rate of natural increase of the Palestine Arabs was so high that the Jews would probably never be able to achieve a majority.

In mid-January we proceeded to London, crossing the Atlantic on the *Queen Elizabeth*. During the passage, which was an extremely stormy one, the members had an opportunity to study their documents and to hold a number of discussions regarding the problems they were faced with. It was then that they began to operate as a single team.

In London, where conditions of austerity still prevailed, the committee held hearings in the underheated, drafty hall of the Royal Empire Society, which some thought an incongruous locale. Again, testimony, much of it repetitious, was taken (among others) from Zionist, non-Zionist, and anti-Zionist witnesses. The Zionist representatives were cross-examined by several members, notably Hutcheson, Crick, and Crossman, as to the implications of the idea of a Jewish state. They had some difficulty in explaining why an American Jew, for example, should have American nationality in the United States and Jewish nationality in Palestine: did this not confer on him a double nationality which other American citizens did not possess?

A feature of the London hearings was the appearance of a number of British officials with experience in Palestine and elsewhere in the Middle East (no similar group of American experts had been invited to testify in Washington). Among these were Lord Samuel, the first British High Commissioner for Palestine, and Sir Ronald Storrs, the first British Governor of Jerusalem, both of whom opposed partition. On the other hand, partition was favored by another former High Commissioner, Sir Harold MacMichael, and by L. S. Amery, former Secretary for India and for the Colonies. An Arab delegation, representing Syria, Iraq, Saudi Arabia, Lebanon, and Egypt, spoke for the Arab point of view. They said that they sympathized with the plight of the displaced Jews but did not see why the Arabs should be forced to "pay the price" of this. They maintained that not a single additional Jew should be allowed to come to Palestine.

The highlight of our stay in London was a luncheon given by Foreign Secretary Bevin, which we all attended. Bevin made a short speech, in the course of which he assured the members of the committee that if they came back with a unanimous report, he would do all in his power to carry it out, a remark that made a profound impression on the members and was very much in their minds when they were writing their report. In view of the controversy that later arose in some quarters over this statement it may be worth recording not only that I heard it, but also that Bevin himself confirmed to the House of Commons in late 1947 that he had made such a pledge to the committee.[4]

While we were in London I had the opportunity to attend one of the sessions of the historic first General Assembly of the United Nations, through arrangements made by George Wadsworth, our Minister to Syria and Lebanon, who was attached to the U.S. delegation.

After the London hearings, the committee split into subcommittees and spent several weeks visiting the displaced persons camps on the Continent. I did not participate in this phase of the mission but instead was sent ahead to the Middle East to prepare for the committee's visit. The members, from all accounts, readily ascertained that the overwhelming majority of the displaced Jews wanted to go to Palestine.

On February 28, the committee reassembled in Cairo to hear the testimony of Arab representatives. These hearings, lasting several days, took place at the Mena House Hotel, near the Pyramids (where the members were staying in conditions of some luxury), in the same room in which Roosevelt, Churchill, and Chiang Kai-shek had met in 1943. Here the members encountered for the first time the security precautions that were to be a constant part of their visit to the area. The principal spokesman for the Arab case was Azzam Pasha, secretary-general of the Arab League. Azzam's eloquent statement of the Arab case, including the reasons why the Arabs considered Zionism to be another form of Western colonialism, greatly impressed the committee. He spoke of the Jews as "brothers," or "cousins," who were no longer close kin:

> Our Brother has gone to Europe and to the West and come back something else. He has come back a Russified Jew, a Polish Jew, a German Jew, an English Jew. He has come back with a totally different conception of things, Western and not Eastern. That does not mean that we are necessarily quarreling with anyone who comes from the West. But the Jew, our old cousin, coming back with imperialistic ideas, with reactionary or revolutionary ideas and trying to implement them first by British pressure and then by American pressure, and then by terrorism on his own part—he is not the old cousin and we do not extend

to him a very good welcome. The Zionist, the new Jew, wants to dominate and he pretends that he has got a particular civilizing mission with which he returns to a backward, degenerate race in order to put the elements of progress into an area which has no progress. Well, that has been the pretension of every power that wanted to colonize and aimed at domination. The excuse has always been that the people are backward and that he has got a human mission to put them forward . . . the Arabs simply stand and say "NO." We are not reactionary and we are not backward. Even if we are ignorant, the difference between ignorance and knowledge is ten years in school. We are a living, vitally strong nation, we are in our renaissance; we are producing as many children as any nation in the world. We still have our brains. We have a heritage of civilization and of spiritual life. We are not going to allow ourselves to be controlled either by great nations or small nations or dispersed nations.[5]

Other Arab representatives who were heard in Cairo included Fadhil al-Jamali, who argued that his government saw no need for another commission to study the problem; Hassan al-Banna, leader of the fanatical Moslem Brotherhood, who claimed that the Koran tolerated Christians but not Jews; Sayed Ahmed Morad al-Bokri, a member of the Sufi sect of Moslem mystics, who declared that his group rejected Zionism in toto; and an Arab labor leader from Tunisia, Habib Bourghiba (later to become president of that country), who urged that the European Jews ought to stay where they were.

While in Cairo, the committee also met privately with Dr. John S. Badeau, president of the American University at Cairo, and with the British military authorities. Some members also held a private meeting with representatives of the local Jewish community, who had no hesitation in expressing their hostility to Zionism, and their desire to stay where they were. Similar views were later expressed to some members in Damascus by a delegation of Syrian Jews.

From Cairo we journeyed overnight to Jerusalem in the well-appointed special train of the High Commissioner for Palestine. As the train crossed the Palestine frontier in the early morning, a rainbow appeared in the sky and we took this as a good omen. It served somewhat to allay our anxiety at the ominous sight of the armed guards posted every two or three hundred yards apart along the entire railway line from the border to Jerusalem.

We soon found, in fact, that Palestine at this time was an armed camp. The security situation dominated everyone's life and the principal British officials traveled about with Jeeps fore and aft containing plainclothesmen with tommy guns. The offices provided for us by the Palestine government were surrounded by barbed wire and guards, and there were barbed wire and guards also at our hotel, the King David, and at the Jerusalem YMCA where the hearings were held, such precautions being considered necessary on account of the widespread Jewish terrorism that had been occurring. The terrorists had, however, announced at the time the Anglo-American Committee was set up that they would suspend operations during the course of the inquiry, and they held to that promise. There were no incidents while we were in Palestine, aside from one bomb threat, which though happily a false alarm, caused the speedy evacuation of our hearing room.

The Palestine government cooperated fully with the committee, providing several senior officials as liaison officers and supplying a large quantity of useful data. Soon after our arrival, the High Commissioner gave a reception in our honor at Government House. The gulf between the two communities became immediately apparent, since the Arabs boycotted the event, not wishing to associate with Jewish invited guests. This pattern came to be a familiar part of the Palestine scene and our activities had to be organized with Arabs and Jews separately, never together. The only exception occurred toward the end of our stay, when we were visiting the Crusader citadel of Acre in northern Palestine, then being used as an asylum for the criminally insane. In reply to our usual question whether these were Jews or Arabs, we were told, to our surprise, "both," leading to the obvious comment that in Palestine you don't have to be crazy to mix with the other community—but it helps.

Both the Arab and Jewish leadership had been of divided opinions on whether or not to cooperate with the committee, and each had decided in favor of cooperation by a fairly narrow margin. The hearings attracted a great deal of attention, on the part not only of the Arab and Jewish communities but of the foreign community, and there were many complaints that the forty-one seats provided for the general public were insufficient.

The atmosphere on the first day of hearings, March 8, was tense. The members sat around the same curved table that had been used by the Peel Commission in 1937. The first witness was Dr. Chaim Weizmann, head of the World Zionist Organization and later to be Israel's first president. He spoke for over two hours and made a deep impression on the committee. He urged that a Jewish state was necessary because it offered the only solution to the problem of anti-Semitism—as he put it, "We Jews carry the germs of anti-Semitism in our knapsack on our backs." He conceded that there was an Arab side to the question, but in view of all that the Jews had been through in Europe he felt compelled to say that the issue was not between right and wrong but between a greater and a lesser injustice.

Other Zionist leaders who testified were David Ben Gurion, Goldie Myerson (Golda Meir), Moshe Shertok (Sharett) of the Jewish Agency, and David Horowitz. Ben Gurion refused to be drawn out on the subject of Jewish terrorism, on which he was repeatedly questioned, saying only that it was "futile" for the authorities to try to stamp out the Jewish resistance movement when it commanded the support of the whole Jewish community.[6]

The Arab case was presented first by Jamal Husseini and Awni Abd al-

Hadi. Their argument was rigid and unimaginative, mostly a repetition of the standard Arab argument that Palestine was Arab and the Jews were interlopers. The Arabs, they said, recognized neither the Balfour Declaration nor the Mandate as valid. They based their stand on the principle of self-determination. When they asserted that the Palestine Arabs still looked to the former Mufti of Jerusalem, Haj Amin al-Husseini, as their leader, Crossman produced a photograph of the Mufti, who was well known as an Axis collaborator, reviewing troops of the Bosnian Moslem SS. This caused a sensation in the hearing room and the two Arab representatives were unable to explain away the picture. But a young Arab intellectual named Albert Hourani, who was director of the Arab Office in Jerusalem, did a brilliant job of presenting the Arab side, comparable to Weizmann's for the Jewish. (Both Ben Gurion and Horowitz in their accounts of the hearings write that Hourani was the best spokesman to appear on the Arab side.) For all his broad-gauged and reasoned approach, however, Hourani had to concede, in reply to a question from Major Manningham-Buller, that he would not agree to the admission of a single additional Jew to Palestine—not even the aged and infirm among the displaced persons. Another Arab who spoke to the committee was Ahmad Shukeiry, who was later to become the first head of the Palestine Liberation Organization.

The best testimony for the moderate position was given by Dr. Judah Magnes, the American-born president of the Hebrew University in Jerusalem, who spoke for the Ihud group which was in favor of cooperation between Arabs and Jews. His views struck us as reasonable and optimistic: he thought it should be possible to find a solution that would combine continued Jewish immigration with self-government for the Arab community. At the end of his testimony, Judge Hutcheson complimented him, in the words from John 1:47, saying that here was "an Israelite indeed in whom is no guile."

The committee also listened to the views of a number of ecclesiastics, Christian, Moslem, and Jewish, all of whom emphasized the role of Palestine as the Holy Land of the world's three monotheistic religions. In a secret session, Lt. General J. C. D'Arcy, the commander of British forces in Palestine, gave the committee some rather sobering details about the security situation and the strength of the Haganah. He said that if the British were to withdraw, the Haganah would immediately take over the entire country; he also said that it would take three army divisions to enforce on the Jewish community any solution that favored the Arabs. The committee then recalled Ben Gurion to question him about the Haganah. As before, Ben Gurion declined to answer any questions that bore on terrorism. He said that the Jewish Agency had nothing to do with the Haganah and that he had no knowledge of who the head of the Haganah was or where its headquarters were. (In a letter to the committee dated March 28, 1946, Moshe Shertok, who was head of the Agency's political department, similarly denied that the

Haganah was under the Agency's control. But, as noted in Chapter 5, the British had almost certain knowledge to the contrary.)

Shortly before the hearings concluded, the committee broke into subcommittees, some of them to go variously to the neighboring Arab capitals, the others to remain for further investigation in Palestine. Members went to Beirut, Amman, Damascus, Baghdad, and Riyadh. The State Department took the precaution of sending a circular telegram to our posts in the area, stressing that these visits were not to be regarded as constituting the consultations to which the two governments were committed.

The members of the committee who remained in Palestine were primarily interested in economic and social conditions there. I was attached to a group which among other things visited several Jewish and Arab schools, had tea with a delegation of Druze sheikhs, all with long white beards, who assured us that they would have preferred to receive us on bended knee, spent one night at a religious *kibbutz*, and were entertained with great pomp by a Bedouin chieftain at an Arab meal in the Jordan valley.

At the end of March, our departure plans ostensibly shrouded in secrecy, we moved on to Lausanne, Switzerland, by way of Malta, to prepare the report.

During our stay in Palestine, events in Iran had come to a head. The Iranian government had brought the question of Soviet intervention before the UN Security Council in January, but the Soviet representative had taken the position that the complaint related to an internal matter with which the Council was not competent to deal, and no effective action had been taken. The date of March 2, when foreign (that is, Soviet) troops were to be withdrawn, came and went. Finally, after two blunt notes from our government to Moscow, the U.S.S.R. announced on March 24 that it was starting to pull out its forces (in exchange, it turned out, for an oil concession in Iran's five northern provinces).

The peaceful surroundings of Lausanne, away from political crises and in such contrast to the turbulent Middle East, were highly conducive to meditation and reflection. The committee members quickly plunged into a series of private meetings in which they hammered out their various specific recommendations. We staff members were not generally included in these sessions except when we were brought in to supply some particular piece of information. A divergence of views soon emerged on the question of the future of Palestine. Certain members, notably Crossman, McDonald, and Crum, favored partition, but it soon became clear that the others would not go along and this proposal was withdrawn in the interest of unanimity. There was considerable discussion of the problem of law and order and how to handle it.[7]

In the process of give and take that preceded the completion of the report, the chief roles were played by Hutcheson, who provided strong leadership; by

Leggett, the veteran conciliator; and by Crossman, who showed great diplomatic skill. At times the discussion grew heated. The members constantly had in mind Bevin's remarks about a unanimous report. An important contribution toward this end was provided by a visit from Philip Noel Baker, Minister of State in the British Foreign Office, who brought a message from Bevin to the British chairman urging unanimity.[8] Eventually all differences were resolved and on April 20, Good Friday, the report was signed, well within the 120-day deadline. The evening before, Judge Hutcheson was host at a dinner celebrating the event and toasts were offered to the success of the mission. I recall that the Judge, who was ever one to indulge in a biblical allusion, compared the twelve members to the twelve men whom Joshua sent into Canaan to spy out the land and the ten recommendations in the report to the Ten Commandments.

There were some aspects of our stay in Switzerland that caused me some concern. The Jewish Agency sent four liaison representatives to Lausanne who maintained close contact with certain members of the committee, notably McDonald and Crum. It has been disclosed since by the Zionists that they managed to keep themselves quite well informed about the discussions within the committee and that they even obtained an advance copy of the report. It is now known also that Crum was often in contact by telephone with David Niles at the White House. It was the possibility of leaks that led me to telegraph to the Department urging the greatest care in the handling of the report when it reached Washington. It appears that McDonald and Crum agreed to the compromise solution proposed in the report for the sake of getting the 100,000 Jews to Palestine and with no real expectation that the rest of the report would be implemented.[9]

While we were at Lausanne, Beeley and I drew up for certain members several papers dealing with the settlement of the Palestine question.[10] One of these proposed a unitary state with considerable autonomy for the two communities. It is clear from a rereading of this paper that Beeley and I were thinking of a binational state, since our memorandum spoke (rather unrealistically as it turned out) of "developing the cooperation between the Arabs and Jews necessary for the eventual creation of a single Palestinian state." Beeley and I also discussed the Department's postwar planning papers for Palestine, which I showed him in strict confidence and with which he indicated his general agreement. Together, we prepared a step-by-step plan of action for our two governments to take regarding the committee's report, on the assumption, which we shared, that they would accept it.

My own impressions were summarized in a memorandum which I prepared in Lausanne under date of April 1 and circulated among the members of the committee and, later, among my colleagues in the Department. On rereading this paper after a lapse of more than thirty years, I must confess that it seems to me that the conclusions I reached were not only pertinent to the situation prevailing at the time, but also have considerable relevance to subsequent developments in the Arab-Israel problem generally. I therefore venture to reproduce this memorandum in full.[11]

April 1, 1946

IMPRESSIONS OF PALESTINE

1. The Basic Issue

The gulf between the two communities and the two points of view with regard to the basic issue is complete. The Arab and Jewish positions have hardened to such a point that absolutely no middle ground exists between these positions as officially put forward.

Socially and economically the gulf is also complete. Economically the situation is characterized by the existence of two economies side by side. Socially, ten years or so ago, Jewish and Arab leaders would meet on common ground, as at government receptions, but now they form distinct groups and do not mix. The Jews tend to despise the Arabs and the Arabs to fear the Jews. In the rural areas and villages there are of course frequent and sometimes friendly contacts between individuals on both sides, but these are rendered very difficult at present by the boycott. The ordinary Arab or Jew moreover finds it hard to maintain amicable relations with his Jewish or Arab neighbor, as the case may be, so long as the rights and wrongs of the Palestine controversy continue to be hotly and endlessly debated by the leaders on both sides and by the press. Every Jewish settlement has at least one member (usually the Mukhtar) who speaks Arabic and is in regular contact with the Arabs of the neighborhood but this does not ordinarily apply to the other members of the settlement.

The basic issue in Palestine today is not so much the question of the future form of the state as the question who is to constitute the majority and so dominate the state. The issue centers about the question whether the Jews shall be allowed to go to Palestine and settle on the land, because both Jews and Arabs realize that the decision on this question will determine the fundamental issue. Many Zionists, of course, insist that in order to ensure the attainment of a majority they must have the Jewish State now. Some Zionist leaders will even go so far as to put the question of the state ahead of the rescue of refugees, like Mr. Ben Gurion when he told the Committee in evidence that he would not give up the idea of the state in exchange for getting the 100,000 displaced Jews into Palestine. Not all Jews, not even all Palestinian Jews, feel so strongly, but they are overwhelmingly convinced of the necessity of having immigration in such numbers as to achieve a majority.

The Arabs say there must not be one further additional Jewish immigrant, not even the elderly and infirm. Nowhere in the questioning of representatives of the Palestine Arabs was the Committee able to shake them from this completely intransigent stand. In London the Committee elicited from Faris Al-Khoury, after some pressing, a concession to the effect that once the people of Palestine (meaning the Arab majority) were given control over their own affairs, it *might* be possible to reconsider the question of further immigration. No such admission was made by the Palestinian Arabs who testified in Jerusalem. Even the Sheikh of the Arab village adjoining Mishmar Ha'Emek, who was obviously on cordial terms with the Jews of the settlement, and who might have been expected to be more friendly disposed toward Jews in general than most Arabs, was adamant on this point. It should be borne in mind that many Arabs demand not only the immediate cessation of Jewish immigration but the repeal of the Balfour Declaration and the liquidation of the Jewish National Home. One has to understand this in order to appreciate how the official Arab witnesses who came before the Committee could describe as a *compromise* solution their proposal for the immediate independence of an Arab Palestine but with the maintenance unimpaired of the existing Jewish population and Jewish National Home.

The Jews, on the other hand, assert with complete determination that there is no power which can prevent any Jew from coming "home" to Palestine and settling freely there. They assert that so long as attempts are made to prevent this, they will oppose such attempts with all the forces at their disposal. In a community as highly organized and well disciplined as the Jewish Community of Palestine, this attitude is something to be reckoned with most seriously. The Jews are completely united on this point (even Dr. Magnes has openly espoused illegal immigration) and their ardor borders on the fanatical. In trying to understand their state of mind one must constantly bear in mind the fact that practically every Jew in Palestine has lost one or more members of his family in the European Holocaust. The effect of this experience upon the Jewish Community has been cataclysmic and has driven many of the Jews to despair. Their determination to bring the surviving remnants of European Jewry to Palestine at all costs is so strong and their disillusionment with the policy followed by the British government in recent years is so profound that they have lost virtually all respect for the normal forces of law and order. This explains why 90 to 95 percent of the Jews of Palestine are back of the terrorists and will do nothing to aid the government in suppressing terrorism.

The terms "Jewish State" and "Arab State" as they are constantly used in this controversy are misleading. What each side really wants is a state in which it will be the majority. The Jews have taken great care to lay down the most complete guarantees for the Arab minority in their Jewish State, and the same is true of the guarantees which the Arabs contemplate for the Jewish minority in their Arab state. Both sides are careful to deny any intention of moving the minority out, and these denials can in all probability be taken at face value. It is quite clear, however, that the minority in each instance, e.g., the Arabs in the Jewish State and Jews in the Arab State, would really be second-class citizens, no matter what their paper guarantees might be. This is only natural but it casts serious doubts on the desirability of having either an Arab or a Jewish State.

What it comes to, then, is that both the Jewish State and the Arab State, as envisaged by their respective protagonists, are really bi-national states, the essential difference being who constitutes the majority and who the minority.

As Mr. Shertok pointed out in his supplementary evidence to the Committee, the term "Jewish State" simply means a state in which the majority would be Jewish and which would be a Jewish State only in the sense that Iraq or Syria are Arab States.

The familiar argument that the age-old homelessness of the Jewish people makes it necessary for them to have a state which they can call their own is naturally seen in a new light when it is realized that, paradoxically enough, the Jewish State will inevitably have so large a non-Jewish element that it cannot really be described as Jewish. Moreover, if the calculations of Professor Notestein are correct—and there seems good reason to believe that they are—the rapid rate of increase of the Moslem Arab population will in all probability render it impossible for the Jews to maintain a majority in Palestine even if they were to achieve it temporarily as a result of large-scale immigration.

The advocates of compromise in both camps are of completely negligible influence. Magnes has only a handful of supporters among the Jews, and no Arab whatever came forward to support him. He himself received threats on his life for daring to testify before the Committee. Bentov and Hashomer Hatzair are in favor of a bi-national state, but only on the basis of the immediate admission of 2,000,000 Jewish immigrants, which would be completely inacceptable to the Arabs. The Arabs in fact regard Magnes and Bentov as more dangerous than the official Zionist spokesman. They know that in any scheme of bi-nationalism on a parity basis they will tend to be out-maneuvered by the more aggressive, more efficient Jews and so they oppose all such proposals quite as vigorously as they do the Jewish state.

A corollary of the foregoing is that while a solution of the basic problem wholly acceptable to either side will of course be resisted by the other side and will have to be imposed on that side by force, a solution inacceptable to both sides, e.g., a compromise solution, will require even more force to implement it, since both Arabs and Jews will oppose it vigorously.

Partition would be wholeheartedly rejected by the Arabs but would probably be accepted by the Jews if they were convinced they could get their Jewish State in no other way. Weizmann, Goldmann, Ben Gurion, Shertok, and Kaplan all admitted as much privately to various members of the Committee. Their eventual acceptance of course would be predicated upon there being the type of partition which would be acceptable to them. This means that partition is now the real objective of the Zionists and that any discussion from now on of a Jewish State in all of Palestine is virtually pointless.

2. American Policy

Everywhere among the Arabs there is an almost complete identification of the United States with Zionism. This is true of the leaders and also of the inhabitants of the remotest village. Whenever the United States is mentioned in connection with the Palestine question, it is taken for granted in Arab circles that we are pursuing a pro-Zionist line. The wonder is that they should be as well disposed toward us as they are.

This raises some fundamental questions regarding the policy which the

Department of State should follow with regard to the Arab world on the question of Palestine. In the Department we like to think that we have a policy which is neither pro-Arab nor anti-Arab, pro-Zionist nor anti-Zionist, but pro-American. But if it is simply a question of not appearing in Arab eyes to be pro-Zionist—and conversely not appearing to the Jews to be pro-Arab—that battle has already been lost long since, in so far as the Arabs are concerned. What the Arabs want to know about America's attitude on Palestine is very simple: are we in favor of letting any more Jews into Palestine or not? There is, of course, only one answer to this question: We are. Even if the Department of State were to try to assert that the protection and promotion of American interests in the Near East required us to base our Palestine policy on the principle that no more Jews at all should be allowed to go to Palestine—which is the Arab policy—the Department would receive absolutely no support from the White House, Congress, any segment of the Jewish community in the United States, or the public at large. We may as well face the fact that according to the Arab definition the entire American people—with the possible exception of the Arab-Americans—have Zionist sympathies.

This brings us to the distinction, on which we sometimes tend to lay considerable stress in the Department, between the differing attitudes of the Zionist, non-Zionist, and anti-Zionist Jews on the question of the Jewish State. Once it is realized that the fundamental issue in the Palestine controversy is the question not of the state but of immigration and settlement, all these distinctions become utterly meaningless in so far as our relations with the Arab world are concerned. The same reasoning applies to Congressional resolutions and party platforms which omit the reference to a "Jewish" state but still call for unrestricted Jewish immigration. It might be argued that such resolutions are relatively innocuous as they simply give expression to our widespread humanitarian desire to do something for the refugees, but at the same time avoid the delicate political issues. Nothing could be further from the truth as far as the Arab reaction is concerned. To the Arabs, such resolutions are different only in degree, not in kind, from say a proposal to settle three million Jews in Palestine at once, move all the Arabs to Iraq, and declare an immediate Jewish State on both sides of the Jordan.

The conclusion to which the foregoing leads is, that there is absolutely nothing to be gained from sending carefully worded assurances to a few Arab leaders pointing out that while it is true that President Roosevelt told Rabbi Wise the United States Government had never approved the White Paper, it is equally true that we had never taken any position on that document, and that in any event we believe Arabs as well as Jews should be consulted before there is what we would regard as a basic change in Palestine. In the first place, such explanations do not reach the ordinary Arab, who will continue to get his impressions of American policy from what he hears in the bazaar or reads in his newspaper. Secondly, even if they did receive the fullest publicity, they would not convince the Arabs in the face of continuing and inevitable manifestations of support for Zionism in our country. And finally, all such explanations contain an element of intellectual dishonesty. No matter how carefully they are worded, they cannot gloss over the fact that there is a real sympathy for Zionism—on any definition—in our country and that this sympathy is constantly making itself known. At best, these explanations succeed only in conveying to a few persons at the top level in the Arab world the impression that the Executive branch of our Government—and sometimes the Department alone—is trying to carry water on both shoulders in defiance of a very strong tendency in American opinion in favor of one of the two sides. At their worst, the explanations give rise to an easily understandable impression that we are trying to conceal from the Arabs the true state of affairs in our country.

In other words, such a Palestine policy as the Department has adopted in recent years does nothing to create good will in the Near East, maintain our prestige, or promote our interests. Nor does it answer the questions the Arabs want answered. To perceive the futility of this line of approach, one has only to ask oneself: how many Arabs, in their testimony before the Committee, or in discussions with members, based their case upon, or even referred to, the assurances they had received to the effect that they would be consulted regarding a settlement of the Palestine question? Of course, not one; but they all declared their opposition to Zionism and their belief that we were supporting the Zionists.

It would seem a more logical as well as a more realistic approach to take for our basic assumption, in formulating our Palestine policy, the indisputable fact that there is a sincere and widespread sympathy in the United States for the Jewish National Home and for the idea that Jews should not be prevented from going to Palestine. We should, of course, make it clear to the Arabs that we fully understand their point of view. But we should seek, not to make the Arabs think we are backing both sides at once—which is impossible—but rather to explain to them the humanitarian reasons which impel us to give our support to Jewish aspirations and the advantages which in the long run can accrue to the people not only of Palestine but of the whole Near East, from the continuing development of the Jewish National Home. Our point of view, moreover, should not be made known to a few leaders only but should be given the widest possible publicity.

This, of course, no more means that the United States should pursue a wholly pro-Zionist course than that it should pursue a wholly pro-Arab course. The foregoing is based on the assumption that it is in the interests of the Arabs and Jews themselves, of Palestine, of the Near East as a whole, and of the United States, that there should be a settlement of the Palestine question under which neither Arab nor Jew will be able to dominate the other. But pending such a settlement, and indeed in any case, the policy of our Government should take more cognizance of the realities of the situation than it has in the recent past.

In connection with our Palestine policy, the Arabs of Palestine are resentful of the importance which seems to be attached by the United States Government to King Ibn Saud as a spokesman for the Arab cause. The Palestine Arabs of course feel great affinity for the Arabs of Trans-Jordan, Syria, and Lebanon. Ibn Saud, however, they tend to regard as an uncivilized desert marauder who has for many years harbored aggressive designs on part of Trans-Jordan and southern Palestine and who has been kept on his throne chiefly by British subsidies. They expect a rapid disintegration of his kingdom and a sharp decline in its influence in Arab and world affairs as soon as the King dies. In many ways it is of course natural that the more educated Arabs in Palestine, for example the graduates of the University of Beirut, should adopt a somewhat scornful attitude toward the Bedouin Arabs. It is also to be expected that they would incline toward the Hashemites rather than the Saudi dynasty. The feeling, however, goes deeper and takes the form of dissatisfaction that there has been so much discussion of Palestine by American and British leaders with Ibn Saud, rather than with the people of the country.

The influence of the American University of Beirut has been of invaluable assistance to the United States and is probably responsible more than any other single factor for such prestige as our country has retained in the Arab world. It seemed that everywhere we went in Palestine, even in the smallest villages, we found one or two graduates of the University and they were always very proud of that fact.

As a final commentary on our Palestine policy, the obvious fact might be pointed out, as far as the reverse side of the medal is concerned, that the Department has been even less successful in convincing the Jews that it is not pro-Arab. This point is too familiar to require any elaboration but it makes a frank restatement of our policy all the more desirable.

Furthermore, the Department, and particularly the Office of Near Eastern and African Affairs, should have much closer and more cordial relations with the Zionists. Too often in the past these relations have taken on the character of a duel, with the Department's Near Eastern officers being put in the position of parrying each Zionist thrust in such a manner as invariably to appear anti-Zionist and pro-Arab. There should be far more frequent contacts and both sides should make a genuine effort to discuss common problems in a frank and sympathetic manner. But if the Department is to cultivate good relations with the Zionists they for their part must give up their irritating practice of going over the heads of the Near Eastern officers to the Secretary or the President when they want to get things done.

3. The Arabs and the Jews

The Arabs of Palestine are badly organized and lacking in leadership. In this they present a sorry contrast to the Jews. Their idea of impressing the Committee with their case seemed to lie more in the direction of a sumptuous luncheon at Katy Antonius' or a ceremonial visit to a large estate rather than any systematic marshalling of facts and figures to make a convincing presentation. An exception of course is Albert Hourani who made a much better impression on the Committee, both in the written material he prepared and in his oral testimony, than the older Arab spokesmen. For the most part the Arab leaders did not appear to take much interest in the Committee's proceedings—which one might have thought would be a matter of life and death to the Arabs of Palestine—and in fact the members of the Arab Higher Committee often did not bother to fill the seats which had been reserved for them at the hearings—and this when hundreds were being turned away daily for lack of space.

The educational facilities accorded the Arab population are simply shocking. Out of a population of one and a quarter million, about 20 boys graduate every year from each of the two technical schools provided for the Arab population. In a town the size of Nazareth, only two or three boys a year (and no girls) are able to go on to advanced schools in other cities. The rest of the boys finish their education at about 14. For girls the situation is worse and only about half the girls of Nazareth are able to go to school at all. In Haifa, out of 8,000 Moslem children, the schools can accommodate only 4,000 and the remainder roam the streets. In the villages, conditions are even worse.

On the Jewish side, Dr. Weizmann gave the impression of a tired old man who knew he no longer commanded the allegiance of his followers. There seems to be some support for the theory that at the Zionist Congress this summer he will be succeeded by Rabbi Silver, rather than Mr. Ben Gurion as might be expected, although Nahum Goldmann may be selected as a compromise between Silver and Ben Gurion. It is probably true that Weizmann does not know all that is going on in the Agency, especially with regard to terrorism, and the Haganah.

Out of the Jewish Agency budget of £P.4,000,000 a year, roughly one-fourth, or £P.1,000,000, goes to the Haganah and other illegal organizations and activities. This money, however, is raised from inside Palestine rather than out, according to an official of the Agency speaking privately. It is thus only indirectly that American Jews are contributing to these activities.

The Jews justify their illegal organizations as being a direct consequence of the policy of the British Government. While Mr. Ben Gurion may in public disclaim any connection with the Haganah, in private Jewish leaders will argue that they have been driven to adopt this course. They will also admit privately that they have not really done much to improve the living conditions of the Arabs, but will justify this on the grounds that their whole accomplishment in Palestine has been an up-hill climb in the face of Arab hostility and Government indifference—or worse—so that it has been all that they could do to hold their gains and look out for their own people.

One must not give too much weight to reports that there is much dissatisfaction among the Jews with the general lines of the Agency's policies or that any substantial number of persons want to leave the country. There are undoubtedly some elements in the community who object to certain policies and who are prevented in various ways from making their opposition felt. But on the main issues the Agency commands the support of almost the entire Jewish community and the number of Jews wishing to leave is probably quite small. It is, however, indisputable that pressures of various types are brought to bear on these individuals.

Certain tendencies in the Jewish community are very disturbing, notably the inward-looking nature of the Jewish national institutions, the way in which the young people are being brought up, and the bad relations prevailing with the mandatory authorities. The Jews have brought many advantages to Palestine but these have been almost entirely for the exclusive benefit of the Jews themselves. Out of 30,000 patients treated per year in Jewish hospitals, over 29,000 are Jewish and only 1,000 non-Jewish. The Jews have a fine University but the instruction is in Hebrew, which effectively bars Arab students apart from the most exceptional instances. The Arabs see the Jews coming to what they have always regarded as an Arab country and bringing in a lot of improvements (desperately needed by the Arab community) for the use of the Jews alone, and they are naturally resentful.

The raising of the young people among the Jews gives rise to the most serious alarm, especially as their parents seem to have very little influence over them. Boys and girls in their teens are absent from home for days at a time, return exhausted as though from marching across country, and refuse to say where they have been—the parents wouldn't understand. Most of the terrorists are under 20 years of age and a remarkably high proportion are girls.

The lack of friendly relations between the Jews and the British officials is also distressing. As Mr. Ben Gurion told the Committee, the Agency decided some time ago to stop cooperating with the authorities. The result is that the relations between the Jewish community and the government are not unlike, say, the relations which existed during the war, between the inhabitants of some German-occupied country and the Nazi occupying force. The telephones of government officials are tapped, documents disappear from government offices, and the ever-present possibility of assassination or violence of some sort is uppermost in every official's mind. In such atmosphere there can be no relaxation, and there is none. Socially there is virtually no contact and while one is apt to encounter a few Arabs at parties given by officials in their homes one never sees a Jew there.

The chief impression of the Jewish community that one takes away is one of vitality. In the United States we are sometimes inclined to think of Zionism as a dying force, as a movement which is on the decline. We are even told that the high point of the movement was reached some years ago, before the virtual annihilation of the Jewish communities in Europe, and that as a result of the drying up of that reservoir of potential manpower the driving force behind the urge to continue the upbuilding of the Jewish National Home is largely spent. There could be no greater misconception as far as the Jewish community in Palestine is concerned. Zionism in Palestine today is a thriving, vibrant movement that is going places in a big way. Its leaders know exactly what they want and how to go about getting it. And they have solidly behind them a people of great talents and great potentialities whose pride in what they have already achieved is matched only by the zeal with which they tackle their next objectives. The Jews of Palestine are at a high pitch of tension and if, as seems inevitable, their hopes are in any respect to be frustrated, the effect on the Jewish community will be shattering.

This does not mean, of course, that the Arabs of Palestine are any less fervent in upholding their side of the case. But after all, the Arabs are on the defensive. It is the Jews who are on the attack and whose aggressiveness is thus more noticeable. On their side, the Arabs do not have the powers of organization, the monetary resources, or the military equipment that the Jews of Palestine possess. If an armed conflict were to occur between the two alone, the Jews would probably occupy the whole country at first, but eventually the Arabs would almost certainly push them into the sea, if allowed free rein. This, however, is not the type of conflict that is likely to take place in Palestine so the point is purely hypothetical. What is of importance as a matter of practical politics is the completely unyielding, passionate way in which both parties adhere to their respective positions.

In spite of everything, Jews and Arabs can and do cooperate in Palestine. An outstanding example is the Haifa Municipal Council, also the Citrus Boards. These are instances where common interests have brought them together. The same is true of the work of Mr. Jardine, the British Council representative in Haifa, who organizes dances and other events where Jewish and Arab boys and girls meet on common ground in a completely friendly atmosphere. One of his groups recently completed a seminar on the solution of the Palestine problem, and came to the conclusion that there should be a bi-national state with its capital at Haifa rather than Jerusalem.

The report of the Anglo-American Committee of Inquiry is a noteworthy document. It certainly deserved more attention than it was to receive from the British and American governments, and its not having been implemented does not make it any less valuable as an analysis of conflicting attitudes and as an effort by men of good will to find a reasonable and moderate solution. I can make this judgment without hesitation because it was the twelve members themselves, not their staff, who wrote the report. [12]

The important thing to bear in mind about the report is that the committee's ten carefully worded recommendations were intended to be integral parts of a single whole, with concessions to one side balanced against concessions to the other. The last thing the members anticipated was that one or two of their recommendations would be accepted and not the entire report.

Thus, a recommendation that 100,000 Jewish displaced persons be admitted immediately to Palestine (this had become an article of faith for the members) was balanced by an assertion that Palestine could not absorb all the homeless Jews and by recommendations designed to raise the standard of living of the Arab population and especially to improve Arab education, the condition of which had shocked the members. The committee sought to resolve the conflicting Arab and Jewish claims by declaring that Palestine should be neither an Arab nor a Jewish state, though they did not say what they had in mind for the future political structure of the country, except that it should not be partition.

The weakness of the report lay in the fact that in order to achieve unanimity it had to be a compromise between differing points of view and was therefore vague on certain key issues. Most important was the failure to be more precise about the future of Palestine, although it is evident that most members were thinking of a binational state. This emerges from what some of them wrote later, as well as from talks that I had with the American members when they were called back to Washington in August 1946.[13] The members of the committee had been greatly impressed by the concept of a binational state as put to them by a number of witnesses, notably Mordecai Bentov of the group known as Hashomer Hatzair, and Dr. Magnes (it was the latter who originated the phrase "no Jewish state, no Arab state").[14] I should add that this line of thinking found a good measure of support in the Department at the time and was shared by most of us who were working on the problem.

The most explicit statement by a member of the committee as to what the members had in mind is to be found in a lecture that Crossman delivered thirteen years afterward—in 1959—at the Weizmann Institute in Rehovoth, Israel. He said on that occasion: "When we drafted the Anglo-American report we were thinking of a bi-national state, but we were more internationalistic in those days. Our idea was to create conditions for co-existence of the two communities . . . I am not sure now that this would have worked." Crossman and others also thought it a weakness in the report that the committee recommended the continuation of the mandatory or trusteeship regime for an indefinite period even though both the Jews and the Arabs of Palestine were fit for self-government.[15] But since the two parties could not agree on the future form of government, it is hard to see what other recommendation was possible. A final comment that should be made is that the committee underestimated the need for force to bring about any solution to the problem.

In spite of the drawbacks, the Anglo-American report had a good deal of influence on our government's later handling of the problem. Truman in his *Memoirs* calls it a "conscientious job," and indeed at the very time that Israel achieved its independence in 1948 he was writing a letter to Crum praising the report.[16] One commentator has aptly characterized the report as follows: "Taken as a whole the report was an honest effort to grapple with a difficult problem. But almost no one took it as a whole."[17]

It has been said that the Anglo-American report offered the last opportunity to find a reasonable solution to the vexing Palestine problem, and thus represented something of a crossroads on the road to partition and a Jewish state.[18] In retrospect it seems clear, however, that by 1946 it was too late for a solution along binational lines. The extremists on both sides had become too strong, and the hope of some members of the committee that their findings would appeal to the moderate elements, and especially the moderates among the Jews, were not borne out.[19] The gulf between the two communities had grown too wide. The Jews, as some of them have recognized, had a lot to do with the widening of this gulf in that, from the very start, they had done nothing to cultivate the good will of the Arab community.

Reaction to the report within the British and American governments differed. The British were immediately worried about its implications, and their worries increased when it became clear that it would take force to impose it, both on the Jewish and on the Arab population of Palestine. After a special Foreign Office committee, appointed to examine the document, came to this conclusion, the British government decided that it would have to have the full cooperation of the United States if the report were to be implemented, and it therefore proposed to Washington that the two governments should follow a joint course of action regarding it.[20]

First reactions to the report in the U.S. State Department were favorable and my superiors shared the hopes which I felt at the time that the report would lead to progress toward a solution.[21] On April 30, however, President Truman, disregarding the British appeals for joint action, issued a statement, written for him by Niles and Crum, in which he welcomed the committee's endorsement of the immediate entry of the 100,000 and one or two other points, but added that the remainder of the report would require careful study.[22] This partial acceptance of the report was unfortunate. It was exactly what the committee had hoped to avoid.

The day after Truman's statement was issued Attlee told the House of Commons (on May 1) that the report involved long-term commitments which the British government was unwilling to undertake before ascertaining the extent to which the United States was "prepared to share the resulting military and financial responsibilities." Attlee also said that Jewish terrorism would have to be ended and the terrorist organizations disbanded before so large a number as 100,000 new Jewish immigrants could be admitted. This statement alienated many Jews, and indeed the Anglo-American Committee had rejected a similar condition in its report because it felt that it was important to get the displaced Jews to Palestine without delay. Apparently the British were worried about indications that many of the Jewish displaced persons were being trained in terrorist tactics.[23]

Thus the structure of cooperation between the two governments, on which the concept of a joint examination had been based, began to collapse as soon as the report was out. British irritation throughout this period was increased by the American tendency to intervene in the Palestine affair without any corresponding willingness to undertake responsibility.[24]

It may be added that a year or so later Bevin told two members of the Jewish Agency Executive (Emmanuel Neumann and Moshe Shertok) that he would have been prepared to accept all ten recommendations of the joint committee had it not been for the way the American government handled the release of the report.[25]

On the morning of May 1, 1946, the front page of the *New York Times* carried a three-column headline proclaiming "Joint Palestine Body Bars a Jewish State but Urges Entry of 100,000 Refugees." An adjoining headline read "Arabs Outraged by Report: Jews are far from Satisfied," while a third ran: "Truman said to plan Start of Jewish Entry 'Forthwith.' " The accompanying article was based on an interview with Bartley Crum. The entire text of the report and appendixes—seven full pages in all—was published in the *Times*. Other front-page stories on that May Day dealt with Austrian demands for the South Tyrol, with a UN Security Council investigation of Franco's Spain, and with an abortive Japanese plot to assassinate General Douglas MacArthur.

As the *Times* indicated, both Arabs and Jews were dissatisfied with the report. The Zionists and their supporters in Congress seized upon the President's endorsement of the recommendation regarding the 100,000 Jews as an opportunity to press for their immediate entry, but they criticized other aspects of the report, particularly its failure to recommend a Jewish state. In Jerusalem, a member of the political department of the Jewish Agency Executive told our Consul General that "Zionist political aims have been sacrificed to philanthropy." Rabbi Silver, at a rally in New York on June 12, declared that negotiations then pending for a U.S. loan to Great Britain ought to be held up until the British agreed to admit the 100,000, but Rabbi Wise opposed this.[26] Only the American Council for Judaism (anti-Zionist) expressed support for the committee's findings.

Arab opinion was overwhelmingly against the report. A special meeting of the Arab League at Bludan in Syria rejected the report and called on all Arabs to oppose it. Fadhil al-Jamali, now the Foreign Minister of Iraq, told one of our representatives that the Arabs were prepared to wage war for 200 years to prevent the report from being carried out. The Arabs found it especially painful that the President in his statement had seen fit to single out the one recommendation that was the most offensive to them—that relating to the 100,000 Jews.[27] The files of the government of Palestine, now a part of the Israel State Archives in Jerusalem, contain several dozens of emotional protests telegraphed to the High Commissioner by Arabs all over the country, using such language as "we will fight the report until death."

Consul General Pinkerton at Jerusalem reported to the Department that the Arab Higher Committee had called for a general strike by Arabs in protest against the report and that the Palestine police were expecting "an immediate uprising of the Arab population." Minister Tuck in Cairo reported that the local reaction to the report was "bitterly critical" and that Azzam Pasha, secretary-general of the Arab League (who had testified before the committee), had called to file a protest on behalf of all the Arab states. Azzam assured Tuck that the Arabs were united in their opposition to the Anglo-American report. Our Chargé in Jidda reported that King Ibn Saud's reaction was "very bad."

On May 10, the Arab diplomatic representatives in Washington, now five in number, called on Acting Secretary of State Acheson and presented identical notes of protest. The essence was that the report had made a "painful impression" on the Arab world. Acheson told his visitors that the President had authorized him to assure them that it was still our government's policy that the Arabs as well as the Jews should be consulted and that this would apply to any decision taken relative to the report.

The United States proposed to the British that the consultations to which the two governments were committed should start at once and that the way to do this was for representative Arabs and Jews to be invited to comment on the committee's report. After some initial delay, the British agreed and consultations began May 20. The State Department wrote to the organizations that had testified at the committee's hearings in Washington, plus the Arab League and certain Arab governments, asking them to submit their views on the report within a month's time.[28] A parallel procedure was followed by the British.[29]

Nothing came of all this, since most of the organizations that were invited to comment, both Jewish and Arab, declined to do so, asserting that they had already made their views abundantly clear. The two governments, however, nonetheless took the position that they had discharged their commitment.[30]

Meanwhile, President Truman had announced in a White House press release of July 2 that the United States had pledged to the British that it would be responsible for the expenses of moving the 100,000 Jews to Palestine once their entry was approved.[31] Although the British had not yet indicated their acceptance of the Anglo-American report or any part of it, our government had already sent a small advance party to London to work out the details of transporting and housing the 100,000. I was a member of this group.[32] Under the chairmanship of Averell Harriman, who was now our Ambassador in London, we met for about two weeks with our British opposite numbers (who included Harold Beeley and responsible officials of the Colonial Office and Ministry of Defense) and at the end of June came up with a tentative report. The British continued to insist they could make no commitment. The total cost of transferring the 100,000 Jews, exclusive of the transport for which the United States government was to pay, was estimated to be $450,000,000, of which Jewish sources were to provide $250,000,000. From London I reported, too optimistically, that I thought the British would eventually agree to the admission of the 100,000, though I doubted that they would accept the entire report. I added that on the future of Palestine they were divided, with the Colonial Office favoring partition and the Foreign

Office continuing to be opposed.[33] On my return to Washington, surmising that in future discussions the British might put forward a proposal for some loose type of partition (as indeed occurred shortly), I urged that if we were going to oppose this we should be ready with our own plan for a binational state.

The initiation of consultations regarding the Anglo-American report was one of two ways in which we sought to keep up momentum on the Palestine question. The other was the appointment of a Cabinet Committee on Palestine and Related Problems composed of the Secretaries of State, War, and Treasury, which was charged with the task of implementing the Anglo-American report. This body was the brainchild of our chief, Loy Henderson, who saw it as a means of giving concrete expression to our government's determination to press for a solution. The idea was that the setting up of a separate group to deal with the problem would be proof of the seriousness with which we viewed the issues raised in the report. The inclusion of the other two departments was natural, in that since both strategic and financial considerations were clearly involved, they both had an obvious interest in the subject. Apparently it was no more than coincidence that the same three Cabinet officers made up the War Refugee Board, which had wound up its activities by this time.

The appointment of the Cabinet Committee was announced on June 11.[34] The committee itself met only once or twice; the actual work was delegated to the alternates of the three cabinet members, under the chairmanship of Henry F. Grady, who had formerly served as Assistant Secretary of State and as head of the American group observing the elections in Greece. Grady agreed to take on the assignment only after he was promised that he would have the rank of ambassador.[35] Neither he nor the other two alternates, Goldthwaite H. Dorr of the War Department and Herbert E. Gaston of the Treasury, had had any previous connection with the Palestine problem. Several members of the staff of the Anglo-American Committee were taken on by the Cabinet Committee but I was asked by Henderson to stay in the Near East Division to backstop the operation from there.

It was agreed with the British that the Cabinet Committee alternates would go to London for talks as soon as possible. Our government remained anxious that something be done promptly to start the movement of the 100,000 Jews to Palestine. It is worth noting that President Truman, in his instructions to the Grady group, affirmed that the United States was willing to accept the Anglo-American report as a whole—a considerable advance over his April 30 statement.[36]

Before the alternates proceeded to London a further rift occurred in the fabric of Anglo-American cooperation. On June 28 Attlee cabled the President informing him that the British had decided to take stern measures to curb Jewish terrorism in Palestine, including the arrest of certain leaders of the Jewish Agency. Attlee added that anything the President might feel able to say in support of the British decision would be welcome. Truman, however, after receiving a group of American Zionist leaders on July 2, issued a statement saying he had not been consulted by the British about this action and expressing the hope that the persons arrested would soon be released.[37]

When the Grady group got to London, the British offered a proposal for provincial autonomy in Palestine—a plan which had already been considered and rejected by the Anglo-American Committee. Specifically, the British proposal provided for the establishment of Jewish and Arab provinces or cantons, with Jerusalem and the Negev (the arid southern part of Palestine) remaining under a central government. The provinces were to have a considerable degree of local self-government, but several powers, including the all-important control over immigration, were reserved for the central authority. It is a reflection of current animosities in Palestine that the stated justification for the plan was that segregation of the Arabs and Jews had become necessary. Ostensibly, the scheme was so devised as to be capable of evolving either toward a unitary state or toward partition. Our report on the technical aspects of the movement of the 100,000 was accepted but this movement was to begin only after the agreement of the Arabs and Jews to the entire plan had been obtained. Grady nonetheless recommended to the President that the plan be accepted, as he saw no other way to get the 100,000 in the near future.[38] As appears from a transatlantic teletype conference that took place on July 26 between Byrnes and Henderson in Washington and Grady and Harriman in London, the Department tried unsuccessfully to get hard-and-fast assurances from the British about the 100,000 Jews. Grady said that the most he was able to elicit from the British was that they would allow the 100,000 Jews to proceed to Palestine as soon as they were "convinced after consultations with the Arabs and Jews that it will not be impossible to carry out the plan without military force." Grady thought that we should accept this assurance, even in this double-negative form. He went so far as to suggest to the Secretary in this conversation that the latter should attempt to persuade the President not to press the issue of the 100,000.[39]

A contretemps developed when Grady cabled from London that the details of the provincial autonomy plan could be found among the papers of the Anglo-American Committee. The Department was obliged to reply with some embarrassment that the papers were not available as they were still in customs, so Grady had to telegraph the full text of the plan.

Unfortunately, the details of the proposal were leaked in London by several members of Grady's staff who opposed it on the grounds that it did not make satisfactory provision for the immediate admission of the 100,000 Jews.[40] In this way the Zionists got wind of the scheme. They mounted an immediate campaign to defeat it. Truman, feeling the pressure, called Grady and his team back from London and told Attlee he would have to defer a decision on the plan pending further consideration. The British, however, went ahead and announced the plan as a joint Anglo-American proposal. The announcement was made in the House of Commons by the Lord President of the Council, Herbert Morrison (acting in place of Bevin, who was ill), and the scheme thus came to be known as the Morrison-Grady plan. Morrison told the House that the British intended to call a conference of Arabs and Jews in London to consider the plan.[41]

Truman asked the six American members of the Anglo-American Committee to come to Washington to confer with the Grady committee. The six unanimously recommended against acceptance of the Morrison-Grady plan on the grounds that it would lead inevitably to partition and therefore could not in any way be considered as an implementation of their report, the ostensible purpose for which the Cabinet Committee had been set up. This certainly appears to have been an accurate interpretation of the scheme.[42]

The Jewish community in our country now launched a full-scale attack on the Morrison-Grady proposals.[43] This time even the American Council for Judaism was in opposition. On August 7 Truman sent word to Attlee that he could not accept the plan. This decision, which Secretary Forrestal in his *Diaries* quotes Byrnes as having attributed chiefly to the influence of Niles and Rosenman, was a great disappointment to the British.[44] It put back even further any prospects for a joint solution. Indeed, it was hard for any of us to see what could be done to retrieve the situation. No wonder Truman himself at this time (July 31) wrote James G. McDonald that he saw no solution for the Palestine problem.[45]

At this point, a new element entered the situation. In early August, an emergency meeting of the Jewish Agency Executive had been convened in Paris to consider what attitude the Zionists should assume, as obviously the Morrison-Grady proposals were not compatible with Zionist aims. One of the participants, Nahum Goldmann, has told how he convinced his colleagues that it was no longer realistic to work for a Jewish state in the whole of Palestine, as foreseen in the Biltmore program. He pointed out that the British could not be expected to impose such a state on a hostile Arab majority. Undoubtedly he also had it in mind that the prospects for wide-scale Jewish immigration had been greatly diminished by the decimation of the Jewish communities in Europe. Goldmann argued that it was wiser to opt for partition. He obtained the agreement of the Executive to press for what became known as a "viable Jewish state in an adequate area of Palestine." This goal was endorsed at a World Zionist Congress later in the year. This was a landmark decision, representing as it did a retreat from the maximalist Biltmore demands.[46]

Goldmann went from Paris to Washington in an attempt to enlist U.S. government support for the "viable state" concept. He was successful to the extent that Truman in a message to Attlee on August 12 urged that the Jewish Agency's plan should be considered at the forthcoming London Conference. Although Truman did not explicitly endorse the Agency's plan, he clearly implied that it might meet with our government's approval. The Cabinet Committee was allowed to disappear gradually and quietly from the scene.[47]

Although we in the Department would have been prepared to go along with the Morrison-Grady plan for the sake of getting some action, even on these unsatisfactory terms, we were surprised that Grady and his colleagues should have agreed so readily to a proposal that had been considered and rejected by the previous committee. In retrospect it does seem clear that the plan would , fact have led to partition, which the United States was not yet ready to accept. At all events the British insistence on making the admission of the 100,000 conditional upon the acceptance by the two parties of the entire scheme—an impossible condition in view of the probable attitudes of both—would not have allowed our government to accept the plan. At the time, however, the Grady group does not seem to have fully grasped the implications of the scheme.[48]

While the Morrison-Grady plan was being first developed in London and then turned down in Washington, other events were taking place that were to have an effect on our foreign relations. In China, Marshall continued to work, without success, for a solution to the tangled military and political situation. The Soviet Union did not relax its pressure on Turkey, and in early August proposed a new regime for the Turkish Straits, from which all non–Black Sea powers would be excluded. This caused apprehension in Ankara, Washington, and London. Truman directed that a stiff protest be delivered to Moscow. Eventually the Turks rejected the Soviet proposals and the crisis passed. Soviet threats, however, against Turkey and Greece were to resume in early 1947, and the continuing instability in the area was to add to the need for finding a solution in Palestine.

"Bridging the Gap":
London Conference Breaks Down

The rejection by our government of the Morrison-Grady plan may have spared us from becoming involved in a scheme that was questionable at best, but it represented a serious blow to Anglo-American cooperation. Though dismayed at our action, the British went ahead with the London Conference, which opened September 10 and adjourned October 2 until December (later postponed to January). The British held formal meetings with the Arabs and informal meetings with the Jews.[1]

The Arabs had taken the position that they would not participate if the Jews, or the United States, attended. The Jewish Agency for its part had refused to participate formally because the conference had been called to discuss the Morrison-Grady plan. The Agency insisted that its participation would be conditional on acceptance of its partition plan as a basis for discussion.[2] The Arabs, incidentally, were irritated by the Zionists' insistence on referring to their proposal for "a viable state in an adequate area of Palestine" as a compromise proposal, that is, by comparison with the Biltmore program calling for a Jewish state in the whole of Palestine. The Arab attitude on this point was again made manifest at the time of the 1947 partition plan. To the Arabs, who regarded Palestine as their land, the Jewish position represented no compromise at all. As the Arab writer Sana Hassan has put it: to offer me half the rooms in my house and tell me you are doing this as a compromise, is like the judgment of Solomon.[3]

The British took the position that they were willing to discuss any proposals, in addition to Morrison-Grady, which either the Jews or the Arabs might wish to place before the conference, but that they could not commit themselves further. This did not satisfy the Jewish Agency.

The wrangling that took place over this issue was illustrative of the extent to which relations between the British and the Agency had worsened by this time. Jewish confidence in the Mandatory authorities had been undermined by a number of British actions, notably the continued detention of leading members of the Jewish community in Palestine (they were not released until November 5) and the introduction of severe measures to combat illegal immigration. The British had announced in August that they were maintaining the monthly quota of 1,500 legal immigrants pending the outcome of the London Conference, but that illegal immigrants would be diverted to Cyprus instead of being deducted from the quota as before. This announcement met with determined resistance on the part of the entire Jewish community in Palestine. From this period can be dated the start of a policy of all-out noncooperation on the part of the Jewish Agency. The subsequent history of Palestine, right up to the end of the Mandate in May 1948, was to be an increasingly dismal story of terrorism, illegal immigration, and repression. The carrying out of countermeasures proved to be a most difficult task for the authorities, both because there was a wide measure of sympathy for the underground throughout the Jewish community and because the British were naturally reluctant to adopt a policy of harsh reprisals (as they were to do, for example, in the Malay Peninsula and in Kenya) against people who had just been through the horrors of the Holocaust.[4]

As far as attendance by the United States at London was concerned, the British had invited us to send an observer to the conference, but we had declined to do so unless both Arabs and Jews participated formally.[5]

At the conference, the Arabs presented their proposal calling for the termination of the Mandate and the independence of Palestine as a unitary state, with a provisional governing council composed of seven Arabs and three Jews, and an immediate halt to all Jewish immigration. Representatives of the Jewish Agency who met with the British on an informal basis spoke of their proposal for "a viable state in an adequate area" of Palestine but declined to give details, nor would they furnish a map of what they had in mind. Because the positions of the Arabs and the Jews were so far apart, the British decided to adjourn the conference in order to allow time for further consideration.

In September, the Department learned that President Truman was being urged by Rabbi Wise and other Zionist leaders to issue a statement in favor of partition. We submitted a memorandum recommending against making any statement at the time, particularly one in favor of partition, and suggested to the President that anything he might say while the London talks were in progress might do more harm than good. The President replied that he hoped not to have to say anything on the subject and in any case would consult the Department before saying anything.[6]

Truman did not take our advice, however. When he learned that the London Conference was being adjourned he cabled Attlee that he felt compelled to issue a statement the very next day. This statement would review the efforts of the United States to find a solution, reiterate the urgent need for the 100,000 to go to Palestine, and urge that an attempt be made to "bridge the gap" between the Morrison-Grady plan and the Jewish Agency plan for a "viable state." The latter plan, the President said, "would command the support of public opinion in the United States." Attlee immediately responded, asking Truman to postpone his statement, but Truman declined to do so and the statement was issued October 4, which happened to be the eve of Yom Kippur.

Attlee, obviously nettled, shot off a telegram to Truman which revealed the extent of his irritation. He complained that Truman had refused to give "even a few hours' grace to the Prime Minister of the country which has the actual responsibility for the government of Palestine." His message ended: "I shall await with interest to learn what were the imperative reasons which compelled this precipitancy." Bevin later declared that Truman's action destroyed all hopes that the British negotiations with the parties would succeed.[7]

There seems to be no question, as Dean Acheson pointed out in his memoirs, that the President had become deeply concerned at the lack of any progress with respect to the Jewish displaced persons—it was now well over a year since he had first written Attlee on the subject and no action had been taken. It must be conceded, however, that Truman also had in mind that the 1946 Congressional elections were approaching. The chairman of the Democratic National Committee, Robert E. Hannegan, had told him that Governor Thomas E. Dewey, the leader of the Republican party, was going to make a statement on the subject at a Jewish meeting October 6, and Dewey did so, calling for the admission to Palestine of "not 100,000 but several hundreds of thousands" of Jews.

That the President's action was politically motivated was the thrust of a column by James Reston which appeared in the *New York Times* for October 7 under the heading "Truman's Palestine Plea Flouted Foreign Advisors." Reston wrote that domestic politics were responsible for the President's appeal. This interpretation is borne out by the fact that the President received letters from a number of prominent Democrats, such as Representative Emmanuel Celler, commending him for having made his appeal and predicting that it would be of material help to the party in the forthcoming elections. A month later, the Democrats lost both Houses of Congress.

The files of the Truman Library show that Truman's Yom Kippur statement was drafted primarily by Eliahu Epstein (later Elath), the Washington representative of the Jewish Agency. Epstein expressed disappointment to his superiors in Jerusalem that his draft had been revised in the State Department by the insertion of the reference to "bridging the gap" between the two plans rather than endorsing the Jewish Agency's plan as he had intended. But though Truman's statement fell short of a commitment to partition, most people who read it probably failed to grasp the fine distinction and the usual interpretation followed the headlines, that "Truman Supports a Jewish State."[8]

On the other hand, Bevin's assertion that the statement destroyed all prospects for a settlement was exaggerated, since the parties, as we have just seen, were not that close to agreement. But certainly there is no question that the appeal was very badly timed and could only have had an adverse effect upon our position in the Middle East.

As usually happened in such situations, the President asked the Department to draft a reply to the British. Our telegram in answer to Attlee's caustic message, which the President approved, expressed regret for embarrassing Attlee, but emphasized the need for speedy action regarding the displaced Jewish persons in Europe before another winter found them still in their camps. The message added that "their feeling of desperation and frustration was, of course, intensified by the approach of their annual Day of Atonement, when they are accustomed to give contemplation to the lot of the Jewish people." There was no further rejoinder from the Prime Minister, but it can hardly be imagined that he was convinced by this explanation, ingenious as it may have seemed to us in NE.

Besides upsetting the British, Truman's Yom Kippur appeal had repercussions in the Department and in the Arab world. My immediate superior, Gordon Merriam, wrote a remarkably perceptive top-secret memorandum under date of October 15 pointing out the implications of the President's statement. Merriam was in favor of our continuing to urge the entry of the 100,000 Jewish DP's into Palestine, on humanitarian grounds. He pointed out, however, that this objective was not likely to be achieved so long as there was no worldwide program aimed at solving the refugee problem and so long as there was no progress in the direction of an acceptable solution to the Palestine question as a whole. As for partition, he urged that "U.S. support for the partition of Palestine as a solution to that problem can be justified only on the basis of Arab and Jewish consent. Otherwise we should violate the principle of self-determination which has been written into the Atlantic Charter, the Declaration of the United Nations, and the United Nations Charter—a principle that is deeply embedded in our foreign policy. Even a United Nations determination in favor of partition would be, in the absence of such consent, a stultification and violation of UN's own charter." (This last comment accurately forecast just what was to occur in the following year.) Merriam continued that if partition were not an agreed solution, it would result in "bloodshed and chaos" (also an accurate prediction). He added that for the United States, in the absence of agreement between the parties, to work actively for partition would "not result in any real benefits to the U.S., the Arabs, or to the Jews, and probably would be disastrous to all." Merriam concluded by quoting from the words used by the Anglo-American Committee of Inquiry concerning partition, that "partition has an appeal at first sight" but that "no partition would have any chance unless it was basically acceptable to Jews and Arabs, and there is no sign of that today"—words which he pointed out were still applicable.[9]

It is worth noting that when Henderson showed this paper to Under Secretary Acheson, Acheson thought it so explosive that he directed that it not be placed in the Department's files and that all copies be destroyed—except for the original which he said the author might keep for himself (and of which Merriam furnished me a copy in connection with the preparation of this book: I had never seen it).

The Arab reaction to the President's Yom Kippur statement was expressed in a letter (dated October 15) which King Ibn Saud wrote to the President, stating his concern that the traditional friendship between the United States and the Arab countries was being endangered and asserting that the United States was not living up to assurances previously made to him and other Arab leaders. The King said he was afraid that the Zionists had designs on his country but, he said, "I am confident that the American people who spent their blood and their money freely to resist aggression, could not possibly support Zionist aggression against a friendly Arab country which has committed no crime except to believe firmly in those principles of justice and equality, for which the United Nations, including the United States, fought, and for which both your predecessor and you exerted great efforts."[10]

The President's lengthy reply, drafted in our Division and dated October 25, is of significance in that it laid it down for the first time as a matter of policy that the United States had a responsibility for the development of the Jewish National Home. The message assured the King that our attitude was still one of consultation and pointed out that "a number of consultations with both Arabs and Jews" had taken place during the year. The King, however, was not satisfied and there was a further exchange of messages which rang the changes on the positions assumed by each side.[11]

In referring to the Jewish National Home, not a Jewish state, Truman accepted our wording, and the fact that he did so would seem to indicate that he was not yet ready to support the idea of statehood. At about the same time, too, he told one of our representatives from the Near East (George Wadsworth, Minister to Syria and Lebanon) that "there could be no Jewish state" in Palestine.[12]

Further Arab anxieties regarding the course of our Palestine policy were voiced by two of Ibn Saud's sons, the Emir Feisal and the Emir Saud, in meetings which they had in Washington with the President and the Secretary of State, respectively (at the time, Feisal was Foreign Minister, Saud was

Crown Prince). Feisal was very harsh in his criticism of the Zionists for attempting, as he said, with our support, to "bring large numbers of Jews to Palestine in order to take away from the Arabs lands upon which they had lived for many centuries." The President assured him that "it was not our purpose in any sense to advocate taking from any person or people what belonged to them or to deal in any way unfairly or unjustly." He was, he told him, seeking a solution to the problem which would be just to all concerned and would make for peace in the Near East. He could not believe that the "pitiful remnant" of the European Jews whom we were trying to help could be the sort of people described by the Emir.

The Emir Saud's complaints to Secretary Byrnes were much the same. Acheson, who was present at both meetings, observed in his memoirs that it seemed to him that the minds of Feisal and the President "crossed but did not meet." Feisal, he added, impressed him as "a man who could be an implacable enemy and who should be taken very seriously." Of the meeting with Saud, Acheson commented that "My abiding memory . . . is of the Crown Prince's immobility."[13]

As 1946 drew to a close, the Near East Division continued to be in the dark as to U.S. policy. Merriam in a memorandum dated December 27 expressed it this way: "Our policy has gradually taken form, though it is still somewhat indefinite, as the result of the pressures that have been applied to us from various directions. We go as far as we can to please the Zionists and other Jews without making the Arabs and the British too angry . . . our policy is one of expediency, not of principle." Merriam argued that this was "an uncomfortable and dangerous" position from which we ought to extricate ourselves with all possible speed. Another point he made was that "the reception accorded by Arabs, Jews, or both, to the report of the Anglo-American Committee of Inquiry, to the Grady Mission plan—indeed, to all schemes and plans proposed by third parties—strongly indicates that no third-party plan has any chance of success unless imposed and maintained by force." As far as the future was concerned, he thought that there should be negotiations between Arabs and Jews looking toward the establishment of a "political entity or entities" in an independent Palestine. In transmitting Merriam's paper to Acheson, Henderson commented: "Of course we have practically been forced by political pressure and sentiment in the U.S. in the direction of a 'viable Jewish state.' I must confess that when I view our policy in the light of the principles avowed by us I become uneasy."[14]

Thus, although the Near East Division was still somewhat uncertain about what the official U.S. Palestine policy was, the thinking in the Division was evidently moving away from a solution based on the Anglo-American report and in the direction of some form of partition. This can be inferred by the fact that Merriam's memorandum, though not endorsing partition as such, did go so far as to refer to a "political entity or entities." Early in the new year, another memorandum carried the Division's thinking a step further, in speaking of "one or more states" rather than "entities." This paper read in part: "Palestine should be neither a Jewish State nor an Arab State, but the people of Palestine should be granted full independence as soon as practicable in one or more states in which the form of government will satisfy as nearly as possible the national aspirations of both Jews and Arabs. Accomplishment of such a solution through a workable partition . . . could be supported by the United States."[15]

It must be understood that a "workable" partition meant to NE a partition that could be carried out peacefully. The Near East Division was not in favor of any policy that would involve enforcing partition in the face of Arab opposition. As it became more and more clear during the year 1947 that the Arabs were adamantly opposed to any form of partition and were prepared to fight to prevent it from being implemented, NE parted company with the Administration.

A little later on, in a talk with the British Ambassador on January 21, Acheson said that he thought "the solution which it would be the easiest for the American Government to support would be one based on partition." He did not define what he had in mind, but on January 27, with the approval of the Secretary of State, he handed the British Ambassador a paper stating that we would find it possible to support a solution "calling for partition and the setting up of a viable Jewish state." If, however, the British, after consulting the Arabs and Jews, should conclude that partition would be unworkable, and if a solution "lying somewhere between partition and the Morrison-Grady plan" could be worked out, we would support that instead.[16]

By this time, the process of communal fragmentation had developed so far in Palestine that it was highly unlikely that a single Palestinian state could emerge as a solution. As one observer (the former official of the Palestine government who wrote under the name John Marlowe) put it: "By February, 1947, the process of communal partition in Palestine, under way for two years, was almost complete. Any possibility of evolution toward a unitary state had ceased to exist."[17]

In December, in Basle, the first meeting of the World Zionist Congress since 1939 had debated the question of participation in the London Conference. Weizmann ran for reelection as president on a platform calling for participation at London and for a partitioned Palestine. Rabbi Silver spoke for the American Zionists, who still wanted a Jewish state in an undivided Palestine and who opposed participation in the conference. (Silver had not attended the August meeting of the Executive which had decided on the "viable state" proposal.) In the end, the Congress could agree only on a resolution calling for a Jewish Commonwealth. It voted down an amendment proposed by Silver forces which would have specified that the Jewish Commonwealth should be in "Palestine as a whole." This outcome was interpreted, rightly it would seem, by those who supported the concept of a "viable state in an adequate area" as an indirect endorsement of their position, that is, of partition. Another resolution called for continued abstention from the London Conference. Out of deference to Weizmann the position of president was left unfilled.[18]

An interesting parallel with contemporary events is provided in an article by David Hirst in the *Manchester Guardian Weekly* for June 15, 1974. Hirst reported that at a meeting of the Palestine National Council (the top policy-making body of the Palestinian Liberation Organization) which had just taken place in Cairo, one of the participants had made the point that at the 1946 Basle Congress Ben Gurion had suggested that it would be possible for the Zionists to adopt the goal of "a viable Jewish state in an adequate area of Palestine" without foregoing their historic claim to all of Palestine. By analogy, this same individual argued, the Palestinians could attend a conference at Geneva on the Arab-Israel conflict without foregoing *their* stated goal of a "secular democratic state" in Palestine. In other words, as Hirst pointed out, the Palestinians had "endorsed a kind of Zionism in reverse."

During the closing months of 1946, the situation in China had been giving rise to increasing anxiety. In October General Marshall had told President Truman that he felt his usefulness was at an end. Certainly it was becoming clear that there was no prospect of bringing about a reconciliation between the warring factions there. Truman therefore recalled Marshall to Washington, on January 3, 1947. By this time Truman was becoming increasingly unhappy over what he considered to be Byrnes's free-wheeling performance as Secretary of State. He decided to replace Byrnes with General Marshall, and Marshall took office as head of the Department of State on January 21. (Later in the year, Robert A. Lovett became Under Secretary.).[19]

In January also, my assignment of four years to the Department expired. Foreign Service Officers were required to return to service abroad after spending four years in the Department, and I was accordingly assigned to our Embassy in Tehran. Fraser Wilkins, a Foreign Service officer with experience in the Near East, who was later to become our first Ambassador to Cyprus, took over the Palestine desk.

In late January, the London Conference resumed. The British met separately with the Arabs and the Jews as before, but it very quickly became evident that no agreement was going to be possible. The reluctance of the Jewish Agency representatives to be explicit about what they meant by "a viable state in an adequate area" was evident throughout the talks. At a meeting on February 11, attended by Sir Norman Brook, Sir Douglas Harris, and Harold Beeley for the British side and David Ben Gurion, Moshe Shertok, and David Horowitz for the Jewish side, the British produced a map showing what they thought such an area ought to comprise, but the Jewish side refused to be drawn out. Ben Gurion declined to do more than draw his finger rapidly across the map. Presumably the Zionists were unwilling to produce their own map or to be too precise because this would have implied that they were waiving their historic claim to all of Palestine.[20]

Finally, as a last resort, the British offered a proposal (which came to be known as the "Bevin Scheme," drafted for Bevin by Harold Beeley) for a five-year trusteeship with substantial autonomy for Jewish and Arab areas and with approximately 100,000 Jews to be admitted over the course of two years. At the end of the five years Palestine would become independent as a single state. Both the Arabs and the Jews rejected this proposal.[21] The atmosphere was gloomy. One of the Jewish Agency participants in the talks, Aubrey, later Abba, Eban, has vividly described the setting of the final confrontation with the British side: "Early in February, 1947 . . . in a chilly room in the Colonial Office, with the electric light repeatedly going out owing to the fuel shortage, the last attempt was made to reach a settlement."[22] The Jews turned down the proposal because, they said, they could not possibly consider any scheme that did not mention the possibility of partition, and the Arabs objected to the provision regarding the 100,000 Jews.

The British concluded that there was no alternative to taking the Palestine matter to the United Nations—this had, in fact, been under consideration for some time. On February 18 Bevin told the House of Commons that the government had decided to submit the Palestine question to the United Nations. Several days later, during the debate on the question, he delivered a sharp attack on American tactics in dealing with the Palestine problem, and mentioned specifically Truman's Yom Kippur statement, obviously still rankled by it even after four months. This brought loud cheers from the benches. The next day (February 26) the White House issued a statement denying that the President's intervention in the matter had been motivated by domestic politics.[23]

The British have been criticized in some quarters for seeming to have washed their hands of this vexing problem by turning it over to the United Nations, but under the circumstances that was probably the only choice possible. Security problems in Palestine were worsening day by day, as widespread Jewish terrorism and illegal immigration added to the thankless task of administration and also to the costs to the British taxpayers. By now, the British had no less than 100,000 troops in Palestine and military casualties were mounting.[24] The seriousness with which the authorities in Palestine were now viewing the situation was reflected in an announcement made on January 13, 1947, that the dependents of British civilian personnel, as well as certain nonessential officials—some 2,000 persons in all—would be evacuated from the country.[25]

The British were also faced at this time with the necessity of adopting a policy of withdrawal from certain parts of the world where they had maintained important strategic interests—India, Greece, Turkey. The problem in the latter two was urgent, and indeed on February 21, only three days after the announcement to the House of Commons, the British informed us that they could no longer bear the burden of financial assistance to the Greek and Turkish governments. It was in consequence of this that President Truman on March 12 told a joint session of Congress that the United States was embarking on a broad program of aid to Greece and Turkey. Loy Henderson, incidentally, played a key role in the development of this policy, which came to be known as the Truman Doctrine. Although the President's message to Congress dealt primarily with Greece and Turkey, the new policy was stated in more comprehensive terms and indeed marked the beginning of our policy of containment.[26]

It should be noted that the British at this time had no intention of giving up the Mandate but simply wanted the United Nations to recommend a solution. The Colonial Secretary, Arthur Creech-Jones, made this clear during the House of Commons debate (on February 25): "Why are we making no recommendation to the United Nations? . . . we are not going to surrender the Mandate—we are going to the United Nations setting out the problem and asking for advice as to how the Mandate can be administered."[27] These words are worth bearing in mind, because the British government was to change its policy later in the year, when, as will be brought out in the next chapter, the decision was taken (in September) to withdraw from Palestine.[28]

There are signs that the Zionists, who had been so adamant, may have been prepared to back down just before Bevin's announcement to the House of Commons that the question was being referred to the United Nations. This shift in the Zionist position has been largely overlooked, but it seems that they were prepared to make concessions to keep the talks from breaking down, suspecting that the next step would be the UN, which they did not want at this time. Ben Gurion in a meeting with the Lord Chancellor, Lord Jowitt, on February 13 offered to agree to a five-year trusteeship during which the Jewish Agency would cease all agitation for a Jewish state, on condition that the 100,000 Jews would be admitted at once and that certain other demands would be met.[29] The offer was too late. When it was put to the Cabinet the next day, Bevin announced that the decision had already been reached to place the matter before the United Nations.

For at least several months, in fact, the Zionists had been worried that if the Palestine question went to the United Nations they would not be able to get the support of the world organization for their program. In November 1946, when Rabbi Silver had a meeting with Foreign Secretary Bevin in New York, Bevin had suggested that the British might find it necessary to turn the whole Palestine question over to the United Nations and Silver had voiced great distress at this possibility.[30] As it turned out, however, the breakdown of the London talks and the transfer of the problem to the United Nations worked in the Zionists' favor, as it led directly to the establishment of the state of Israel a little over a year later.

Characteristically, it was Dean Acheson who most aptly summed up the reaction in the Department to this course of events when he predicted to Henderson at this time that it looked as though 1947 was going to be a "bad year" for the U.S. in Palestine and the Middle East.[31]

Palestine before the United Nations

Following Bevin's announcement in the House of Commons that the British were referring the Palestine question to the United Nations, there was a delay of several weeks during which the manner of presenting the issue to the UN was discussed between Washington, London, and New York. In early April, the British submitted a formal request to the Secretary-General of the United Nations asking that a special session of the General Assembly be convened for the purpose of setting up a special committee to prepare recommendations for submission to the regular session of the Assembly in September.

When the special session of the General Assembly met on April 28, the Arab states proposed that the Mandate should be terminated at once and Palestine declared an independent state. This was voted down. The United States then proposed the creation of a committee of investigation composed of disinterested member states (the Soviet Union wanted the five permanent members of the Security Council to be members of the committee, but this was not accepted).[1]

The Arab Higher Committee and the Jewish Agency were permitted to appear before the First Committee of the Assembly, which was considering the American proposal. During the debate in committee, the Soviet Union advocated the immediate independence of Palestine as a binational state, but eventually went along with the U.S. proposal for an investigation. The United States did not endorse any particular solution and this continued to be our position for some months to come. The British representative, Sir Alexander Cadogan, made it clear that his government would not carry out any decision of the Assembly of which it did not approve—which in his words, "we cannot reconcile with our conscience." He provided an insight into what the British attitude was to be during the coming months by declaring that His Majesty's Government would not be a party to enforcing on the two communities in Palestine any solution which was not acceptable to both of them. This was a warning of difficulties to come.

The Assembly adjourned on May 15 after adopting, by a vote of 45 to 7, the report of the First Committee, the negative votes being the five Arab members—Egypt, Iraq, Syria, Lebanon, and Saudi Arabia—and Afghanistan and Turkey. A Special Committee on Palestine (which became known as UNSCOP) was set up with broad powers to investigate all aspects of the problem and with a mandate to submit a report to the Assembly not later than September 1. The eleven member states represented on the Special Committee were Australia, Canada, Czechoslovakia, Guatemala, India, Iran, the Netherlands, Peru, Sweden, Uruguay, and Yugoslavia—in Secretary Marshall's words, "eleven relatively neutral states not including the Great Powers or an Arab state." During the discussion regarding the composition of the Special Committee, the Zionists were extremely active in putting forward the names of certain countries which they wanted to see included, notably Guatemala. The reason for this last choice became clear when the committee embarked on its mission. As will be explained below, Guatemala was represented on the committee by Jorge Garcia-Granados, the head of its UN delegation, who proved to be an outspoken supporter of the Zionist cause.[2]

The Assembly also passed a resolution calling upon "all governments and peoples and particularly upon the inhabitants of Palestine, to refrain, pending action by the General Assembly on the report of the Special Committee, from the threat or use of force or any other action which might create an atmosphere prejudicial to an early settlement of the question of Palestine." In the light of conditions prevailing in Palestine at the time, this seems somewhat unrealistic. The Assembly's resolution was paralleled by a statement issued on June 5 by President Truman, appealing, in similarly grandiloquent terms, to "every citizen and resident of the United States, in the interests of this country, of world peace, and of humanity, meticulously to refrain, while the United Nations is considering the problem of Palestine, from engaging in, or facilitating, any activities which tend further to inflame the passions of the inhabitants of Palestine, to undermine law and order in Palestine, or to promote violence in that country."[3]

The Department, in a circular telegram dated June 13, told our representatives in the field that they should explain, in discussing the Palestine question, that the United States was not supporting any particular solution. Secretary Marshall, in a letter to Ambassador Austin at the United Nations on the same date, made the same point, adding that it looked as though an agreed settlement in Palestine no longer seemed possible and that "at least a certain degree of force" would be required to implement any solution of the problem.[4]

A more detailed statement of our attitude was set out in a July 7 memorandum by Loy Henderson.[5] This outlined four alternative plans: (1) a "uninational" state; (2) a binational state; (3) partition, with a Jewish state of some 1,500 square miles comprising those areas where the Jews were in a clear majority; and (4) a variant of partition which would add to the Jewish state the virtually uninhabited Negev desert to the south. Henderson supported solution No. 1 as conforming to UN Charter principles, but conceded that this might be considered unattainable as being too idealistic. Of course solution No. 2 (a binational state) might be unacceptable to both Arabs and Jews, but he thought that either of these would be preferable to No. 3 or No. 4.

Other points brought out in Henderson's very perceptive July 7 memorandum were that UNSCOP would probably be unable to achieve unanimity and would come up with a majority report and one or more minority reports; that the U.S. should not take a public position until UNSCOP had submitted its report and the British, the Arabs, and the Jews had been given an opportunity to comment; that the debate on UNSCOP's findings in the General Assembly would be very heated, with the United States coming under intense pressure to adopt a pro-Zionist position; and finally that our delegation to the Assembly should take care that any final plan not be labeled an American plan. We should, he thought, retain the greatest possible flexibility so as to be able to "exert an ameliorating influence" on the parties.

Henderson summarized past and current statements of U.S. policy on Palestine as showing that the Mandate, which incorporated the Balfour Declaration, was recognized by us as an international instrument; that we were in favor of continued Jewish immigration to Palestine; and that we might favor partition provided it gave promise of being workable. He added that it now appeared it would not be possible, except through the use of force, to continue Jewish immigration or to establish a Jewish state. The situation, he pointed out, was now totally different from that prevailing earlier. It no longer looked as though a peaceful solution could be found.

Meanwhile, important developments had been taking place with regard to Europe. Secretary Marshall had returned in late April from the Moscow Conference of Foreign Ministers convinced that the European nations were facing severe economic difficulties and that the Soviet Union was determined to exploit these difficulties to advance Communist aims. In a landmark speech at the Harvard University commencement exercises on June 5 Marshall announced that the United States was prepared to cooperate with the countries of Europe in a program of economic recovery, but he stressed that the initiative would have to come from the Europeans themselves. This led to the calling in July, under British and French auspices, of a conference at Paris, to which governments from Eastern as well as Western Europe were invited. The Soviet Union, however, decided not to cooperate with the proposed recovery effort and went so far as to bring pressure on Czechoslovakia, Poland, and Hungary to withdraw their acceptances of the invitation to the Paris meeting. Nonetheless, the European Recovery Program, generally known as the Marshall Plan, went into action and in the succeeding years, with considerable American help, was credited with restoring the economic well-being of the Western European nations, and along with the North Atlantic Treaty Organization, with keeping those nations from falling under Communist domination.[6]

UNSCOP held its first meeting at Lake Success on May 26 and arrived in Jerusalem June 16.[7] Out of deference to Arab opinion, the committee had decided not to hold hearings in New York or to visit the displaced persons camps, but even so, the Arab Higher Committee boycotted the committee, although the members met Arab representatives outside Palestine. The Jewish Agency, on the other hand, engaged in an elaborate program of briefing and entertainment. It soon became clear that the two Latin American members, Jose Garcia-Granados of Guatemala and Enrique Rodriguez Fabregat of Uruguay, held pronounced pro-Zionist views (so much so, indeed, that streets were later named after these two gentlemen in Tel Aviv).[8]

The period of the committee's visit to Palestine was marked by continuing acts of terrorism, kidnapping, and sabotage by the Jewish underground. As the committee's report aptly put it, "the atmosphere in Palestine today is one of profound tension." The already tense situation was made worse by the incident of the *S.S. Exodus*, a former Chesapeake Bay excursion steamer which, greatly overloaded, took off at this time from a port in France with a shipload of illegal immigrants bound for Palestine. The ship was intercepted by the British and sent back to France, where the authorities were willing to allow the passengers to disembark, but they refused. Eventually the British forcibly transported the refugees to camps in Germany, an action which was almost universally condemned by world opinion.[9] On several occasions the United States took this matter up with the British government in an effort to work out a satisfactory settlement, but to no avail. Relations between us and the British throughout this period were strained by the fact that many American citizens were engaged in helping the Zionist underground in Palestine, chiefly by supplying arms and financing illegal immigration.

A number of British and Jewish witnesses testified at the UNSCOP hearings in Jerusalem, including, of course, Ben Gurion, who had some difficulty justifying Zionist aims in Palestine in terms of self-determination and majority rule, and the aging Weizmann, who had to be helped to the witness chair and whose testimony was so confused on some points as to cause obvious consternation among his Jewish Agency colleagues seated near him. When Dr. Magnes appeared before the committee, he called for implementation of the Anglo-American report. The members traveled around Palestine, but because of the Arab boycott were able to visit only Jewish installations. On one occasion when they were passing through an

Arab village, the signal had been given to evacuate the inhabitants and they found only deserted buildings. [10]

After a visit to Beirut to meet Arab representatives, the members proceeded to Geneva to prepare their report. [11] The earlier decision that the group as a whole would not go to the displaced persons camps was sustained, but a subcommittee (including Garcia-Granados and Fabregat) did so. As was the case with the earlier Anglo-American Committee at Lausanne, the Jewish Agency assigned liaison officers to Geneva to maintain contact with the members. Richard Crossman, a member of the Anglo-American Committee, came to Geneva to speak before the UN committee and it was said that the two books that influenced the members the most were his recently published book on the earlier committee (*Palestine Mission*) and the Peel Report, both of which advocated partition. On August 31, one day before the Assembly's deadline, the report was completed and signed. [12]

In an introductory section, the members of UNSCOP confirmed the judgment of the Peel Commission in 1936–37 that the Mandate was unworkable. In terms similar to Loy Henderson's words, quoted above, they added that "the history of the last 25 years has established the fact that not only the creation of a Jewish state but even the continuation of the building of the Jewish National Home by . . . immigration could be implemented only by the use of some considerable force."

The members were able to agree on eleven recommendations, including termination of the Mandate, granting independence to Palestine, provision of a transitional period before independence, continuing United Nations responsibility, safeguarding the Holy Places, international action to solve the problem of the Jewish displaced persons in Europe (now grown to 250,000), democracy, peace, economic unity, termination of the capitulary regime, and an appeal against acts of violence. A twelfth finding, to the effect that Palestine could not be expected to provide a solution to what was called "the Jewish problem in general," was adopted with two dissenting votes (Guatemala and Uruguay).

On the vital question of the future of Palestine, the committee split. A majority of seven members—Canada, Czechoslovakia, Guatemala, the Netherlands, Peru, Sweden, and Uruguay—called for the partition of Palestine into an Arab state, a Jewish state, and an internationalized Jerusalem, in economic union with one another. The Arab and Jewish states were to become independent within two years from September 1, 1947. During this period, Great Britain was to continue to administer the country, under the auspices of the United Nations, and was to admit into the proposed Jewish state 150,000 Jewish immigrants. Jerusalem was to be placed under the international trusteeship system, with the United Nations as the administering authority.

Three members (India, Iran, and Yugoslavia) proposed an independent federal state. The eleventh member of the committee, the Australian, did not endorse either plan.

Ralph Bunche, an American member of the UN Secretariat who had been detailed to UNSCOP and who later was to achieve prominence as the second UN Mediator for Palestine, was the author of both majority and minority plans. This was quite a feat in itself, but his task was rendered even more difficult by the fact that the members of the majority group were unable to agree among themselves on the details of the partition until the last minute. As a result, Bunche and one of his colleagues spent most of the night before the report was signed putting the finishing touches on the draft. They had time only to draw rough boundaries on a map, using colored pencils. This led to some confusion on the ground later on: for instance, villages were inadvertently separated from their fields.[13]

The majority report rejected either a single Arab state or a single Jewish state in the whole of Palestine. It was impossible to satisfy both parties fully, and "indefensible" to satisfy one party at the expense of the other. Both the binational and the cantonal types of solution were dismissed as unworkable. This left either partition under some form of confederal arrangement, or a federal state.

Starting from the basic premise that the conflicting claims of Arabs and Jews were irreconcilable, the majority report argued that only through partition could the necessary "finality" be attained. Arab objections could be anticipated but these would be tempered by a solution which would definitively fix boundaries and thus set a limit to Jewish immigration. The fact that the solution would carry the sanction of the United Nations should allay Arab fears. The partition that was being proposed was in any event a "qualified" one since the two states would be part of a single economic entity.

A principal defect in the UNSCOP majority report, as many observers have pointed out, is that it is difficult to reconcile the concept of partitioning Palestine, against the wishes of the majority of its inhabitants, with commonly accepted principles of self-determination, democracy, and majority rule. Indeed, the recommending of partition appeared to be inconsistent with the support for democratic principles avowed elsewhere in the report.[14]

It should be borne in mind that at the time the population of Palestine comprised 1,200,000 Arabs and 650,000 Jews, or an Arab majority of about two to one. The task of drawing workable boundaries for the proposed Jewish state was complicated because the population was so distributed that any Jewish state was bound to have a sizable Arab minority. In other words, even though the Jews were largely concentrated in certain areas, mainly the coastal plain, it was hard to devise a Jewish state that made any sense without incorporating large numbers of Arabs in it. The result was that the boundaries suggested for both states were gerrymandered to say the least. The distribution of population as recommended in the UNSCOP majority report was as follows:

	Jews	Arabs	Total
Jewish state	498,000	407,000	905,000
Arab state	10,000	725,000	735,000
Jerusalem	142,000	68,000	210,000
Total	650,000	1,200,000	1,850,000

These figures did not tell the whole story, however. The report made the revealing statement in an aside that "in addition there will be in the Jewish state about 90,000 Bedouins, cultivators and stock-owners who seek grazing further afield in dry seasons." In other words, as these additional 90,000 persons could hardly be Jews, the Arab population of the Jewish state would total 497,000, as compared with 498,000 Jews—a very slim margin indeed. This immediately raised the prospect, given the rapid rate of natural increase of the Palestine Arabs, that the Jewish state would soon have an actual Arab majority.

Economic union was proposed as a means of sweetening the pill to the Arabs, but it presupposed a degree of cooperation between the two communities that did not exist and was little heard of after the report came out. And yet the scheme depended for its success upon some form of economic union: without it, the two proposed states would not be economically viable. In fact the entire plan, with its checkerboard-like division of the country into six different zones (not counting Jerusalem) converging at only two meeting points, and with its four separate entities—Jewish state, Arab state, internationalized Jerusalem, and the economic union—was far too complex to be workable without a maximum of good will on all sides.

Implementation of the majority plan was made dependent on acceptance by the two parties, since it was provided that each of the proposed states would become independent only upon its own request. It was reasonably certain that the Arabs, whose position rested on a claim to independence in an undivided Palestine, would never make such a request. In such event, the plan provided that the entire matter would be referred back to the General Assembly, thus starting the cycle all over again. The Arabs could also be expected to oppose the proposal that 150,000 Jewish refugees be admitted within two years.

On matters of detail, it may be noted that the majority report did not provide a suitable seaport or a suitable capital for the Arab state; that Jaffa, a wholly Arab city, was included in the Jewish state; and that Jerusalem would be an isolated enclave dependent for its road and rail connections and its water supply on the Arab state. Also, the proposed Jewish state would have

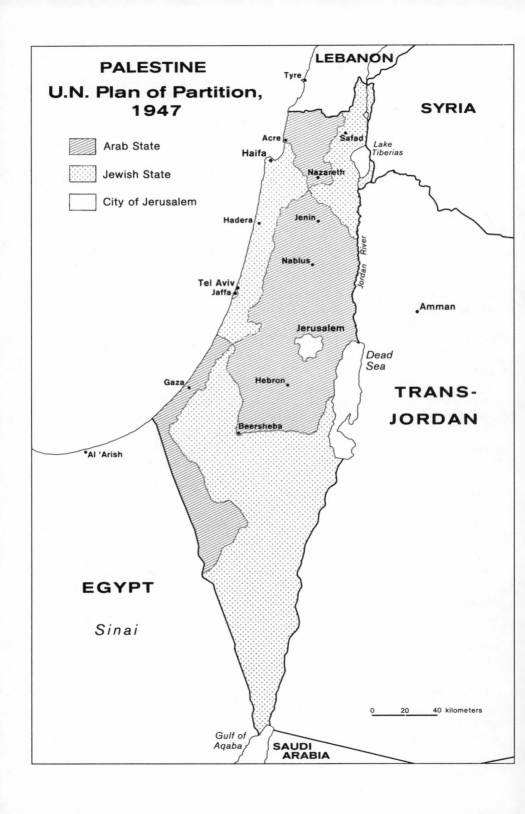

frontiers that would be extremely difficult to defend. Thus the plan was probably not going to satisfy either the political demands of most Zionists or the humanitarian needs of the Jewish displaced persons, and it might well lead to an intensification of expansionist pressures on the part of the Jews. No wonder one commentator calls the report a "desperate solution for a situation which had thus far defied reason." [15] All these arguments against the partition plan had cogency, but they carried little weight compared to the political realities of the day, which compelled a solution favorable to the Zionists.

There seems no need to dwell at length on the minority plan of UNSCOP, calling for an independent federal state, since it was clear from the outset that this plan (although preferable in many ways to the majority plan) would appeal neither to Arabs nor to Jews and in any event had little chance of success in the prevailing political climate at the United Nations.

When the UNSCOP report came out, the Arabs voiced strong objections to the majority plan. An exception was King Abdullah of Trans-Jordan, who confided to a Greek diplomat that he was planning to annex the Arab portion of Palestine to his domains. [16] This was confirmed also to a member of the staff of our General Assembly delegation by a Trans-Jordanian official at the United Nations. The Jewish Agency accepted the majority plan reluctantly. Rabbi Silver and the American Zionists at first opposed the plan, but later accepted it, as did the American Jewish Committee and all other Jewish organizations in the United States except the American Council for Judaism. Press reaction in the United States was largely in favor of partition.

British officials in London and Jerusalem said that they considered the majority plan unworkable and unfair, while in Washington, the Department of State and the Pentagon were also opposed to it.

The Administration was now subjected to intense pressure as public opinion in the United States became more and more pro-Zionist. An illustration of this pressure is provided by an analysis of communications regarding Palestine received at the White House during this period. In the third quarter of 1947, approximately 65,000 items (telegrams, postcards, letters, petitions, and so on) were received, and in the fourth quarter of that year about 70,000 such items were received. [17] The diaries of Secretary of Defense Forrestal record that at two cabinet meetings during this period, on September 4 and again on October 6, Postmaster General Robert E. Hannegan, who was also chairman of the Democratic National Committee, brought up the subject of Palestine, calling attention to the "very great influence" that Administration support for the Zionist position had on fund-raising for the party. [18]

At a meeting on September 15 of our delegation to the United Nations General Assembly, Henderson was asked to express his views. He warned that the majority plan, if accepted by the Assembly, would have to be implemented by force, that this would result in much bloodshed and suffering, and that many people throughout the world would lose their trust in the United States. He predicted that the existence of a Jewish state in Palestine would cause injury and damage to the United States for many years to come.

Our delegation included two persons, Mrs. Eleanor Roosevelt, widow of the late President, and Major General John H. Hilldring, Assistant Secretary of State for Occupied Areas, who were regarded as pro-Zionist. Both of them expressed support for the majority report at this meeting of the delegation. Recapitulating the meeting for me nearly thirty years later, in an interview in March 1976, Mr. Henderson recalled that after he spoke Mrs. Roosevelt intervened and declared: "Come, come, Mr. Henderson. I think you're exaggerating the dangers. You are too pessimistic. A few years ago Ireland was considered to be a permanent problem that could not be solved. Then the Irish Republic was established and the problem vanished. I'm confident that when a Jewish state is set up, the Arabs will see the light; they will quiet down; and Palestine will no longer be a problem."[19]

General Hilldring had been appointed to the delegation in place of Dean Virginia Gildersleeve of Barnard College, who had served as the only woman member of our delegation to the San Francisco Conference but had been unable to accept the appointment in 1947 owing to ill health. As early as July 29 David K. Niles, the Presidential Administrative Assistant, was urging the President to put Hilldring on the delegation in order to have the Zionist point of view represented.[20] It would appear that had Miss Gildersleeve been able to serve she would have brought a different approach, as her public statements had tended to favor the Arab side. She was later one of the founding members of the American Friends of the Middle East, a group generally regarded as pro-Arab. During the entire session of the Assembly, Hilldring was in direct touch with the White House, frequently with Niles and on at least one occasion with Truman himself. The Department often did not know what was being reported to the White House or what instructions Niles was passing on to Hilldring.[21]

The General Assembly met on September 16 in an atmosphere of growing international tension characterized by such events as the Soviet Union's rejection of the Marshall Plan and the formation of the Cominform. Discussion of the Palestine issue tended to overshadow all others in the Assembly. Because of its crowded agenda, the Assembly set up an ad hoc committee, composed of all the member states, to consider the Palestine question. The Arab Higher Committee and the Jewish Agency again testified, the Arabs rejecting both the majority and the minority plans of UNSCOP and the Jews indicating acceptance of the majority plan as "the indispensable minimum." It seems likely that the Zionists took this position in the hope that they would be able to expand their state beyond the borders provided in the plan.

On September 17 Secretary Marshall appeared before the General Assembly. He stated that the United States "gives great weight" both to those of the recommendations of the committee which had been unanimous and also to the majority report. This was interpreted by many as an endorsement of the majority report by our government, although in fact a decision to this effect had not yet been reached. In the Assembly the United States came under great pressure from both Arabs and Jews.[22]

Henderson's misgivings with regard to partition were amplified in a memorandum which he submitted to the Secretary of State under date of September 22, entitled "Certain Considerations against Advocacy by the U.S. of the Majority Plan." Henderson began by saying that his views not only were those of the entire Near East Division but were shared by "nearly every member of the Foreign Service or of the Department who has worked to any appreciable extent on Near Eastern problems." He then expressed the view that it would not be in the national interest of the United States for it to advocate the partition of Palestine or the setting up of a Jewish state there. I think it worthwhile to give his memorandum in full, because of the cogent way in which he outlined his position and because of the important place this paper holds in the context of our government's developing Palestine policy.[23]

In summary, Henderson's main points were that support of the majority plan would undermine our relations with the Arab and Moslem worlds; that we would be expected to make a major contribution to the implementation of the plan; that any plan for partitioning Palestine was unworkable; that adoption of the plan would not dispose of the Palestine problem; and finally that the proposals in the plan were "not only not based on any principles of an international character . . . but in definite contravention of . . . the Charter as well as principles on which American concepts of government are based." Henderson urged that the United States should not play too active a role in the General Assembly debate but should concentrate on trying to get the agreement of the parties to a period of temporary trusteeship which could be followed by a plebiscite.

CERTAIN CONSIDERATIONS AGAINST ADVOCACY BY THE U.S. OF THE MAJORITY PLAN

1. *An advocacy on our part of any plan providing for the partitioning of Palestine or the establishment in Palestine of a Jewish state would be certain to undermine our relations with the Arab, and to a lesser extent with the Moslem, world at a time when the Western World needs the friendship and cooperation of the Arabs and other Moslems.*

Without at least a degree of Arab cooperation we shall encounter numerous difficulties in connection with any support which we may give to the efforts of the British to find bases which will enable Great Britain to remain as a stabilizing power in the Eastern Mediterranean. We shall need the confidence and cooperation of the Arabs in the near future if we are to achieve any success in forestalling violent Arab nationalist uprisings against the French in Tunisia, Algeria and Morocco. The resources and geographical position of the Arab countries are of such a character that those countries are necessarily factors of importance in the international economic field. Arab friendship is essential if we are to have their cooperation in the carrying out of some of our vital economic programs. During the next few years we are planning to draw heavily on the resources of the area, not only for our use, but for the reconstruction of Europe. Furthermore, we are intending to make important use of the communications facilities in the area. Already, partly as a result of our policies regarding Palestine, the attitude of the Arab Governments towards American firms has changed sharply and their demands on the firms are becoming more and more truculent and extravagant. Loss of confidence in the sense of justness and in the impartiality of the United States has been accompanied during the last two years in the Arab world by a growing suspicion of our overall motives and by increasing doubts as to our national integrity. Although the Arabs have in general no use for Communism, they feel so emotional with regard to the problem of Palestine that if an attempt should actually be made to set up a Jewish State in Palestine in pursuance of decisions supported by us, they may consider the United States as their foremost enemy and enter into at least temporary cooperation with the Soviet Union against us just as we cooperated with the Russians during the war years against common enemies.

If we press for a Jewish state, we shall undoubtedly weaken the position of the moderate Arabs who are friends of the western world and strengthen that of the fanatical extremists. Just last week, for instance, one of the moderate Arab leaders was slain in Palestine by followers of the fanatical Mufti.

2. *If we advocate a plan providing for partitioning and the setting up of a Jewish State, we shall certainly be expected to make major contributions in force, materials and money to the implementation of such a plan if it is adopted.*

We are under tremendous pressure at the present time to advocate such a plan. If we do, and if the plan is adopted, we shall be under still greater pressure to contribute to its implementation. We shall be lacking in courage and consistency, it will be argued, if after a plan supported by us has been adopted we do not do our part in carrying it out. Furthermore, we shall be expected to bear the main burden of implementation. We have shown more interest in the Palestine problem than any other great Power, except Great Britain, and Great Britain is beginning to weary of the Palestine burden. Furthermore, the execution of a partition plan such as that in the majority report will be a task lasting over a period of many years. Differences arising from attempts to carry out such a plan will arise to plague every session of the General Assembly. As one of the sponsors for the execution of the plan, we shall be the target for bitter attacks by both Arabs and Jews.

3. *Any plan for partitioning Palestine would be unworkable.*

Of all the previous committees which have ever studied the Palestine problem, only the Royal (Peel) Commission 1937 recommended partition as a solution.

The Partition (Woodhead) Commission set up in 1938 to carry out the Peel proposals was unable to devise a practicable plan for partition, so the Peel recommendations fell to the ground. The Anglo-American Committee of Inquiry, composed of six prominent Britishers and six well-known Americans, stated in their report of April 20, 1946:

> Partition has an appeal at first sight as giving a prospect of early independence and self-government to Jews and Arabs, but in our view no partition would have any chance unless it was basically acceptable to Jews and Arabs, and there is no sign of that today. We are accordingly unable to recommend partition as a solution.

If complete partition would be unsuccessful unless acceptable to Jews and Arabs, how much chance of success in the face of fierce Arab opposition has the UNSCOP majority plan which provides for an economic union of the two states—a union which cannot possibly succeed without Arab-Jewish friendship and cooperation? Irrigation ditches, railways, roads, telephone and telegraph lines, etc. must pass through both states. These facilities cannot function if the population of one state is hostile to that of the other. If political partition providing for the incorporation of 400,000 Arabs in a Jewish State is forced on the population of Palestine, this hostility will exist and will increase.

4. *The UNSCOP Majority Plan is not only unworkable; if adopted, it would guarantee that the Palestine problem would be permanent and still more complicated in the future.*

Some of the reasons for the unworkability of the Majority Plan are:

(a) It is not possible for the two states to have political individuality and economic unity if the population of one or both of these states objects to such a partnership and refuses to cooperate;

(b) In case economic unity is found to be unworkable, it would not be possible to have complete economic individuality since the terrain of the country and the nature of the communications are such that the two states are inextricably meshed economically;

(c) In spite of the arguments advanced to the contrary in the report, an Arab state of the type envisaged would not be viable even if subsidized by receiving half of the revenues derived from the customs and other services;

(d) The cost of policing, in view of both extreme Arab and Jewish irredentism, would be more than the combined national budget could bear.

5. *The Majority Plan does not dispose once and for all of the Palestine problem because:*

(a) It provides for an economic union to be presided over by a Joint Economic Board, the members of which shall consist of three representatives of each of the two States and the foreign members appointed by the Economic and Social Council. An organ of the United Nations must, therefore, indefinitely act as an economic umpire between these two States. Will representatives of the Great Powers serve on this Board? If so, will an American serve? In case important Jewish interests are involved, is the American Government to be put under constant internal political pressure to order its representative to side with the Jewish State? Is the Soviet Union or a Soviet satellite to be represented by one of the three members? If so, what kind of a role would such a representative be likely to play?

(b) The Majority Plan provides that if either of the two states should fail to take the steps suggested in the plan, including the calling of a constituent assembly, the setting up of a provisional government, the making of a Declaration, etc., that fact will be communicated to the United Nations for such action by the General Assembly as may be deemed proper.

It is likely that the Arab State will not take the steps suggested and that, therefore, the whole Palestine problem will be back on the doorstep of the General Assembly at least within two years.

We are convinced that no plan can be found which will completely dispose of the Palestine problem so far as the United Nations is concerned at this session. I have stressed the fact that the majority plan does not rid us of this problem merely because there has been some thinking in the Department to the effect that if it is adopted, we can finally wash our hands of this disagreeable matter.

6. *The proposals contained in the UNSCOP plan are not only not based on any principles of an international character, the maintenance of which would be in the interests of the United States, but they are in definite contravention to various principles laid down in the Charter as well as to principles on which American concepts of Government are based.*

These proposals, for instance, ignore such principles as self-determination and majority rule. They recognize the principle of a theocratic racial state and even go so far in several instances as to discriminate on grounds of religion and race against persons outside of Palestine. We have hitherto always held that in our foreign relations American citizens, regardless of race or religion, are entitled to uniform treatment. The stress on whether persons are Jews or non-Jews is certain to strengthen feelings among both Jews and Gentiles in the United States and elsewhere that Jewish citizens are not the same as other citizens.

The United States is undoubtedly honor bound to take steps to make sure that the Jews in Palestine are not discriminated against and that they participate on at least an equal basis with other peoples in the Government of Palestine. We are under no obligations to the Jews to set up a Jewish State. The Balfour Declaration and the Mandate provided not for a Jewish State, but for a Jewish national home. Neither the United States nor the British Government has ever interpreted the term "Jewish national home" to be a Jewish national state.

7. *Tactics which the United States should pursue in the handling of the Palestine problem before the present session of the General Assembly.*

In our opinion, there is no ready solution of the Palestine problem to which both Jews and Arabs would acquiesce to such an extent as to render it workable. Any kind of an imposed solution opposed by the majority of either the Arabs or the Jews is bound to result in failure, involving much loss of property and bloodshed and loss of prestige to the supporters and executors of the plan, as well as to the whole United Nations. If a solution is found which is workable, it will, we believe, be evolved only after long and protracted discussions during the course of which the moderate Jews and moderate Arabs would find common ground. If we at the beginning take either the Arab or the Jewish side of the controversy, it will be extremely difficult for either the moderate Arabs or the moderate Jews to get together.

Our Government has already stated that we give serious weight to the majority proposals. On an early occasion, we should repeat this statement, making it clear at the same time that our minds are by no means closed and that we shall also give due weight to the views of other nations and particularly of the interested parties.

During the debates regarding the merits of the various plans, we should not play too active a role. We should create the respect of all fair-minded persons by being, so far as possible, strictly impartial. We should concentrate our efforts primarily on working out agreements of all parties with regard to as many points as possible. It seems to us that there is a possibility that the moderates in both camps might be led to acquiesce in a sufficient number of points to enable the setting up of a trusteeship for a period of years which would be instructed to function in such a neutral manner as not to favor either partition or a single state. At the conclusion of this term of years, there could be a plebiscite on the question of partition, in the light of which the General Assembly could make its final decision on this fateful question. Any kind of a temporary arrangement should probably provide for immediate Jewish immigration of at least 100,000 persons.

It may be impossible even to work out a delayed solution such as that outlined above. If so, the Palestine problem will probably become even more of a world problem than at the present time.

It is realized that the tactics outlined above are not likely to appeal to those of us who prefer to approach all problems with energy and decisiveness. There are times, however, when energy and decisiveness are not appropriate.

The reader will note that in this memorandum Henderson, like Merriam in his memorandum of October 15, 1946 (see Chapter 7 above), quoted from the Anglo-American Committee of Inquiry with respect to partition. These are only two examples of the way in which the report of that committee, in spite of its not having been accepted, had an influence on our policy makers.

In the light of current discussion of the issue of dissent in government, and particularly in the Department of State and the Foreign Service, it is worth calling attention to the fact that in transmitting this memorandum to the

Secretary, Henderson said that in spite of the position which he outlined, he and his staff would loyally carry out any decision which the Secretary might reach in the matter.

The chief justification for Henderson's statement that any partition of Palestine would be unworkable was, of course, the complex distribution of the population between Arabs and Jews. Subsequently, this difficulty was taken care of in a rather drastic fashion by the flight of some 726,000 Arab refugees, an event which very few observers foresaw at this time and which Weizmann was later to call "a miraculous simplification of Israel's tasks." For all the logic of Henderson's arguments, however, the views of the Near East Division were not to prevail.

At the United Nations on September 26 the British Colonial Secretary, Arthur Creech-Jones, announced in the Ad Hoc Committee that the British would not implement any policy recommended by the Assembly that was not acceptable to both Arabs and Jews. Since it was clear that no plan, certainly not the majority report of UNSCOP, was likely to meet this condition, Creech-Jones's statement could only be interpreted as an indication that the British would not cooperate in carrying out the majority plan if it were adopted by the General Assembly. The Colonial Secretary also said that the British accepted the unanimous recommendation of UNSCOP regarding the termination of the Mandate and were prepared to withdraw from Palestine. This represented a change of policy from that announced in February.[24]

On October 3, the leaders of the Arab delegations in New York met with Ambassador George Wadsworth, who was serving as an adviser to our delegation. They told Wadsworth that they had had overtures from Soviet representatives, offering support for the Arab position on Palestine, and that they would have to respond affirmatively unless they could be assured that the United States was not going to come out for partition. Wadsworth undertook to seek instructions from Washington. In commenting on this Arab *démarche*, Henderson pointed out to Lovett that to the Arabs Palestine was "the most important question in their international life" and that there was a real danger that they would turn to the Soviet Union for support unless they could be reassured. He added (with some reason, as it turned out) that the Soviet delegation was probably also in touch with the Zionists.[25]

Henderson's advice, however, was not heeded. On October 11, the U.S. delegation, on instructions from President Truman, announced its decision. Herschel V. Johnson, the Acting U.S. Representative at the United Nations, informed the Ad Hoc Committee that the United States would support the majority plan, with some territorial modifications. This was the key decision in the U.S. government's adoption of a policy favoring the establishment of a Jewish state in Palestine.

Truman says in his *Memoirs* that one element in his decision to support partition was that he had received reports of belligerent statements and military preparations on the part of the Arabs, indicating that they were prepared to defy the United Nations and oppose partition by force. He also says (rather unconvincingly) that partition with economic union impressed him as "the most practicable way" to achieve the development of the entire Middle Eastern region for the benefit of both Jews and Arabs, while at the same time continuing our support for the Balfour Declaration and the Jewish National Home. An additional factor, to which indeed he refers later on, must have been the unremitting pressure to which he was subjected throughout this period by the Zionist advisers: in his words, "I do not think I ever had as much pressure and propaganda aimed at the White House as I had in this instance."[26]

The hostile Arab reaction to which Truman refers was greatly heightened by our announcement that we were in favor of the majority plan. Our posts in Damascus, Baghdad, and elsewhere in the Middle East reported an intensification of recruiting for an "Army of Liberation" to fight for the Arabs in Palestine, the movement of troops toward the Palestine frontier and calls for a *Jihad* or Holy War. King Ibn Saud decided to make one more appeal to President Truman, arguing that U.S. support for partition was an "unfriendly act" which would strike a "deathblow to American interests in the Arab countries." A Jewish state, he declared, would be a "menace to peace in the Near East." Truman replied that the United States had no desire to appear unfriendly toward the Arabs, but would abide by whatever decision was taken by the UN.[27]

Two days after Johnson's statement, the U.S.S.R. announced that it, too, was supporting partition. The decision seems to have been due not to any change in the Soviet Union's traditional position of opposing Zionism but rather to the belief that partition would lead to continuing unrest in the Middle East and a decline in Western influence in the Arab world that would serve Soviet interests in the Cold War. Subsequent events have borne out this interpretation.[28]

As tension grew in Palestine and neighboring countries, the State Department on November 10 imposed an embargo on the export of arms and ammunition to the area. During this period the Near East Division encountered increasing difficulty in finding out what was going on at the United Nations, or in learning how the President wanted the Palestine problem to be handled. The confusion, in fact, was shared by our UN delegation itself. A memorandum from Secretary Marshall to Ambassador Johnson saying that the delegation was to "line up the vote" in support of certain of our proposals was endorsed by a member of our staff in New York as being "the only written and express instructions" ever received by the delegation as to the position it should take with other delegations; in any event, these instructions were limited in scope.[29]

A particularly egregious instance of how the problem was being handled occurred in mid-November in connection with the Negev. The majority plan of UNSCOP had awarded to the Jewish state the entire Negev, in spite of the fact that such population as there was in this sparsely populated area consisted of seminomadic Bedouin tribes. In discussions between the Department and our delegation in New York it was agreed that one of the changes in the majority plan which we would support would be the inclusion of the Negev in the Arab state. But the Jewish Agency very much wanted to have this territory in the Jewish state because of its potential for development. Just as Ambassador Johnson was about to go into a meeting of the subcommittee which was to consider the matter, President Truman, who had just seen Dr. Weizmann, telephoned General Hilldring from Washington to say that he agreed with the position taken in the majority report and supported by the Jewish Agency. Thus the Negev, except for a small strip awarded to the Arabs, was left in the Jewish state.[30]

At about this time, our Consul General in Jerusalem reported that the Jewish Agency Executive had decided to set up a Jewish state within the boundaries of the UNSCOP majority plan regardless of whatever decision the General Assembly might take.

Just before the Palestine matter came to a vote, Henderson again expressed his grave anxiety regarding the course that our government was following. In a memorandum dated November 24 to Acting Secretary of State Lovett he observed: "I wonder if the President realizes that the plan which we are supporting for Palestine leaves no force other than local law enforcement organizations for preserving order in Palestine. It is quite clear that there will be wide-scale violence in that country, both from the Jewish and Arab sides, with which the local authorities will not be able to cope."[31] He warned against the consequences of sending American troops to Palestine to enforce partition, as was being discussed in some quarters. Mr. Lovett made a notation on this paper that he had read it aloud to the President during a meeting at the White House.

On November 25 the Ad Hoc Committee approved the partition plan by a vote of 25 to 13, with 17 abstentions. The vote was just short of the two-thirds majority that would be required for passage by the Assembly. By one vote, the committee defeated an Arab proposal to seek an advisory opinion from the International Court of Justice as to whether the General Assembly had the power to partition Palestine against the wishes of the majority of its inhabitants, so this legal issue was never resolved. It is worth noting in passing that in one of the subcommittees of the Ad Hoc Committee, the United States voted against a resolution urging the absorption within the territories of member states of such Jewish displaced persons as could not be repatriated to their original countries of origin.[32]

Intensive efforts were now begun by the Zionists and their sympathizers to persuade certain delegations to shift to a position favoring partition. Meanwhile they were successful in getting the meeting of the Assembly postponed several times. The greatest pressure was brought to bear on three delegations—those of Haiti and Liberia, which had abstained, and the Philippines, which had not participated.[33] All three were to vote for partition when the matter finally came before the General Assembly on November 29. Of the seventeen countries that abstained on November 25, seven voted affirmatively on November 29, and in this way the necessary margin for partition was achieved.

Former Assistant Secretary of State Adolph A. Berle worked on the Haitians, while former Secretary of State Edward R. Stettinius and economist Robert R. Nathan worked on the Liberians and Supreme Court Justices Felix Frankfurter and Frank Murphy, who had been High Commissioner in Manila, worked on the Filipinos. Nathan, who was particularly active in behalf of the Jewish Agency, conceded afterward that "we used any tools at hand," such as telling certain delegations that the Zionists would use their influence to block economic aid to any countries that did not vote the right way. Nathan also revealed that the representatives of the Jewish Agency were able to use delegates' passes lent to them by various members of the United States delegation so that they could circulate freely on the floor of the Assembly.[34]

The Zionists worked hard to cultivate certain of the Latin American delegates, presenting mink coats to their wives and even offering to get the Cuban ambassador to the United Nations elected president of Cuba if he would vote for partition (he declined).[35] William C. Bullitt, former ambassador to the Soviet Union and to France, who had good contacts in the Chinese government, was asked by Presidential confidant Bernard M. Baruch, a Zionist sympathizer, to approach the Chinese regarding partition, and he did this (though the Chinese ultimately abstained).[36]

However, though there seems no doubt that pressure was brought to bear on certain delegations in New York to vote in favor of the Zionist position, the extent to which the representatives of the United States government were involved in this activity has been a matter of some controversy. Truman's denial in his *Memoirs* that there was any pressure does not seem entirely convincing: he remarks that some had suggested that we apply pressure at the UN but that he "never approved of the practice of the strong imposing their will on the weak, whether among men or among nations."[37] In a memorandum to Secretary Marshall dated December 11, 1947, Truman said that allegations of pressure by the U.S. were "most interesting," and he added, "as you very well know, I refused to make statements to any country on the subject of its vote in the United Nations."[38]

Other sources do not agree. It seems certain that between the two votes, in the Ad Hoc Committee and in the General Assembly, orders went out from the White House to make every effort to rally support for partition, and it is hard to believe that Truman himself did not have a hand in this. Nahum Goldmann and David Horowitz of the Jewish Agency, both of whom were present as observers at the General Assembly, state flatly in their books that Truman was personally involved. Goldmann's words are: "President Truman himself lent a hand by conferring with various delegates," while Horowitz says: "As a result of instructions from the President . . . the United States exerted the weight of its influence almost at the last hour, and the way the final vote turned out must be ascribed to this fact."[39] Jonathan Daniels, Truman's press secretary, says in his biography of the President that Truman "had a personal part" in the passage of the partition resolution.[40] And Truman's intimate friend Eddie Jacobson says in his diary that Truman told him afterward that "he [Truman] and he alone, was responsible for swinging the vote of several delegations."[41]

Aside from the President's own role, the intervention of the White House staff is mentioned in a number of sources. Sumner Welles writes: "By direct order of the White House every form of pressure, direct and indirect, was brought to bear by American officials upon the countries outside the Moslem world that were known to be either uncertain or opposed to partition."[42] Herbert Feis, the former economic adviser to the Secretary of State, writes that "it has become known" that Truman's subordinates in the White House had intervened in the matter.[43]

The whole matter was complicated by the different instructions sent at different times to our delegation in New York as to the position it was to adopt with other delegations. I have already mentioned the instructions given by Secretary Marshall to Ambassador Johnson on October 22 to "line up the vote." But these instructions were specifically limited by Marshall to cover only "amendments to the majority plan on partition and the manner of implementation." As said earlier, they constituted the only written instructions received by our delegation.

On November 24, the President told Lovett that he "did not wish the United States Delegation to use threats or improper pressure of any kind" with respect to other delegations. These instructions were immediately telephoned to Johnson and Hilldring in New York by Lovett.[44] Henderson explained to me in March of 1976 that on the same day, Lovett authorized him to inform several of the Arab representatives in Washington that this was our government's attitude. Later, when some of these individuals reported to

Henderson that our delegation in New York was applying strong pressure on other delegations, Henderson telephoned Johnson and learned that this was indeed true and that Niles had called him (Johnson) to say that the President wanted the delegation to "get the necessary votes or there would be real trouble."

Representative Emmanuel Celler, according to the record in the Truman Library, telegraphed the President on November 27, two days before the vote, asking that the delegation be instructed to intervene actively with certain delegations that might be wavering in their support for partition. November 27 in 1947 happened to be Thanksgiving Day, and it would appear from several sources that it was on this day that Truman, after attending church services, instructed Acting Secretary Lovett to "contact the representatives of countries that were wavering."[45] That this was indeed done seems to be borne out by a statement made by General Hilldring, who as previously mentioned was generally considered to be pro-Zionist and who was a part of our delegation, that "certainly we tried as best we could to persuade other countries of the logic and justice of our position."[46]

It is no wonder that Truman in his 1973 interviews with Merle Miller (published under the title *Plain Speaking*) was to say that not even at the time of General MacArthur's dismissal had he been under such pressure.[47] Lovett for his part was reported by Secretary of Defense Forrestal as telling a Cabinet meeting on December 1 with respect to the vote that "he had never in his life been subject to as much pressure as he had been in the three days beginning Thursday morning and ending Saturday night" (that is, November 27 through 29).[48]

On the day of the Assembly's vote, 10,000 persons tried to gain admittance to the meeting hall and tension was at a high pitch. When the vote was taken, partition was supported by 33 votes to 13, with 10 abstentions and one delegation (Siam) absent. The thirteen negative votes were cast by Afghanistan, Cuba, Egypt, Greece, India, Iran, Iraq, Lebanon, Pakistan, Saudi Arabia, Syria, Turkey, and Yemen. Abstaining were Argentina, Chile, China, Colombia, El Salvador, Ethiopia, Honduras, Mexico, the United Kingdom, and Yugoslavia. It was said that the delegate of Haiti voted "with tears in his eyes," and the Canadian representative was heard to say that his country supported partition "with a heavy heart and many misgivings."[49]

As the vote was announced, pandemonium and hysteria broke out in the hall. The Arab delegations walked out. That night, Weizmann addressed an ecstatic Zionist rally of 5,000 persons in New York City. In Palestine, there was dancing in the streets of Tel Aviv, while the Arabs declared a three-day general strike. The very next day after the vote, November 30, an Arab attack was launched against Jews near Tel Aviv.[50]

President Truman received hundreds of congratulatory telegrams from

Zionists and their supporters in Congress.[51] He was accused by several Arab leaders, including King Farouk of Egypt and Prime Minister Nuri Said of Iraq, of having been responsible for exerting undue pressure to bring about an outcome favorable to partition.[52] Dr. Judah Magnes was quoted in the *New York Times* as gloomily predicting that "it looks like trouble" ahead.

It is important to note that the resolution passed by the General Assembly on November 29 was in the form of a recommendation to the Mandatory Power, Great Britain, and to all other members of the United Nations, that the plan of partition with economic union be adopted.[53] The Assembly could only *recommend* that this be done. The resolution provided that the UN Security Council should determine as "a threat to the peace or act of aggression" any attempt to alter by force the program outlined in the resolution. A commission of five members of the United Nations was elected by the Assembly to implement the partition plan and to take over the administration of Palestine progressively, as the British relinquished it. The transitional period foreseen by UNSCOP was greatly curtailed: the Arab and Jewish states were to become independent not later than October 1, 1948, which was also the date on which the economic union and the internationalized city of Jerusalem were to come into being. The Jewish state would include roughly 53 percent of the total land area of Palestine, in spite of the fact that Jews owned only 7 percent of the land in the proposed state. The most significant territorial changes, as compared with the majority plan of UNSCOP, were the allocation to the Arab state of Jaffa and of a small portion of the Negev.[54]

And so the die was cast.

The State of Israel
Is Born

In the immediate aftermath of the General Assembly's November 29 resolution, it looked as though the course of action to be followed in implementing the partition of Palestine was clear. A five-member United Nations commission was to be set up and provided with a sizable secretariat of administrative officials and technical experts. After consultations with representatives of the Mandatory Power and other interested parties, the commission with its staff was expected to proceed to Palestine in the latter part of December 1947. Once arrived in Palestine, it was to take over administrative responsibility from the British as they evacuated their troops, beginning at the Egyptian border and moving northward. The British withdrawal and the termination of the Mandate were to take place not later than August 1, 1948. During the interim period, the commission was to work with the Jewish Agency and the Arab Higher Committee with a view to forming provisional councils of government in the two proposed states, as well as a Joint Economic Board. The provisional councils were to be established by April 1, and administrative authority was to be progressively turned over to them by the UN Commission, so that the two states could come into being not later than October 1. Each of the states was to have an armed militia which would be under the general control of the United Nations Commission until independence was achieved. The resolution also provided that by February 1 the British should make available in the territory of the Jewish state a port and hinterland so as to allow "substantial" Jewish immigration.

Almost at once it became evident that these elaborate plans were going to prove highly difficult, if not impossible, to carry out. The British informed us confidentially at the end of November that their withdrawal from Palestine was being accelerated and that the Mandate would end by May 15, 1948. They also told us that it would be impossible, for administrative reasons as well as considerations of security, for the UN Commission to arrive in

Palestine earlier than two weeks before the end of the Mandate—in other words, around May first. This, as we shall see, was to pose an insuperable obstacle to the orderly implementation of the partition plan. The British government's attitude and timetable for withdrawal were made public in mid-December during a debate in the House of Commons.[1]

There were other indications that partition was not going to enjoy smooth sailing. The Arab reaction to the passage of the partition resolution was prompt and vigorous. Arab assaults against Jewish installations in Palestine, which had begun on the very morrow of the UN action, continued, and there were attacks against American diplomatic missions in Damascus and Baghdad. King Farouk told our Ambassador in Cairo that the Arab states were prepared to resist partition by force of arms. The consequences for American relations with the Arab world were obvious. King Abdullah warned us that Trans-Jordan might have to send the Arab Legion into Palestine following the British evacuation, to preserve order, and that this might involve his army in clashes with Jews.[2]

On the Jewish side, there were those outside the Zionist leadership who saw beyond the euphoria of the partition resolution and realized that the Jewish community was going to have to fight to secure the Jewish state. Menachem Begin, leader of the Irgun Zvai Leumi, the underground force which was not yet a part of the Zionist establishment, has written that he warned the Jewish Agency that war was coming, and that he began to prepare for it at this time.[3] His group's first operation against the Arabs was launched December 11, at Haifa.

President Truman, too, had a premonition of trouble ahead. To messages which he had received regarding the partition resolution from Henry Morgenthau, now head of the United Jewish Appeal, and from Dr. Weizmann, the President wrote in virtually identical terms that the resolution was only a beginning and that the Jews in Palestine must show restraint and tolerance toward their Arab neighbors.[4] The official United States position at this time is contained in a telegram, drafted in the Near East Division and initialed by all concerned, including Acting Secretary Lovett and the President, telling Ambassador Tuck in Cairo how to reply to King Farouk's warning. The message (dated December 26, 1947) took the line that our government had been "practically forced" by public opinion in this country to support partition. This did not mean that we harbored any unfriendliness toward the Arabs: on the contrary, we wanted the best of relations with the Arab world and a peaceful resolution of the Palestine question. We hoped that the Arabs would not use force to oppose the carrying out of the United Nations decision.[5] Tuck later reported that he had made these points to Farouk but did not think they had made the slightest impression.

As the year drew to a close, our Consulate General at Jerusalem sent in a report which summarized the fast-deteriorating security situation and offered a gloomy prognosis for the year 1948, for Arabs, Jews, British, and the United Nations alike.[6] The message, written by Vice Consul William J. Porter, commented that the task of the UN Commission would be well-nigh impossible and predicted with considerable prescience that there would be no Arab state in Palestine. During the next few months, the reports from the Consulate General were to prove invaluable to the Department in following the situation in Palestine.

In spite of urging by Secretary-General Trygve Lie, the UN Commission was slow in getting started. It was not until late in December that all five members were appointed by their respective governments (Czechoslovakia, Bolivia, Denmark, the Philippines, and Panama), and the commission did not hold its first meeting until January 9. It then became clear that the commission's task, already one of great difficulty, was to be compounded by its members themselves. As Pablo de Azcarate, a UN official who was secretary to the commission, put it: "If the plan of November was defective, and if its adoption by the Assembly took place in conditions that were far from ideal, what barred the last hope of seeing it executed was the Palestine Commission itself."[7] The members were an undistinguished and timorous lot who feared, with some justification, for their safety if they were to set foot in Palestine. They were determined not to budge from New York, in spite of the terms of their mandate from the General Assembly. Aside from the Czechoslovak chairman, Lisicky, none of them had any knowledge of the Palestine problem.

In addition, the attitude of the British authorities greatly hampered the work of the commission. The Permanent Representative of Great Britian, Sir Alexander Cadogan, appeared several times before the commission. He repeated that the British would not permit the commission to arrive in Palestine before May 1. The members of the commission pointed out that this would seriously impede their appointed task of "progressively" taking over the administration from the Mandatory authorities. Eventually a small advance party from the commission's staff, headed by Azcarate, was allowed to proceed to Palestine but it was able to accomplish little.

Cadogan also told the commission that it would be impossible for the British to make available a port and its hinterland to facilitate Jewish immigration, though this was specified in the partition resolution. This unhelpful attitude was consistent with the largely negative stance which the British displayed throughout the last months of the Mandate. They seem to have had no policy other than an overriding desire to get out of Palestine. They continued, however, to send arms to the various Arab states, as they were bound to do by treaty in many instances, and this was to help the Arab governments in arming the Arabs of Palestine.[8]

The Jewish Agency cooperated with the United Nations Commission but the Arab Higher Committee declined to do so, informing the Secretary-General that the November 29 resolution was totally without validity and that the only way to achieve partition was to "wipe out the Arabs of Palestine, man, woman, and child."[9]

Shortly after the passage of the resolution, the Arab League had met to consider how to carry out the announced Arab determination to oppose the partition of Palestine by force. It was decided that all possible assistance, chiefly in the form of arms, would be sent to the Arabs of Palestine and that the armed forces of the Arab states would be stationed on the borders of the country, although these forces would not actually enter it until the departure of the British. By the end of February, the newly established CIA estimated that some 8,000 Arab "volunteers" had slipped into Palestine.[10]

These developments naturally led to increased clashes between Arabs and Jews. The first Arab guerrilla raid from neighboring territory into Palestine took place on January 15 and was repulsed by the Jews with many casualties. Heavy fighting continued and by the middle of February over 1,000 persons (the majority of them Arabs) had been killed since November 29, the date of the UN resolution. (By mid-May the casualty figures were to rise to roughly 2,500 persons killed and 5,000 wounded, of whom 1,500 of the dead and 3,000 of the wounded were estimated to be Arabs.) Our Consul General at Jerusalem reported to the Department on February 9 that a significant development had been "the influx of uniformed and trained Arabs from Iraq and Syria." He stated that Jews traveling from Jerusalem to Tel Aviv were now having to use armored buses because of constant Arab attacks along the way.[11]

All three of the Jewish paramilitary organizations, the Haganah or "official" military arm of the Jewish Agency, and the "unofficial" Irgun and the Stern Gang, participated in the fighting against the Arabs. To finance these operations, Mrs. Myerson of the Jewish Agency was sent to the United States on a fund-raising trip. Within six weeks she managed to raise no less than $50,000,000, which was turned over at once to the Haganah for the secret purchase of arms in Europe. This earned for her the following tribute from Agency chairman David Ben Gurion: "Some day when history will be written, it will be said that there was a Jewish woman who got the money which made the State possible."[12] Ben Gurion also told his biographer Moshe Pearlman that "the major preparations to convert the Haganah into an army were begun three years before the birth of the state." He added that "as soon as World War II ended we began acquiring surplus military equipment, especially in the U.S.A."[13]

The Palestine Commission reported to the Security Council on February 16 that partition could not be implemented without an international police force. Otherwise, the commission foresaw "a period of uncontrolled, widespread strife and bloodshed" on the termination of the Mandate.[14]

By the time the Security Council met to consider the commission's first report, on February 24, there was some speculation that the United States was about to abandon partition. In fact, the subject had begun to be intensively debated within the U.S. government. As early as December 17, a draft policy paper was prepared by the Department of State for circulation to the members of the National Security Council, taking the position that partition was "impossible of implementation." This was the forerunner of a paper distributed by the Department's Policy Planning Staff under date of January 19. This paper concluded that there were serious doubts as to the workability of partition owing to the intense Arab opposition that had emerged since the November 29, 1947, resolution and had invalidated the assumptions on which U.S. support for the resolution was based; therefore the U.S. should urge that the matter come back to the General Assembly for further study and elaboration of an alternative solution.[15]

Dean Rusk, director of the Department's Office of Special Political Affairs, dealing with the United Nations, advanced similar arguments in a memorandum to Acting Secretary Lovett on February 3. These views were shared by Loy Henderson and his colleagues in the Near East Division and by Secretary of Defense Forrestal. In mid-January Forrestal told a subcommittee of the House of Representatives that partition was contrary to U.S. interests, and his diaries show that he frequently took the same position at Cabinet meetings.[16] The subject came up in the National Security Council on February 12, when Forrestal stated that any attempt on our part to enforce partition would lead to partial mobilization and to a return to the draft. In reaching the conclusion that partition was going to prove unworkable, these officials were influenced by a series of reports from our posts in the Middle East, forecasting Arab military intervention on a large scale. The possibility that this might force us to send U.S. troops to Palestine in defense of the Jews was a contingency that the State and Defense Departments wished to avoid at all costs.[17]

A CIA assessment prepared at the end of February concluded that partition could not be implemented in the face of certain Arab opposition, without the use of considerable force. The paper discussed various alternatives for the composition of an international force but considered none of them to be acceptable.[18]

It is clear that in initiating a reconsideration of our attitude toward Palestine our policy makers had the prevailing international climate very much in mind. There was a growing concern in Washington about Soviet intentions in several areas, stemming from the recent show of force in Czechoslovakia which culminated on February 25 in President Benes's agreement to install a pro-Soviet cabinet and with the subsequent death, allegedly by suicide, of Foreign Minister Jan Masaryk. This was accompanied by continuing threats and pressure against Iran, Turkey, and Greece, as well as against Austria and Hungary. It was feared that a real confrontation might be developing with the Soviet Union.

Against this background the U.S. Representative, Warren Austin, addressed the Security Council on February 24. The main thrust of his remarks was that the Council did not have the power under the charter of the United Nations to enforce a resolution of the General Assembly such as the partition resolution. He proposed that the five permanent members of the Council should try to come to some agreement about what to do next.[19] Though Austin did not specifically disavow partition on this occasion, his remarks were widely interpreted as a hint that the U.S. was having second thoughts. One result of his statement was that Lie and Bunche decided not to submit to the Security Council at this time a plan which they had drawn up for an international force to implement the partition resolution.

The Council voted in favor of Austin's proposal. However, when the five permanent members met they were unable to reach unanimous agreement, although a majority of three (the United States, China, and France) reported back to the Council that partition could not be implemented peacefully.[20]

The Zionists, fearing a lessening of support for partition on the part of our government, now opened an intensive campaign. In one week in February, over 22,000 communications respecting Palestine were received in the Department. The United Jewish Appeal raised $35,000,000 in two weeks. There was steady agitation for repeal of the arms embargo and growing criticism of the Administration on the part of the American Jewish community. American Jews were active in smuggling arms to the Jews in Palestine, and many volunteered to fight with the Jewish forces. The Arabs naturally welcomed Austin's statement in the Security Council and declared that they were prepared to talk if partition were dropped.[21] As before, the Arab-Americans did little to support the Palestine Arabs.

In early March, General Lucius D. Clay, the commanding officer of U.S. forces in Germany, submitted an alarming report regarding Soviet intentions.[22] This had the effect of reinforcing the views of those who believed that we should proceed with caution in the Middle East (from this time can be dated the start of the Berlin crisis, which became acute in June). There was also concern in Washington about the forthcoming elections in Italy and the possibility of Communist gains. Meanwhile, Presidential Counsel Clark Clifford was still recommending to Truman that we should continue to support partition. In a memorandum of March 8, which he claimed was "completely un-influenced by election considerations," Clifford urged that support of the Arabs was "much less valuable" than support of the Jews and that we should not put ourselves in the position of "trembling before a few desert tribes."[23]

Truman was showing signs of increasing irritation at the Zionist campaign, however, and vowing that he would see no more Zionist leaders. But his old haberdashery partner Eddie Jacobson, in an emotional meeting, persuaded him to see Weizmann. Both Truman and Jacobson have left accounts of this conversation, in which Jacobson burst into tears as he compared his hero Weizmann with Truman's hero Andrew Jackson. Truman finally relented, and when he received Weizmann on March 18 (unknown to the State Department) he assured him that he was still for partition.[24]

The very next day, March 19, Austin announced in the Security Council that we had concluded that under existing circumstances partition could not be carried out without the use of force and that we therefore were calling for an immediate truce and for a special session of the General Assembly to consider a plan for placing Palestine under temporary trusteeship. Austin made it clear that the trusteeship proposal was not intended to prejudice the character of an eventual solution of the problem.[25]

The main concern of our government at this stage seems to have been that there was not sufficient time before May 15 to proceed with an orderly resolution of the problem and that if we continued to press for immediate partition, the result would be a chaotic situation from which only the Soviet Union would benefit. This in fact was the explanation for our shift in policy offered by Marshall at a closed session of the Senate Foreign Relations Committee a few days later (March 24).[26]

In his *Memoirs* Truman implies that the Austin statement caught him by surprise.[27] This is also implied in a paper that Clark Clifford read to a meeting of historians in Washington, D.C., in December 1976.[28] A number of officials, however, including both Marshall and Lovett, have gone on record saying that the President had approved the statement in advance, although it does appear that he was not aware just when it would be made, any more than Marshall and Lovett knew he was seeing Weizmann on March 18. Secretary Marshall wrote under date of March 22 that on that day the President "said the reason he was so much exercised in the matter was the fact that Austin made his statement without the President having been advised that he was going to make it at that particular time. He had agreed to the statement but said that if he had known when it was going to be made he could have taken certain measures to have avoided the political blast of the press." On the same day, March 22, Under Secretary Lovett wrote, referring to the statement: "There is absolutely no question but what the President approved it. There was a definite clearance there."[29]

Austin's statement caused consternation in Zionist circles, and our government was charged with betrayal. Pressure on the Administration intensified, especially from Congress. Mrs. Roosevelt expressed dismay and offered to resign as U.S. representative on the United Nations Commission on Human Rights, but Marshall persuaded her to remain.[30] The Jewish Agency issued a statement in Jerusalem declaring that trusteeship was a step backward from the partition resolution, which had recognized the right of the Jewish people to statehood. Zionist leaders assured the Department that a truce would solve nothing. They were prepared to fight indefinitely to secure their state.[31] In his memoirs, Dr. Weizmann comments that following Austin's proposal the Zionists "had no choice but to create facts." (It is worth noting that these same words "create facts" have been used by Moshe Dayan and other Israeli leaders to justify Israeli actions in the occupied territories since the Six Day War.) In a letter of April 9 to Truman, Weizmann characterized the choice as being "between statehood and extermination."[32]

A few moderate Jews such as Magnes hailed our announcement, as did most Arab leaders, but the reaction in the American press to the new policy was mainly adverse. The *New York Times,* for example (March 21), characterized it as the "climax to a series of moves which has seldom been matched for ineptness in the handling of an international issue by any American administration," as a "surrender to the threat of force," and as being likely to incur the "very hazards it is intended to circumvent." At the White House, Clifford and Niles resolved to mount a campaign against the trusteeship proposal. Niles went so far as to recommend to the President that Loy Henderson be replaced at the State Department as being anti-Zionist. Acting on this advice, the President a little later on appointed General John H. Hilldring as Special Assistant to the Secretary of State for Palestine Affairs, but he was unable to take up the appointment because of ill health. Niles's proposal would of course have had a profound effect on our Palestine policy in view of Hilldring's strongly pro-Zionist views. (The President must have realized this, for in a conversation with Dean Rusk on April 30 he inquired if Rusk thought the Hilldring appointment would "complicate things.")[33]

On March 25, the President issued a statement, written for him by Clifford and others, which attempted to explain the shift in policy.[34] The statement pointed out that we had proposed the trusteeship plan only after we had exhausted every effort to carry out partition by peaceful means. Trusteeship, it said, was being proposed not as a substitute for partition but in an effort to "fill the vacuum" that would be created by the forthcoming termination of the Mandate. It repeated Austin's statement that our proposal did not prejudice the character of a final settlement and that the most pressing need was to bring about a truce between the Arabs and Jews in Palestine. In his *Memoirs* (II, 163) Truman described his position as follows: "This was not a rejection of partition but rather an effort to postpone its effective date until proper conditions for the establishment of self-government in the two parts might be established." Assuming that this accurately reflects the President's thinking at the time, one must conclude that, unlike his advisers in the State and Defense Departments, Truman was still in favor of a solution based on partition, regardless of what he said on March 25 about the nonprejudicial nature of the trusteeship proposal.

When Austin queried the Department as to whether the United States would contribute armed forces to enforce the proposed truce and trusteeship, the working level wanted to reply in the affirmative, but Lovett turned this down on White House instructions. Later Forrestal wrote Marshall that we would be unable to provide forces for such a task without affecting our commitments elsewhere. In other words, our government was as unwilling to use force to carry out the new policy as it had been in the case of partition. This meant, as we shall see, that the United States was to find itself in the position of being unable effectively to achieve the solution in Palestine that it was seeking. Our problem was made more difficult by the likelihood that a greater degree of force would be required to implement truce-with-trusteeship than partition. Ironically, as Secretary-General Lie was to point out, since Palestine was in the process of *de facto* partition, had we nonetheless decided to employ our armed forces to carry out trusteeship, this would have involved us in using force *against* partition—a course of action that we certainly would not have wanted to pursue.

The bankruptcy of our policy was summed up by Henderson at about this time in conversation with the Saudi Arabian minister. Henderson told him that "the position was very different last fall." Now we were unwilling to push trusteeship in the absence of Arab and Jewish acquiescence, nor would we take any responsibility with respect to trusteeship if it would have to be imposed.[35]

At the United Nations, it soon became clear that our truce and trusteeship plan was in difficulty. On April 1, the Security Council, acting on Austin's March 19 proposal, voted to call a special session of the General Assembly and meanwhile to invite the Jewish Agency and the Arab Higher Committee to send representatives to New York to discuss a truce. The president of the Council, however, had to report on April 15 that no progress had been achieved in these talks. The Council then passed a resolution calling again for a cessation of all acts of violence in Palestine. A Consular Truce Commission consisting of the Consuls General in Jerusalem of Belgium, France, and the United States was appointed to help implement this resolution. The appointment of this commission was the result of an initiative by the State Department, which throughout this period was anxious to avoid involving the Soviet Union in the handling of the Palestine question. Since there was no Soviet career consular officer in Jerusalem, this device conveniently excluded Soviet participation.[36]

The UN Palestine Commission reported to the General Assembly that it had been prevented from discharging its functions by Arab hostility, by lack of cooperation from the Mandatory power, by the disintegrating security situation in Palestine, and by the fact that the Security Council had not furnished the commission with the "necessary armed assistance." In an echo of its earlier gloomy forecast, the commission warned the Assembly that "in the absence of forces adequate to restore and maintain law and order in Palestine following the termination of the Mandate, there will be administrative chaos, starvation, widespread strife, violence and bloodshed in Palestine, including Jerusalem."[37]

A position paper prepared in the Department as of April 13 recommended the following course of action for our delegation at the special session: (1) if the Assembly were to vote to amend the partition resolution, our delegation should support changes which would permit its peaceful implementation; (2) if our plan for a temporary trusteeship were approved, we should seek the "suspension" of the partition resolution; and (3) if any other proposal for a settlement were approved, we should seek the "withdrawal" of the partition resolution. This would imply that we saw the period of temporary trusteeship as one in which partition would be merely suspended, not rescinded.[38]

When the special session of the Assembly met on April 16 the United States submitted a plan for a temporary trusteeship which was intended to provide a government and essential public services in Palestine pending further negotiations. This plan was modeled on the draft Statute for Jerusalem which the Trusteeship Council had been preparing under the terms of the partition resolution. The Arabs indicated a conditional acceptance of this proposal but the Jews strongly opposed it, asserting that they had implemented the partition resolution to such an extent that a retreat was now impossible.

The special session spent the next month bogged down in a debate which produced little in the way of accomplishment. Virtually no enthusiasm was shown for our trusteeship plan, which was generally considered to have come too late. The representative of New Zealand, Sir Carl A. Berendsen, showed his impatience with the slow pace of the proceedings when he declared "what the world needs today is not resolutions, it is resolution."[39] In the event, although a number of resolutions were passed by the Assembly at the eleventh hour before the end of the Mandate, as will be recounted below, the partition resolution was never rescinded or amended in any way. (Under date of May 4 Acting Secretary of State Lovett had instructed our New York Mission not to concern itself any longer with how to deal with the November 29 partition resolution but to concentrate on getting a truce.)

In Palestine, conditions grew worse and worse as the end of the Mandate drew closer and as the British hastened their pell-mell withdrawal. That there was an almost complete breakdown of law and order as well as a collapse of the machinery of government is apparent from the accounts of persons on the spot, including American consular officers, senior British officials such as Sir

Henry Gurney (the last Chief Secretary of the Mandatory government), missionaries, representatives of the United Nations and of the International Red Cross, and many others. During this period, for example, our Consul General at Jerusalem telegraphed to Washington that the British "cannot get out of Palestine too soon." Later he reported that "the Palestine Government has generally ceased to function and central public services no longer exist."[40]

The representative of an American oil company, on arriving in Beirut from Jerusalem shortly before the end of the Mandate, told one of our officials that "complete lawlessness" prevailed there. A German Quaker, a former employee of the Palestine government, who also reached Beirut from Jerusalem at this time, spoke of "anarchy" and "panic." He said that many official files had been unceremoniously dumped in the street near the King David Hotel (used as government offices) while other streets in the neighborhood were littered with half-burned documents.[41]

One incident, at the beginning of March, involved our own Consulate General. This was the explosion of a booby-trapped car in the compound of the Jewish Agency in the heart of the Jewish section of Jerusalem, in which thirteen persons were killed. The car belonged to our Consulate General and had been brought into the Agency by one of our Arab drivers who, unknown to his employers, had been suborned by Arab terrorists. He was admitted to the compound without question by the Jewish guards, as he came to the Agency daily, and managed to escape unscathed. A typical bureaucratic hassle ensued when the Consulate General, understandably enough, asked the Department to replace the sedan which had been blown up. The reply was that steps could not be taken to provide a replacement until the Consulate General could supply the serial number of the destroyed vehicle. It was therefore necessary for someone from our office to go to the Jewish Agency compound and search through the wreckage until he found the charred engine block with the missing number.[42]

In late March, the Jewish Agency announced that it was making preparations to set up a provisional government in the Jewish portion of the country as soon as the British withdrew. The process of partitioning Palestine on the ground was already in full swing. Weeks before the date of May 15, blue and white Zionist flags were hoisted over public buildings in Tel Aviv and elsewhere, and the Jewish authorities began to issue their own stamps and levy their own taxes. These well-orchestrated preparations contrasted with the disorganization and lack of leadership within the Palestine Arab community. Again, the Jews, with their European background and training, showed their superiority over the native Arabs.[43]

The Department had Consul General Thomas C. Wasson query the Agency as to whether the authority of the proposed provisional government would be limited to the area set aside for the Jewish state in the partition resolution. Wasson was given an affirmative reply, but in reporting it to the Department he cautioned that Ben Gurion (who as I have previously explained was widely expected to be the prime minister) was known to be in favor of a Jewish state in all of Palestine. On April 29 Epstein of the Jewish Agency, in a conversation with Henderson, asserted that "the Jewish state already exists." Azcarate says in his book that early in 1948 the consular officers in Jerusalem started to deal direct with the respective Jewish and Arab community organizations for many purposes.[44]

In mid-April, a particularly brutal massacre of some 250 Arab residents of the village of Deir Yassin (many of them women and children) by a combined force of the Irgun and Stern Gang led to savage reprisals, and more importantly, to the start of the exodus of Arabs from Palestine. The incident was widely publicized and caused a panic among the Arabs, many of whom fled from their homes in fear of their lives. Jacques de Reynier, the representative in Jerusalem of the International Red Cross, visited Deir Yassin as soon as he was permitted to do so by the Jewish authorities and gives in his book an eyewitness account of a number of the atrocities that were committed. As Consul General Wasson had predicted in reporting the incident, the Arabs retaliated almost at once. The next day, they ambushed a Jewish convoy on its way to Hadassah Hospital on Mount Scopus with the loss of many Jewish lives.

The Jewish leadership was not slow to grasp the significance of this movement of population in terms of the opportunity it offered for expansion of the Jewish-held area. Ben Gurion was quoted as saying "without Deir Yassin there would be no Israel," and later Dr. Weizmann was to speak of the Arabs' flight as "a miraculous simplification of Israel's tasks."[45] It seems clear that in the first few months after the partition resolution, the leaders of the Jewish community did not follow a deliberate policy of driving the Arabs from Palestine even though they must have been aware that their razor-thin majority in the Jewish state under the partition plan might well pose problems for the future. Two observers have recently advanced the hypothesis, which strikes me as plausible, that after Austin's Security Council statement on March 19 had indicated that the United States was rethinking its support for partition, the Zionists must have seen that in order to achieve their Jewish state they would have to redouble their efforts and lead from a position of strength—hence the shift in the direction of ridding Palestine of its Arab inhabitants that was to characterize Zionist policy in the last weeks of the Mandate.[46]

The exodus of Arabs was stimulated not only by incidents such as Deir Yassin (and there were others) but also by a series of military operations launched in April and early May by the Haganah (with some assistance from the Irgun) aimed at gaining control of certain portions of Palestine before the entry of the forces of the Arab states which was expected to take place as soon as the British left. These operations were known as "Plan Dalet" (from the fourth letter of the Hebrew alphabet). Some of them had as their objective areas that had been allocated to the Jewish state under the partition plan; others were carried out against areas that had been allocated to the Arab state, or the proposed international zone of Jerusalem. As a result, the Jews were able, before the end of the Mandate, to occupy considerable territory, including most of the important cities and towns in the country, notably Tiberias, Haifa, Safad, Jaffa, Acre, and most of the New City of Jerusalem (the primarily Jewish part of the city). The importance of these little-known operations in adding to the areas actually held by the Jews at the termination of the Mandate can hardly be exaggerated.[47]

The Consular Truce Commission reported to the Security Council on April 30 that the security situation was steadily deteriorating, government departments were closing daily, normal activities were coming to a standstill, and the intensity of the fighting was increasing. Meanwhile, outside Palestine, the Arab states continued their military preparations and there was open talk of invading Palestine. Strident calls for action were heard from Arab capitals and tanks rumbled through the streets of Damascus on their way to the frontier. Early in May we asked the British to urge Abdullah of Trans-Jordan to restrain the Arab Legion from invading Palestine but this proved unavailing.[48]

The United States, still intent on achieving a truce, offered to fly Arab and Jewish representatives to Jerusalem in the President's plane the *Sacred Cow* to try to get agreement on a ceasefire but both parties declined.[49] Marshall and Lovett then tried to persuade the Jews to postpone their plans to proclaim a Jewish state, but they refused.[50] The decision to go ahead with plans for the state was taken at a meeting of Ben Gurion's "Council of Thirteen" in Tel Aviv on May 12 and was carried by a single vote. Some members of the Zionist inner circle advised delay, especially in view of the fact that Nahum Goldmann had reported from Washington that he had had feelers from Egyptian diplomats there that they were prepared to negotiate with Jewish representatives in Malta or Rhodes.[51] Mrs. Myerson, who had just returned from the second of two clandestine meetings she had had with King Abdullah of Trans-Jordan, reported at this session that she had failed to make any headway with the King, who now seemed bent on war.[52] The representatives of the Haganah told the meeting that there was only a 50–50 chance of success if war came. Nevertheless, the pressure for independence was very strong, and so the decision was taken.

The Department sent out instructions at this time to our posts in the Near East expressing anxiety that Jews resident in Arab or Moslem countries might be subjected to attack in reaction against events in Palestine. I happened to be

Chargé d'Affaires in Tehran and called upon the Shah, who assured me that the Iranian Jews were in no danger, which turned out to be the case. I recall that His Imperial Majesty said: "Don't worry, Mr. Wilson—you know, one of our kings married a Jewish girl"—a reference to the biblical story of Esther and Ahasuerus (Xerxes).[53]

Pressures mounted on the President to announce that the United States would recognize the new Jewish state as soon as it was proclaimed. This course of action had been recommended to him for some time by Jacobson, Clifford, and Niles, among others. The various memoranda urging prompt recognition, to be seen in the Clifford papers at the Harry S. Truman Library, contain endorsements to the effect that they must be closely held, describing their contents as "dynamite" and the like. The line taken is that the Democrats need Jewish support, that the Republicans are already taking up the issue, and that the repercussions in the Arab world can be safely disregarded. One such paper, which is particularly critical of the State Department and of our handling of the matter in the United Nations, asserts: "We should not seek to retrieve the reputations, to satisfy the *amour propre,* of a few State Department officials. We cannot afford to live in a bygone day."[54]

To consider what should be done, Truman called a meeting of his advisers on May 12. Present were Marshall, Lovett, Robert McClintock, and Fraser Wilkins from the State Department and Clifford, Niles, and Matthew Connelly from the White House.[55] As Wilkins reconstructed the scene for me nearly thirty years later, the President was sitting at his desk in the Oval Office, with Marshall seated at his right. On the same side of the room were the three members of the White House Staff, with Clifford in the middle, sitting slightly forward of the other two. Lovett sat across the room, on the President's left, with McClintock and Wilkins seated behind him.

Lovett outlined the position at some length from the Department's standpoint, calling attention to the critical situation in the Middle East and the risks that we would run if we were to recognize the new state immediately. Clifford rose to his feet to reply, stressing the importance of keeping the support of Jewish opinion and urging the desirability of acting promptly. He then read a statement which he proposed that the President should make at his press conference the following day, which would have announced that the early recognition by the United States of the new state, upon its being proclaimed. Both Lovett and Marshall voiced strong objection to this suggestion. Marshall then sharply rebuked Clifford for trying to interject domestic politics into what was an international issue, and he told the President bluntly that if the election were being held tomorrow he would not vote for him. Truman quickly brought the session to a close, initialing the draft of a proposed resolution in the General Assembly, prepared in the State Department, calling for the appointment of a UN Mediator for Palestine.

According to Wilkins, the State Department representatives came away from the meeting at the White House with the impression that recognition of the new Jewish state would be put off indefinitely. Indeed, at his May 13 press conference, the President did not make the announcement prepared by Clifford but said in reply to a question on the subject, "I will cross that bridge when I come to it." He was coming to it quickly, as we shall see. The next day the pendulum swung in the opposite direction.

On May 14, The British High Commissioner and last few British officials and military personnel left Jerusalem for Haifa, where they embarked on the British cruiser *Euralyus* at nightfall. The Mandate was to expire officially at midnight. For security reasons, the British had not announced the details of their departure. The UN representative, Azcarate, was much surprised when he returned from a brief visit to Amman later in the day and found them gone. The diary of Chief Secretary Gurney contains many details of the final rather confused evacuation. At police headquarters, for example, the authorities locked the doors and then tried to hand the keys to a United Nations representative, who refused to accept them. They were therefore left on the doorstep, to be picked up by Arabs or Jews as the case might be.[56]

As soon as the British forces left Jerusalem, Arab and Jewish troops moved forward to extend their occupation of portions of the city. This division of the city was to last for nineteen years, until the Six Day War of 1967. From now on, there were in effect two Jerusalems, one Jewish and one Arab, separated by a no-man's-land with barbed wire and land mines and having no contact with each other: two water and electric systems, two languages, in essence two cultures. This was the divided Jerusalem, the Jerusalem of the Mandelbaum Gate, which I was to know when I arrived there as American Consul General in 1964.[57]

On the evening of May 14, 1948, just before the start of the Jewish Sabbath, a group of Zionist leaders met at the Tel Aviv Art Museum and proclaimed the establishment of the State of Israel as from midnight. In deference to the solemnity of the occasion, the nude statues in the museum were modestly draped and Ben Gurion, the chairman of the meeting, wore a necktie. (It was an article of faith among the Zionist pioneers never to wear a necktie and Ben Gurion, while Prime Minister, had a rule that none should be worn at cabinet meetings.) With emotion and while many of those present wept, he read a proclamation rehearsing the long struggle of Jewish people for a state of their own and citing as its authority the November 29 partition resolution of the General Assembly (see Appendix L).[58] It may be pointed out in passing that although the independence proclamation cited as its authority the November 29 partition resolution, it was actually a violation of that resolution for the state to be proclaimed immediately upon the British withdrawal rather than sixty days later.[59]

The proclamation did not specify that the boundaries of the new state would be those provided in the UN resolution. This point, and the name of the new state, had been decided at a meeting of the Zionist leadership earlier in the day. Ben Gurion had taken the position that just as the American Declaration of Independence had not set any frontiers for the new American state, neither was it necessary for the Jewish proclamation to do so. On the question of the name of the state, there had been quick agreement that it should be Israel, rather than Zion, which was the only alternative considered.

And thus the dream of Herzl was fulfilled, in the fifty years he had predicted.

Simultaneously with the British departure, the armies of the four neighboring Arab states—Egypt, Trans-Jordan, Syria, and Lebanon—entered Palestine and joined the Arab irregular forces already there in fighting with Jewish units, a development which Secretary-General Lie branded as aggression and a "brazen defiance" of the UN. The Palestine War was on. Just before dawn on the morning of the fifteenth, as Ben Gurion was making an Independence Day broadcast to American Jewish supporters, the first Egyptian air raid hit Tel Aviv.

Heavy fighting broke out in Jerusalem and elsewhere in the country. A few days later, our Consul General, Thomas C. Wasson, who had only recently arrived in Jerusalem, was killed by a sniper's bullet as he was returning from a meeting of the Consular Truce Commission; his assailant was never identified.

Wasson, a bachelor, had been assigned to the position of Consul General at Jerusalem in April 1948, in succession to Robert B. Macatee. Wasson had been provided with a bullet-proof vest and was wearing it when he was shot while passing along the alley to the immediate west of the premises of the Consulate General on Mamillah Road (now Rehov Agron), on May 22. The bullet struck him in the armpit and ricocheted through his chest in spite of the protective vest. Wasson showed great courage and dedication in taking up the post in the light of the dangers that it entailed. Loy Henderson recalls warning him before he went out to Jerusalem of the hazards to which he would be exposed, but Wasson's reply was that this represented a challenge which he could not bring himself to turn down. In a press release dated May 22, the Department paid high tribute to his "great ability, judgment, and courage" and pointed out that although in carrying out his duties he had had to pass constantly through "bullet-swept streets and battle lines," he had never once mentioned in his reports the physical dangers to which he was exposed.

In Washington, where the time was six hours behind Tel Aviv, Henderson and Clifford had both been in touch early on the fourteenth with Eliahu

Epstein, the Washington representative of the Jewish Agency, to discuss the mechanics of how U.S. recognition would be extended to the new state, should there be a decision to grant immediate recognition.[60] Clifford had been designated by the President to handle this matter for him, and there is no question that he was the individual most responsible for the swiftness of our recognition. Henderson and Clifford told Epstein that diplomatic usage demanded that there be a request for recognition. Although Epstein did not have authority from Tel Aviv to submit such a request, he nonetheless did so, in the name of the provisional government of the new state.[61] When Henderson inquired whether the boundaries of the state would be the same as in the partition resolution, Epstein assumed the responsibility of giving an affirmative reply. He confirmed to Clifford that the new state would come into existence at one minute after midnight, Palestine time, or 6:01 P.M. Washington time.

In the early afternoon, Clifford telephoned Lovett to say the President was under "unbearable pressure" to recognize promptly. Lovett asked if recognition could not be delayed but Clifford told him it was "of the greatest possible importance from a domestic point of view." Later on, after he and Lovett had agreed on the wording of Epstein's letter requesting recognition, Clifford called Epstein and read him the draft over the telephone. Not knowing at that time what the name of the state would be, Epstein began to prepare his letter, referring simply to the "Jewish state," and stating that its boundaries would be as in the November 29 resolution. Lovett and Clifford also prepared a statement for White House Press Secretary Charles G. Ross to give to the press, assuming a decision to recognize. During the afternoon, Lovett again urged delay, at least until after the adjournment of the session of the UN General Assembly which was under way at Flushing Meadows, but Clifford indicated he did not think this would be possible.

At about twenty minutes to six, Clifford called Lovett and said that the President had reached his decision, that Epstein's letter was on its way, and that the announcement would be made shortly after six o'clock. He authorized Lovett to inform our UN Mission and our posts in the field (Lovett had wanted to do this earlier but Clifford had said the President was anxious to avoid any leaks).[62]

After Epstein had sent off his letter to the White House (and an identical letter to Secretary Marshall), he heard on the radio that the proclamation of independence had been issued in Tel Aviv and that the name of the new state was Israel. He thereupon dispatched a second messenger, who overtook the first at the White House gate, where the name "Israel" was substituted for "Jewish state" (see Appendix M). The White House announcement, signed by the President, was issued at 6:11 P.M. after Ross had amended it to give the correct name. A few days later, Secretary Marshall addressed a formal reply to Epstein's request for recognition. This letter, backdated to May 14, is now to be found framed in the latter's home in Jerusalem.[63]

It was not only in Tel Aviv and Washington that dramatic events were taking place on this day of May 14. At the United Nations the General Assembly, which as we have seen had been debating the Palestine question for the past several weeks, was meeting. A member of the U.S. delegation, Francis B. Sayre, was actually addressing the Assembly on the problem of Jerusalem when word began to spread in the corridors, soon after six o'clock, that we had recognized Israel. Another member of the delegation, Philip C. Jessup, has told the story of what then occurred.[64] At first, the delegation refused to believe the rumors, as no instructions had been seen from Washington (later it developed that Rusk had telephoned Austin about 5:45 P.M. to give him the word and Austin had been so upset that he had gone straight home without informing anyone). Finally, as the rumors persisted, Jessup sent a secretary to check the news tickers and she returned with a crumpled piece of paper, taken from Secretary-General Lie's wastepaper basket, with the President's announcement. Jessup then mounted the rostrum and read the announcement to the Assembly.

A few days previously it had become evident that the U.S. proposal for trusteeship would not be approved by the Assembly. Our delegation had been authorized, once this had become clear, to introduce in its place a resolution providing for the appointment of a United Nations mediator with the dual mandate of seeking a settlement of the Palestine dispute and assisting in bringing about a truce. This was done on May 13, and around eight o'clock on the evening of the fourteenth the resolution in question was passed by the Assembly, which adjourned soon afterward. A resolution relieving the Palestine Commission from further exercise of its duties was also approved. It was originally envisaged that Paul Van Zeeland of Belgium would be the Mediator but when he declined the appointment the choice fell on Count Folke Bernadotte of Sweden—with tragic consequences, as Bernadotte was to be assassinated in Jerusalem that September.[65]

Before the General Assembly adjourned, another instance occurred of a country's representative taking it upon himself to speak for his government. Jorge Garcia-Granados of Guatemala, who as a member of UNSCOP had displayed markedly pro-Zionist sentiments, had been determined that his country should be the first to recognize the Jewish state. After Jessup had upstaged him by announcing the American decision, Garcia-Granados rose in the Assembly to announce, acting on his own responsibility as he later conceded, that Guatemala, too, had recognized Israel.[66] It became the second nation to do so. A few days later, on May 17, the Soviet Union accorded *de jure* recognition: ours had been merely *de facto* and was not made *de jure* for another year.[67]

Austin, Jessup, and the other members of our delegation joined in composing a telegram to the Department protesting the position in which they had been placed in the Assembly by the lack of prior notice regarding the decision. Mrs. Roosevelt also wrote Marshall, saying that the way in which the matter had been handled had caused "consternation" among the delegates of many countries. She received a brief reply, explaining that Austin, but no one else in our delegation, had been informed and adding "more than this, I am not free to say."[68]

A few days later, Marshall, in conversation with the President, learned that he had been unaware of the lack of communication between Washington and New York on the fourteenth. Marshall told the President that quite a few members of our delegation and of the Department had thought of resigning over the Palestine issue but had been dissuaded from doing so. The President expressed surprise. (The only official who ever did resign over our Palestine policy was Colonel Eddy, Roosevelt's interpreter in the Ibn Saud meeting in 1945; he resigned in late 1947 while serving as Special Assistant to the Secretary for Intelligence.)

On the morning of May 15, the *Washington Post* headline read: "Recognition of Israel Stuns U.N. Delegates," while the *New York Times* said "U.S. Moves Quickly." the *Times* also carried an article quoting Lessing J. Rosenwald of the American Council for Judaism (anti-Zionist) as terming the recognition episode a "sordid affair"; the *Washington Daily News* called it "irresponsible" and "inexcusable." The reaction in the Arab countries was, of course, overwhelmingly unfavorable.

To summarize events following May 15, 1948: fighting continued in Palestine throughout 1948 and into 1949, when Israel signed armistice agreements with its four Arab neighbors. By this time, the Arabs, overconfident from the start, had suffered a shattering defeat. The Israelis, fighting with great efficiency and tenacity, had been able to seize some 40 percent more territory than had been awarded to the Jewish state in the partition plan, including a portion of Jerusalem and a corridor leading to the city. By this time also, the West Bank, representing the bulk of the remaining territory of the proposed Arab state, had been annexed by Trans-Jordan (now known as the Hashemite Jordan Kingdom), putting an end for the foreseeable future to the possibility of an independent Arab state in Palestine. The number of Arab refugees had risen by 1949 to an estimated 726,000, according to UN figures. Thus were sown the seeds of the Palestinian problem of today—a problem compounded by the Israeli occupation of the whole of Palestine in 1967.[69]

In September 1948, the Mediator, Count Bernadotte, was assassinated by Jewish irregulars in Jerusalem as he was submitting to the Security Council a report recommending certain territorial changes unfavorable to Israel. This report became an issue in the Presidential campaign of 1948, when Truman refused to endorse it in spite of Marshall's having done so.

In subsequent years the United States continued to work for a settlement of the Arab-Israeli dispute but these efforts have proved fruitless up to the present time. In 1956, 1967, and 1973 there were further wars between the parties and the problem remains.

EVALUATION OF TRUMAN'S CONTRIBUTION

President Truman was largely responsible for bringing the state of Israel into being, through the support that he gave to the partition plan. Starting from a humanitarian desire to alleviate the plight of the displaced Jews of Europe, he ended up by endorsing the creation of a Jewish state in Palestine, which the Zionists constantly argued was the only way that the Jewish refugee problem could be solved. He kept hoping that the professionals in the State Department would be able to produce evidence to show that a Jewish state could be established without bloodshed. When such proof was not forthcoming, he decided in the fall of 1947 to support partition nonetheless. In the spring of 1948, as it became clear that the Zionists were determined to set up their Jewish state regardless, he opted for immediate recognition.

In reaching both these decisions, Truman was greatly influenced by his pro-Zionist advisers in the White House, whose advice was admittedly based on domestic political considerations. Chief among their arguments was the need for Jewish support to get Truman elected in 1948, in the face of widespread doubts as to his prospects (a *Newsweek* poll of fifty Washington correspondents shortly before the election showed that not one of them believed Truman would win).[70] In siding with the Zionists, the President discounted the advice which the professionals had repeatedly tendered him regarding the consequences of such a policy as far as American standing in the Middle East was concerned. Ironically, in seeking to solve one refugee problem he contributed to the creation of another.

The decisions that Truman took were his own, and to the end of his days he maintained that he was right. And yet for all of his decisiveness he never gave a clear set of instructions to the Department or to our delegation in New York as to how to proceed. As a recent biographer of Truman (Robert J. Donovan) has remarked, he was "tormented" on this issue—an exception to his habit of making quick decisions.[71]

The inescapable conclusion of my examination of our Palestine policy during these six years is that many of our present problems in the Middle East must be attributed to Truman's decisions regarding partition and recognition—decisions that have drastically affected American interests in the area to this day.

I began this study with the opinion, which I had held since my days on the Palestine desk, that Truman's principal motivation had been humanitarian, but after examining all the evidence, including data that were not available to us in the State Department at the time, I have been forced reluctantly to the conclusion that on certain key occasions (October 1947 and May 1948) he was more influenced by domestic political considerations than by humanitarian ideals.

EPILOGUE

I have now carried the story of our Palestine policy through the six fateful years from May 1942 to May 1948, from the first official endorsement by the Zionist movement of the idea of a Jewish state to the creation of such a state in Israel, with the strong backing of the United States. I have discussed the conflicting pressures to which President Roosevelt and President Truman were subjected and I have explained the background of the decisions that they took with respect to Palestine. It is now time to go back to the three main themes stated in the Preface, to examine them, and to advance some reflections regarding past events.

THE THREE MAIN THEMES RESTATED

THEME NO. 1.   The steady trend in our Palestine policy toward the Jewish side in the conflict was inevitable in the years 1942–48. In the circumstances, there was no other way in which the basic dilemma in our policy could have been resolved. The pressure for such a solution was just too strong—the combination of the humanitarian imperative and of what was viewed (rightly or wrongly) as a domestic political imperative was irresistible. To cite one trenchant comment on this point:

> Leaders of all major American institutions: trade unions, colleges and universities, Protestant and Catholic church bodies, state and local governments, the courts, and the U.S. Congress had rallied to the cause. The Zionists won because there was no opposition, no alternative being advanced. Who was there who would stand up and say that the Jewish question would not be solved by creating a separate Jewish state in Palestine for the Jews?[1]

Indeed, there were some who stood up against this powerful phalanx. There were, as I have shown, the career men in the State Department and officials in the defense establishment (like Secretary Forrestal) who tried to see the problem in the broader context of the overall American interest. There were also the anti-Zionist Jews, though their influence, as explained, was slight; and also elements (also relatively uninfluential) that could be described as pro-Arab: the Arab-Americans; a handful of individuals, former missionaries and the like, with personal experience of the Arab world; and of course the oil industry.

On this last point, a curious thing is that the archives contain little or no evidence of the oil company pressure which is so often alleged by the Zionists to have taken place. It was to be expected that the companies having an interest in petroleum concessions in the Arab countries, particularly Saudi Arabia, would be opposed to the creation of a Jewish state in Palestine. They undoubtedly were, but I recall no instances where the representatives of ARAMCO or of any other oil company came into the Department and urged that our government follow a particular line regarding Palestine, nor could I find any letters to that effect in the files. Those of my colleagues whom I have consulted on this point, notably Loy Henderson, Gordon Merriam, and Fraser Wilkins, likewise can recall no pressure on the part of the oil companies. It is of course possible that the oil companies made oral representations at a higher level, but if they did so we were not aware of it.

It may be noted, too, that King Ibn Saud's close adviser for many years, H. St. John Philby, has written that in spite of United States support for the Zionists, the King never considered abrogating the ARAMCO concession, because he feared the Saudi Arabian economy would suffer if he did so.[2] A number of Zionist or pro-Zionist writers have made similar statements. One Israeli writer on the subject (Golding) agrees that although Ibn Saud was urged by the Arab League to use his oil as a lever against the United States, he always refused. Golding says in his dissertation on U.S. foreign policy in Palestine that Ibn Saud told C. L. Sulzberger of the *New York Times* in November 1946 that he would never withdraw the ARAMCO concession because of the Palestine question. He also adds that the influence of the oil companies on U.S. policy is hard to trace.[3] Another work which approaches the subject from the Zionist point of view also finds that adequate confirmation of the role of the oil companies is lacking.[4]

A third source points out that although the oil companies could have "made trouble" for the advocates of a Jewish state they did not do so, because they did not feel unduly threatened by Zionist policy. This writer says that Benjamin Akzin of the American Zionist Emergency Council reported, after a series of meetings with oil company representatives in New York, that they had a generally pro-Arab viewpoint but declared themselves neutral on Zionism and that Ibn Saud and other Arab leaders were in fact more dependent upon the United States than vice versa.[5] Several other pro-Zionist writers have alleged that the oil companies were active in urging the United States government to pursue an anti-Zionist policy, but they have not provided details.[6] In any event, if there was oil company pressure, it failed of its objective.

Rather much the same can be said about the influence of domestic politics on our Palestine policy. That is, if, as some cynical observers have contended, our most important decisions on Palestine were purely political in motivation, it is ironic that the policy did not always pay off. Granted that Roosevelt did make some gestures to the Zionists in 1944, he had in three earlier elections got about 90 percent of the votes of the American Jewish community, and he got a similar percentage in 1944. But two years later, despite Truman's Yom Kippur statement which so infuriated the British, the Democrats lost both houses of Congress. And in the Presidential election of 1948, after the United States had, largely because of Truman (and his adviser Clifford), recognized Israel, the Democrats failed to carry New York and several other states with a large Jewish vote—Pennsylvania, New Jersey, Michigan, and Maryland—though Truman himself managed to win the Presidency.[7]

American Jews, of course, can bring considerable political pressure to bear, and they have done so on occasion. It is undeniable, as I have earlier suggested, that Jews hold a pivotal position in certain cities, hence in certain states. It is also undeniable that Americans of the Jewish faith tend to be influenced in their voting behavior by what candidates have to say about Palestine. The strength of the Jewish vote, however, is apt to be exaggerated in the minds of our political leaders. Unfortunately, this misconception some-times leads them to make the wrong decisions.

Jimmy Breslin sums it up very accurately, I think. "All political power is primarily an illusion," he says. "If people think you have power, then you have power. If people think you have no power, then you have no power. . . . For those who take their politics from a book . . . this same proposition has been advanced in print by Thomas Hobbes, who wrote in England in the 1660's: 'The reputation of power is power.' "[8]

THEME NO. 2.   Although our policy in the years 1942–48 was slanted toward the Jewish side, this does not mean that we tried to adopt an all-out pro-Zionist policy, nor could we have done so, because of our stake in the Arab world. For many reasons, we had always to work for the greatest possible accommodation between the two opposing points of view. The result was that our policy often seemed to be one of pure expediency. Much the same thing can be said about our policy today.

There are two other comments that might be made regarding our policy in the 1940s. First, there was a basic inconsistency, never thought through, between our support for the Zionist position and our often repeated determination not to use force to achieve our objective. As early as 1943, Roosevelt agreed with Colonel Hoskins that a Jewish state could only be established in Palestine by applying force, but he frequently spoke of the necessity of finding a solution that would not result in bloodshed. The same was true of Truman, as, for example, in August 1945 when at a press conference he said that we wanted "to let as many Jews into Palestine as possible" but "had no desire to send half a million American soldiers to keep the peace" there.[9] Neither Roosevelt nor Truman seemed to be fully aware of the inherent inconsistency.

A second observation that might be made is that regardless of what we might say, it was to our actions that the people of the Middle East looked for an indication of our real attitude. (See my April 1946 memorandum, which is included in Chapter 6.)

THEME NO. 3.   The professionals in the State Department did not exert a dominant influence on Presidential decision making, especially from mid-1945 on, when control over Palestine policy passed from the State Department to the White House. Under the system prevailing in Washington, this was probably inevitable, since not all the factors that went to make up the final decision were in the province of the career men. The information that the professionals gave the Presidents, however, was complete and their advice was sound. Subsequent events have borne them out. It is no exaggeration to say that our relations with the entire Arab world have never recovered from the events of 1947–48, when we sided with the Jews against the Arabs and advocated a solution in Palestine which went contrary to self-determination as far as the majority population of the country was concerned. Both President Roosevelt and President Truman were fully aware of these potential consequences but discounted them.

The record (as I have reviewed our diplomatic correspondence in preparing this book) shows that the career men, with a few exceptions, managed to preserve their objectivity, at the cost of being attacked by both sides. The volume and high degree of excellence of my colleagues' reporting was matched only by their dedication.

In many ways the experience of these officials in connection with the Palestine question paralleled that of the Foreign Service officers who were dealing with China in these same years. In both cases, the Presidents heard what they wanted to hear and ignored many of the recommendations of the professionals. In both cases, a powerful lobby often exerted decisive influence in the White House and the Congress.

Those of us who were concerned with the Near East were at least fortunate in not suffering the fate of some of our colleagues in the Far Eastern Division who were pilloried for their beliefs and even forced out of the service. For this we can be thankful, but some of us were scarred by the Palestine experience. I have already told how the Zionists all but succeeded in having our chief, Loy Henderson, replaced by a man (General Hilldring) who was completely sympathetic to their point of view. Shortly after the events related in this book, the time came for Henderson to go back to the field. The Department wanted to have him appointed ambassador to Turkey but some members of the Senate committee informally objected, having been persuaded by the Zionist lobby that an alleged anti-Zionist ought not to be sent to a country so close to the Arab-Israel complex. He was sent to India instead. Gordon Merriam, who bore the brunt of the day-to-day work on Palestine longer than any of us in NE, developed ulcers and took an early retirement in 1949. James E. Keeley, an outspoken critic of Zionist policy whose reports while serving as Minister to Damascus had made him unpopular in certain circles, was relegated to a consular post at Palermo, Sicily.

SOME REFLECTIONS ON THE MANDATE

The failure of the British Mandate in Palestine was, like the coming of the Jewish state, inevitable. The Mandate failed, essentially, because the British were unable to find a solution that would satisfy the Jews without provoking the Arabs. As soon as it became apparent that there was no common ground between the Arabs and Jews in Palestine, the Mandate was no longer workable.

There is no doubt that the British tried. For years they did all they could to carry out the Mandate, but the conflicting claims of Arabs and Jews, and later on the upsurge of Jewish terrorism and the unhelpful attitude of the United States became too much for them. As I showed in Chapter 7, the growth of Jewish underground activity made the British position more and more intolerable. There were repeated incidents in which British officers and men and civilians were kidnapped, flogged, and even put to death. Illegal immigration was almost impossible to prevent when, as was the case by the mid-1940s, the entire Jewish community was behind it. It is no wonder that the British threw up their hands and passed the problem to the United Nations.

There might have been a chance, just after the end of the Second World War, for the British, though only with considerable use of force and with the acquiescence of the United States, to have put through a solution along the lines of partition. Even then, however, it was too late for a compromise solution along the lines of a binational state; the gulf between the two communities was already much too wide. The Jews, as some of them have themselves recognized, contributed significantly to the creation of this gulf, by failing, right from the start, to make an adequate effort to cultivate the good will of the Arab community.[10]

Even partition, it must be emphasized, could only have been imposed by the use of force. By 1945, the Arabs were firmly opposed to any form of partition, and the Jews were equally opposed to the only kind of partition that the British could have been expected to put forward, on the grounds that it did not sufficiently meet Jewish needs. It would have been a bitter fight, with the outcome by no means predictable.

A great deal has been said in the years since 1945 on the matter of the failure to allow the 100,000 Jewish displaced persons to go to Palestine. Our government repeatedly urged that this be done, and it seems obvious that it would have solved the most pressing problems of relocating the displaced Jews of Europe. What the consequences would have been so far as Arab opinion is concerned is another question, of course. An even more intriguing question is how such an action might have affected the establishment of a Jewish state—if the 100,000 had been admitted in 1945, or 1946, or even 1947. No less an authority than Abba Eban has said that it is doubtful that there would have been a Jewish state if this had happened.[11] He suggests that if the 100,000 had come to Palestine as urged by Truman, it would have removed the pressure to such an extent that the advocates of a Jewish state would no longer have enjoyed wide popular support in our country and elsewhere. Possibly this is what might have happened, but it seems much more likely to me that the Jewish state was bound to come.

WHERE WE WENT WRONG

In retrospect, there were a number of events that we in NE did not anticipate. First, none of us foresaw the Holocaust, the almost total extermination of the Jews of Nazi-occupied Europe. Neither did the Zionists: as already explained, the famous Weizmann *Foreign Affairs* article in 1942, written just before the Biltmore Conference, spoke in terms of at least two million Jews who were expected to go from Europe to Palestine after the war, and the Biltmore program was drawn up on the same assumption. The virtual disappearance of European Jewry not only has resulted in the greater prominence of the American Jewish community among the Jews of the world but also has had deep-seated consequences on the social structure of the state of Israel. Since independence, the bulk of the immigrants going to Israel has come from the Oriental (Arab) countries, mainly North Africa, to such a degree that the country now has a majority of Oriental Jews. This means that the Jewish state today is very different from the state that Herzl had in mind, or any of the Zionist leaders who fought for its establishment.

Second, most of us predicted that once they got their state and had absorbed the remnants of the displaced persons camps, 100,000 or whatever number would eventually come, the Israelis would voluntarily begin to place restrictions on immigration.[12] No one thought that there would be a mass exodus of Palestine Arabs,[13] aided and abetted in many instances by the

Jewish paramilitary organizations along the lines described in Chapter 9. This exodus not only created the Arab refugee problem and the problem of the Palestinians but also made it possible for Israel to take in a much larger number of immigrant Jews than had been expected.

Third, though all of us who were dealing with Palestine affairs at the time expected that there would be considerable fighting in connection with the creation of the Jewish state, none of us thought that the Jews would achieve such an overwhelming victory or that by the end of the fighting they would have conquered as much as 40 percent more territory than was allotted to the Jewish state under the United Nations partition plan. Everyone, except the Jews themselves, tended to downgrade the Jews and upgrade the Arabs as fighting men. The catastrophic Arab defeat came as a surprise.

A fourth point on which we were surprised was the attitude of the Soviet Union toward a Jewish state. Although the Zionists told us that the U.S.S.R. was on their side, we did not believe them. We continued to rely on reports from our Embassy in Moscow to the effect that the U.S.S.R. would support the Arabs. As explained in Chapter 8, it is generally supposed that the Soviet advocacy of the United Nations partition plan was based on a desire to contribute to instability in the Middle East and thus frustrate the "imperialists." Since 1947–48, however, the Soviet attitude has changed completely and the U.S.S.R. has become an outspoken supporter of the Arabs.

Fifth, although we in the Department had reason to be aware of the force of the Zionist drive toward a Jewish state, we continued until the end of 1946, at least, to think in terms of a compromise solution in Palestine. We thought there should be a solution under which, in the words of the Anglo-American Committee of Inquiry, Jew would not dominate Arab and Arab would not dominate Jew. In other words, we were thinking of a binational state long after the conflict between the parties had become so complete, and their opposing positions so intractable, as to put this out of the question. As men who tried to be reasonable, we thought that it should be possible to achieve a compromise, but the hard fact was that neither of the two parties in the dispute wanted a compromise; the depth of the nationalistic feeling on both sides precluded this.

Finally, as a study of the diplomatic correspondence for these years will confirm, we were too confident of the ability of the new United Nations Organization to solve disputes between nations. Unfortunately, our optimism has not been borne out.

LESSONS FOR TODAY

Since 1948, the struggle for Palestine, the conflict between two rights, has shifted to the Middle Eastern scene as a whole. The story of the years since

1948, the search for an elusive peace which still escapes us, illustrates the depths of the passions that have been aroused on both sides. The hatreds are more intense now, after four Arab-Israeli wars. But this should not deter us from pressing the search to a successful conclusion. Otherwise, the Middle East, and the world, face the prospect of continuing violence and bloodshed, instead of the peace that we all desire.

Photographs

✡✡✡✡✡✡✡✡✡✡✡✡✡✡✡✡✡✡✡✡✡✡✡✡✡✡✡

The Old State Department Building *(National Archives #VS 320-13-53)*

President Roosevelt and King Ibn Saud aboard the cruiser *Quincy*, with Fleet Admiral William D. Leahy, Chief of Staff to the President, and Colonel William A. Eddy, U. S. Minister to Saudi Arabia, February 14, 1945. *(Courtesy of Mrs. William A. Eddy.)*

Chaim Weizmann, head of the World Zionist Organization, testifying before the Anglo-American Committee of Inquiry in Jerusalem, March 1946. (The author appears in the background at the end of the table.) *(Courtesy of the author.)*

A session of the UN Special Committee on Palestine in Jerusalem, June 1947, with David Horowitz (left) and Moshe Shertok of the Jewish Agency testifying. (Jorge Garcia-Granados of Guatemala is second from the right at the table.) *(National Archives #306-NT-21270v)*

Syrian irregulars [of the] Arab Liberation A[rmy] on guard in north[ern] Palestine, April 19[48]. *(National Archives #306-NT-1190-2)*

Haganah recruits drilling openly near Tel Aviv before the end of the British Mandate. *(National Archives #306-NT-1190-14)*

Damage caused at the headquarters of the Jewish Agency in Jerusalem, March 1948, by the explosion of a booby-trapped vehicle brought in by the Arab driver of the American Consulate General. *(National Archives #306-NT-1189-39)*

David Ben-Gurion reading the proclamation of Israel's independence at the ceremony at the Tel Aviv Art Museum, May 14, 1948, with members of the Jewish Agency Executive ranged on either side and a portrait of Herzl on the wall behind. *(National Archives #306-NT-1189-17)*

The Union Jack is lowered for the last time in Palestine, at a ceremony in Haifa harbor, June 1948. *(National Archives #306-NT-1188-21)*

President Truman with Clark Clifford, William Hassett, Matthew Connelly, and Charles G. Ross in the Oval Office at the White House. *(Marion Carpenter for UPI)*

This Government has been informed that a Jewish state has been proclaimed in Palestine, and recognition has been requested by the *provisional* Government thereof.

The United States recognizes the provisional government as the de facto authority of the new ~~Jewish~~ *State of* ~~state.~~ *Israel.*

Harry Truman

Approved
May 14. 1948.

6:11

Original draft of the White House statement for the press announcing recognition of Israel, with handwritten corrections by Press Secretary Charles G. Ross, and signature, date, and time added by President Truman. (*Harry S. Truman Library, from the Papers of Charles G. Ross*)

Secretary of State George C. Marshall's letter to Eliahu Epstein announcing U.S. recognition of the new state of Israel. (*Courtesy of H. E. Eliahu Elath.*)

ADDRESS OFFICIAL COMMUNICATIONS TO
THE SECRETARY OF STATE
WASHINGTON 25, D. C.

DEPARTMENT OF STATE
WASHINGTON

May 14, 1948

Dear Mr. Epstein:

I have the honor to acknowledge the receipt of your letter of May 14, 1948 and to inform you that on May 14, 1948 at 6:11 p.m., Washington time, the President of the United States issued the following statement:

"This Government has been informed that a Jewish state has been proclaimed in Palestine, and recognition has been requested by the provisional government thereof.

"The United States recognizes the provisional government as the de facto authority of the new State of Israel."

Sincerely yours,

Mr. Eliahu Epstein,
2210 Massachusetts Avenue, N.W.,
Washington 8, D.C.

Appendixes

Order (No. 21) Establishing the Dept. of State Division of Near Eastern Affairs

It is hereby ordered that there shall be established in the Department of State a Division of Near Eastern Affairs, which shall have charge of correspondence, diplomatic and consular, on matters other than those of an administrative character in relation to Germany, Austria-Hungary, Russia, Roumania, Serbia, Bulgaria, Montenegro, Turkey, Greece, Italy, Abyssinia, Persia, Egypt, and colonies belonging to countries of this series. Mr. Evan E. Young, formerly Consul at Saloniki, is hereby designated as Chief of the Division of Near Eastern Affairs.

All correspondence in relation to the countries named, except routine correspondence relating to deaths, marriages, citizenship, passports, sanitary reports, invoices, applications for Section 6 certificates, bills of health, and similar subjects, will be sent by the Index Bureau direct to the Division of Near Eastern Affairs, subject to such special instructions as the Secretary or Assistant Secretary may issue from time to time.

The Chief Clerk of the Department will provide room for the new Division and will assign such clerks as the work of the Division may require.

P. C. KNOX

Department of State
Washington, December 13, 1909

B

Responsibilities of the
Near East Division*

The Office is responsible for formulating plans and over-all policies for the conduct of United States relations with the countries and areas under its jurisdiction, and for coordinating and reviewing policy matters originating within other geographic or functional offices of the Department or other Federal agencies; and performs the following functions: (a) develops basic country and area policies to guide the conduct of United States relations with the countries and areas under its jurisdiction; (b) directs the conduct of foreign relations with the countries under its jurisdiction, taking the initiative in affairs primarily political, and, in other affairs, stimulating the initiative of functional divisions within the Department and other agencies charged with primary responsibility in specialized fields; (c) draws into consultation all appropriate functional offices and divisions of the Department and all appropriate agencies of the Government in the formulation of policy; (d) keeps other offices and divisions of the Department and other departments and agencies of the Government adequately informed on emerging problems, policy decisions, and actions with respect to other countries, so that all United States programs in such countries may be coordinated with over-all United States foreign policy; (e) reviews and evaluates programs and activities of functional and other offices of the Department and of other agencies of the Government as they affect the political situation in a particular area; (f) directs and instructs United States Foreign Service establishments in the countries and areas within the jurisdiction; (g) advises on the type and number of personnel required in Foreign Service establishments in the countries and areas within its jurisdiction; (g) advises on the type and number of personnel required in Foreign Service establishments in collaboration with the Office of the Foreign Service, interested offices and divisions of the Department, and other Government agencies and departments; (h) maintains contact with appropriate foreign diplomatic missions in the United States; (i) provides representation on appropriate intra- and inter-departmental committees; (j) in conformance with the standards set by the Advisory Committee on Intelligence, directs the planning and implementation of a program of

---

*As set forth in the 1946 *Registrar of the Department of State* (p. 20).

basic research and analysis to provide evaluated positive intelligence on problems in the area; and (k) advises on matters relating to the United Nations and its auxiliary organizations, working in close relationship with the Office of Special Political Affairs.

C

Extracts from Theodor Herzl's Der Judenstaat (The Jewish State), 1896

    The idea which I have developed in this pamphlet is a very old one: it is the restoration of the Jewish State. . . . We are a people—one people. . . . Let the sovereignty be granted us over a portion of the globe large enough to satisfy the rightful requirements of a nation; the rest we shall manage for ourselves. . . . Shall we take Palestine or Argentina? We shall take what is given us and what is selected by Jewish public opinion.

SOURCE: Translation of the original, issued by the American Zionist Emergency Council, New York, 1946, p. 69 and p. 95.

D

Program of the First World Zionist Congress, Basle, August 1897

Zionism seeks to create for the Jewish people a home in Palestine secured by public law. The Congress contemplates the following means to the attainment of this end:

1. The promotion by appropriate means of the settlement in Palestine of Jewish agriculturalists, artisans and manufacturers.

2. The organization and binding together of the whole of Jewry by means of appropriate institutions, both local and international, in accordance with the laws of each country.

3. The strengthening and fostering of Jewish national sentiment and national consciousness.

4. Preparatory steps toward obtaining the consent of governments, where necessary, in order to reach the goal of Zionism.

SOURCE: J. C. Hurewitz, *The Middle East and North Africa in World Politics: A Documentary Record*, vol. I (New Haven and London: Yale University Press, 1975), p. 466.

E

The Balfour Declaration

Foreign Office
November 2nd, 1917

Dear Lord Rothschild:

I have much pleasure in conveying to you, on behalf of His Majesty's Government, the following declaration of sympathy with Jewish Zionist aspirations which has been submitted to, and approved by, the Cabinet:

His Majesty's Government view with favor the establishment in Palestine of a national home for the Jewish people, and will use their best endeavors to facilitate the achievement of this object, it being clearly understood that nothing shall be done which may prejudice the civil and religious rights of existing non-Jewish communities in Palestine, or the rights and political status enjoyed by Jews in any other country.

I should be grateful if you would bring this declaration to the knowledge of the Zionist Federation.

Yours,

ARTHUR JAMES BALFOUR

SOURCE: J. C. Hurewitz, *The Middle East and North Africa in World Politics: A Documentary Record*, vol. II (New Haven and London: Yale University Press, 1979), p. 106. Pp. 103–6 contain useful background data. (Lord Rothschild was Honorary President of the Zionist Federation; Balfour was the British Foreign Secretary.)

F

The Zionist (Biltmore)
Program May 11, 1942

1. American Zionists assembled in this Extraordinary Conference reaffirm their unequivocal devotion to the cause of democratic freedom and international justice to which the people of the United States, allied with the other United Nations, have dedicated themselves, and give expression to their faith in the ultimate victory of humanity and justice over lawlessness and brute force.

2. This Conference offers a message of hope and encouragement to their fellow Jews in the Ghettos and concentration camps of Hitler-dominated Europe and prays that their hour of liberation may not be far distant.

3. The Conference sends its warmest greetings to the Jewish Agency Executive in Jerusalem, to the Va'ad Leumi, and to the whole Yishuv in Palestine, and expresses its profound admiration for their steadfastness and achievements in the face of peril and great difficulties. The Jewish men and women in field and factory, and the thousands of Jewish soldiers of Palestine in the Near East who have acquitted themselves with honor and distinction in Greece, Ethiopia, Syria, Libya and on other battlefields, have shown themselves worthy of their people and ready to assume the rights and responsibilities of nationhood.

4. In our generation, and in particular in the course of the past twenty years, the Jewish people have awakened and transformed their ancient homeland; from 50,000 at the end of the last war their numbers have increased to more than 500,000. They have made the waste places to bear fruit and the desert to blossom. Their pioneering achievements in agriculture and in industry, embodying new patterns of cooperative endeavor, have written a notable page in the history of colonization.

5. In the new values thus created, their Arab neighbors in Palestine have shared. The Jewish people in its own work of national redemption welcomes the economic, agricultural and national development of the Arab peoples and states. The Conference reaffirms the stand previously adopted at Congresses of the World Zionist Organization, expressing the readiness and the desire of the Jewish people for full cooperation with their Arab neighbors.

SOURCE: J. C. Hurewitz, *The Middle East and North Africa in World Politics: A Documentary Record*, vol. II (New Haven and London: Yale University Press, 1979), pp. 595–97.

6. The Conference calls for the fulfillment of the original purpose of the Balfour Declaration and the Mandate which "recognizing the historical connection of the Jewish people with Palestine" was to afford them the opportunity, as stated by President Wilson, to found there a Jewish Commonwealth.

The Conference affirms its unalterable rejection of the White Paper of May 1939 and denies its moral or legal validity. The White Paper seeks to limit, and in fact to nullify Jewish rights to immigration and settlement in Palestine, and, as stated by Mr. Winston Churchill in the House of Commons in May 1939, constitutes "a breach and repudiation of the Balfour Declaration." The policy of the White Paper is cruel and indefensible in its denial of sanctuary to Jews fleeing from Nazi persecution; and at a time when Palestine has become a focal point in the war front of the United Nations, and Palestine Jewry must provide all available manpower for farm and factory and camp, it is in direct conflict with the interests of the allied war effort.

7. In the struggle against the forces of aggression and tyranny, of which Jews were the earliest victims, and which now menace the Jewish National Home, recognition must be given to the right of the Jews of Palestine to play their full part in the war effort and in the defense of their country, through a Jewish military force fighting under its own flag and under the high command of the United Nations.

8. The Conference declares that the new world order that will follow victory cannot be established on foundations of peace, justice and equality, unless the problem of Jewish homelessness is finally solved.

The Conference urges that the gates of Palestine be opened; that the Jewish Agency be vested with control of immigration into Palestine and with the necessary authority for upbuilding the country, including the development of its unoccupied and uncultivated lands; and that Palestine be established as a Jewish Commonwealth integrated in the structure of the new democratic world.

Then and only then will the age-old wrong to the Jewish people be righted.

G

Statement for Issuance by the Governments of the U.S. and the U.K. Regarding Palestine*

The Governments of the United States and of the United Kingdom, having in mind the terms of the United Nations declaration of January 1, 1942, are agreed that while public discussions on controversial international questions are in general desirable, in order to promote an informed public opinion and clarification of the issues involved, it is undesirable that special viewpoints should be pressed while the war is in progress to such an extent as to create undue anxiety among United Nations and other friendly governments and peoples.

In this connection, the Governments of the United States and of the United Kingdom have taken note of public discussions and activities of a political nature relating to Palestine and consider that it would be helpful to the war effort if these were to cease. As in the case of other territorial problems, it is not, in their view, essential that a settlement of the Palestine question be achieved prior to the end of the war. Nevertheless, if the interested Arabs and Jews can reach a friendly understanding through their own efforts before the end of the war, such a development would be highly desirable. In any case, the British Government has already stated that no decision affecting the basic situation in Palestine would be reached without full consultation with all concerned, including both Arabs and Jews. But the British Government wishes to make it clear that it has no intention of permitting or acquiescing in any changes brought about by force in the status of Palestine or the administration of that country. The United States Government is in full accord with that policy.

SOURCE: *FRUS 1943*, IV, 799–800.
*(Never issued).

H

Proposed Congressional
Resolutions (1944)

In January, 1944, identical resolutions were introduced into the House of Representatives and Senate pertaining to Palestine. In the House, one resolution was presented on January 27 by Representative James A. Wright (Democrat, of Pennsylvania) and one by Representative Ranulf Compton (Republican, of Connecticut). In the Senate a single resolution was introduced on February 1 by Senators Robert F. Wagner (Democrat, of New York) and Robert A. Taft (Republican, of Ohio). The bipartisan nature of the resolutions was emphasized by their endorsement by the entire Democrat and Republican leadership of both Houses.

The text of all these resolutions was the same, reading:

Resolved, that the United States shall use its good offices and take appropriate measures to the end that the doors of Palestine shall be opened for free entry of Jews into that country, and that there be full opportunity for colonization, so that the Jewish people may ultimately reconstitute Palestine as a free and democratic Jewish Commonwealth.

SOURCE: *FRUS 1944*, V, 560.

I

President Roosevelt to Senator Robert F. Wagner

Washington, October 15, 1944

Dear Bob:

Knowing that you are to attend the forty-seventh annual convention of the Zionist Organization of America, I ask you to convey to the delegates assembled my cordial greetings.

Please express my satisfaction that, in accord with the traditional American policy and in keeping with the spirit of the "four freedoms," the Democratic Party at its July convention this year included the following plank in its platform:

> We favor the opening of Palestine to unrestricted Jewish immigration and colonization, and such a policy as to result in the establishment there of a free and democratic Jewish commonwealth.

Efforts will be made to find appropriate ways and means of effectuating this policy as soon as practicable. I know how long and ardently the Jewish people have worked and prayed for the establishment of Palestine as a free and democratic Jewish commonwealth. I am convinced that the American people give their support to this aim and if re-elected I shall help to bring about its realization.

FRANKLIN D. ROOSEVELT

SOURCE: *FRUS 1944*, V, 615–16.

J

Palestine (A Summary)

March 17, 1944

1. With the failure of twenty-five years of government in Palestine, a radically different settlement, freed from the commitments arising from World War I, seems to be required.

2. *A Trusteeship for Palestine exercised by the three religious groups would be a failure.* However, there is moral and political justification for the proposal that the three principal religious groups should be associated with the future plan of government.

3. It is recommended that Palestine be constituted as an International Territory under a charter; that a great power be appointed a Trustee; that a Board of Overseers representing the three world religions be set up as an advisory body. The reasons and conditions that support this recommendation are as follows:

  a. The administrator of Palestine must be capable of firm, decisive and prompt action. This requires experienced officials under central control.

  b. Firm, decisive and prompt action cannot be taken if sectarian and political differences are allowed to exercise their divisive and delaying influences.

  c. The political and economic problems being highly complex and interwoven with hitherto irreconcilable religious differences, only a centralized and experienced rulership will guarantee justice.

4. It is recommended that the Trusteeship should be awarded to Great Britain by the United Nations Organization under the charter. This charter would recognize the interest in Palestine of Christians, Jews, and Moslems. It would establish the Arab and Jewish communities as autonomous political entities with wide powers of self-government.

5. The advantages of the proposed settlement are:

  a. It would eliminate the difficulties that arise because of conflicting commitments in the past.

SOURCE: *FRUS 1944*, V, 594.

b. It would place Palestine outside the bounds of both nationalist and imperialist ambitions.

c. It would provide means by which to solve the basic economic problems.

d. It offers a better prospect than any other plan yet proposed for cooperation in the government of Palestine and for eventual self-determination of the people of Palestine.

K

President Roosevelt's Letter to King Ibn Saud, April 5, 1945

April 5, 1945

Great and Good Friend:

I have received the communication which Your Majesty sent me under date of March 10, 1945, in which you refer to the question of Palestine and to the continuing interest of the Arabs in current developments affecting that country.

I am gratified that Your Majesty took this occasion to bring your views on this question to my attention and I have given the most careful attention to the statements which you make in your letter. I am also mindful of the memorable conversation which we had not so long ago and in the course of which I had an opportunity to obtain so vivid an impression of Your Majesty's sentiments on this question.

Your Majesty will recall that on previous occasions I communicated to you the attitude of the American Government toward Palestine and made clear our desire that no decision be taken with respect to the basic situation in that country without full consultation with both Arabs and Jews. Your Majesty will also doubtless recall that during our recent conversation I assured you that I would take no action, in my capacity as Chief of the Executive Branch of this Government, which might prove hostile to the Arab people.

It gives me pleasure to renew to Your Majesty the assurances which you have

---

SOURCE: *FRUS 1945*, VIII, 698.

received regarding the attitude of my Government and my own, as Chief Executive, with regard to the question of Palestine and to inform you that the policy of this Government in this respect is unchanged.

I desire also at this time to send you my best wishes for Your Majesty's continued good health and for the welfare of your people.

Your Good Friend,
FRANKLIN D. ROOSEVELT

L

Declaration of the Establishment of the State of Israel, May 14, 1948*

ERETZ-ISRAEL† was the birthplace of the Jewish people. Here their spiritual, religious and political identity was shaped. Here they first attained to statehood, created cultural values of national and universal significance and gave to the world the eternal Book of Books.

After being forcibly exiled from their land, the people kept faith with it throughout their Dispersion and never ceased to pray and hope for their return to it and for the restoration in it of their political freedom.

Impelled by this historic and traditional attachment, Jews strove in every successive generation to re-establish themselves in their ancient homeland. In recent decades they returned in their masses. Pioneers, *ma'pilim*‡ and defenders, they made deserts bloom, revived the Hebrew language, built villages and towns, and created a thriving community, controlling its own economy and culture, loving peace but knowing how to defend itself, bringing the blessings of progress to all the country's inhabitants, and aspiring towards independent nationhood.

---

*I Laws of the State of Israel 3–5(1948). Published in the Official Gazette, No. 1 of the 5th Iyar, 5708 (May 14, 1948).

†*Eretz-Israel* (Hebrew): the Land of Israel, Palestine.

‡*Ma'pilim* (Hebrew): immigrants coming to Eretz-Israel in defiance of restrictive legislation (generally referred to elsewhere as illegal immigrants).

In the year 5657 (1897), at the summons of the spiritual father of the Jewish State, Theodore Herzl, the First Zionist Congress convened and proclaimed the right of the Jewish people to national rebirth in its own country.

This right was recognized in the Balfour Declaration of the 2nd November, 1917, and re-affirmed in the Mandate of the League of Nations which, in particular, gave international sanction to the historic connection between the Jewish people and Eretz-Israel and to the right of the Jewish people to rebuild its National Home.

The catastrophe which recently befell the Jewish people—the massacre of millions of Jews in Europe—was another clear demonstration of the urgency of solving the problem of its homelessness by re-establishing in Eretz-Israel the Jewish State, which would open the gates of the homeland wide to every Jew and confer upon the Jewish people the status of a fully-privileged member of the comity of nations.

Survivors of the Nazi holocaust in Europe, as well as Jews from other parts of the world, continued to migrate to Eretz-Israel, undaunted by difficulties, restrictions and dangers, and never ceased to assert their right to a life of dignity, freedom and honest toil in their national homeland.

In the Second World War, the Jewish community of this country contributed its full share to the struggle of the freedom and peace-loving nations against the forces of Nazi wickedness and, by the blood of its soldiers and its war effort, gained the right to be reckoned among the peoples who founded the United Nations.

On the 29th November, 1947, the United Nations General Assembly passed a resolution calling for the establishment of a Jewish State in Eretz-Israel; the General Assembly required the inhabitants of Eretz-Israel to take such steps as were necessary on their part for the implementation of that resolution. This recognition by the United Nations of the right of the Jewish people to establish their State is irrevocable.

This right is the natural right of the Jewish people to be masters of their own fate, like all other nations, in their own sovereign State.

ACCORDINGLY WE, MEMBERS OF THE PEOPLE'S COUNCIL, REPRESENTATIVE OF THE JEWISH COMMUNITY OF ERETZ-ISRAEL AND OF THE ZIONIST MOVEMENT, ARE HERE ASSEMBLED ON THE DAY OF THE TERMINATION OF THE BRITISH MANDATE OVER ERETZ-ISRAEL AND, BY VIRTUE OF OUR NATURAL AND HISTORIC RIGHT AND ON THE STRENGTH OF THE RESOLUTION OF THE UNITED NATIONS GENERAL ASSEMBLY, HEREBY DECLARE THE ESTABLISHMENT OF A JEWISH STATE IN ERETZ-ISRAEL, TO BE KNOWN AS THE STATE OF ISRAEL.

WE DECLARE that, with effect from the moment of the termination of the Mandate, being tonight, the eve of Sabbath, the 6th Iyar, 5708 (15th May, 1948), until the establishment of the elected, regular authorities of the State in accordance with the Constitution which shall be adopted by the Elected Constituent Assembly not later than the 1st October 1948, the People's Council shall act as a Provisional Council of State, and its executive organ, the People's Administration, shall be the Provisional Government of the Jewish State, to be called "Israel."

THE STATE OF ISRAEL will be open for Jewish immigration and for the Ingathering of the Exiles; it will foster the development of the country for the benefit of all its inhabitants; it will be based on freedom, justice and peace as envisaged by the prophets of Israel; it will ensure complete equality of social and political rights to all its inhabitants irrespective of religion, race or sex; it will guarantee freedom of

religion, conscience, language, education and culture; it will safeguard the Holy
Places of all religions; and it will be faithful to the principles of the Charter of the
United Nations.

THE STATE OF ISRAEL is prepared to cooperate with the agencies and representatives
of the United Nations in implementing the resolution of the General Assembly of the
29th November, 1947, and will take steps to bring about the economic union of the
whole of Eretz-Israel.

WE APPEAL to the United Nations to assist the Jewish people in the building-up of
its State and to receive the State of Israel into the comity of nations.

WE APPEAL—in the very midst of the onslaught launched against us now for
months—to the Arab inhabitants of the State of Israel to preserve peace and
participate in the upbuilding of the State on the basis of full and equal citizenship and
due representation in all its provisional and permanent institutions.

WE EXTEND our hand to all neighbouring States and their peoples in an offer of
peace and good neighbourliness, and appeal to them to establish bonds of cooperation and mutual help with the sovereign Jewish people settled in its own land. The
State of Israel is prepared to do its share in a common effort for the advancement of
the entire Middle East.

WE APPEAL to the Jewish people throughout the Diaspora to rally round the Jews of
Eretz-Israel in the tasks of immigration and upbuilding and to stand by them in the
great struggle for the realization of the age-old dream—the redemption of Israel.

PLACING OUR TRUST IN THE ALMIGHTY, WE AFFIX OUR SIGNATURES TO THIS
PROCLAMATION AT THIS SESSION OF THE PROVISIONAL COUNCIL OF STATE, ON THE SOIL
OF THE HOMELAND, IN THE CITY OF TEL-AVIV, ON THIS SABBATH EVE, THE 5TH DAY OF
IYAR, 5708 (14TH MAY, 1948).

DAVID BEN-GURION

DANIEL AUSTER	ZVI LURIA
MORDEKHAI BENTOV	GOLDA MYERSON
YITZCHAK BEN ZVI	NACHUM NIR
ELIAYAHU BERLIGNE	ZVI SEGAL
FRITZ BERNSTEIN	RABBI YEHUDA LEIB HACOHEN FISHMAN
RABBI WOLF GOLD	DAVID ZVI PINKAS
MEIR GRABOVSKY	AHARON ZISLING
YITZCHAK GRUENBAUM	MOSHE KOLODNY
DR. ABRAHAM GRANOVSKY	ELIEZER KAPLAN
ELIYAHU DOBKIN	ABRAHAM KATZNELSON
MEIR WILNER-KOVNER	FELIX ROSENBLUETH
ZERACH WAHRHAFTIG	DAVID REMEZ
HERZL VARDI	BERL REPETUR
RACHEL COHEN	MORDEKHAI SHATTNER
RABBI KALMAN KAHANA	BEN ZION STERNBERG
SAADIA KOBASHI	BEKHOR SHITREET
RABBI YITZCHAK MEIR LEVIN	MOSHE SHAPIRA
MEIR DAVID LOWENSTEIN	MOSHE SHERTOK

M

The Agent of the Provisional Government of Israel (Epstein) to President Truman

Washington, May 14, 1948

My dear Mr. President:

I have the honor to notify you that the state of Israel has been proclaimed as an independent republic within frontiers approved by the General Assembly of the United Nations in its Resolution of November 29, 1947, and that a provisional government has been charged to assume the rights and duties of government for preserving law and order within the boundaries of Israel, for defending the state against external aggression, and for discharging the obligations of Israel to the other nations of the world in accordance with international law. The Act of Independence will become effective at one minute after six o'clock on the evening of 14 May, 1948, Washington time.

With full knowledge of the deep bond of sympathy which has existed and has been strengthened over the past thirty years between the Government of the United States and the Jewish people of Palestine, I have been authorized by the provisional government of the new state to tender this message and to express the hope that your government will recognize and will welcome Israel into the community of nations.

Very respectfully yours,

ELIAHU EPSTEIN

SOURCE: *FRUS 1948*, V, Part 2, 989, from the Truman Library, President's Secretary's file. An identical letter sent to the Secretary of State is in the 1948 Departmental files at the National Archives.

Notes

INTRODUCTION

1. For a description of the building, see an article, "State, War, and Navy Building, July 1875–April 1947," by Lee H. Burke of the Department's Historical Office, Department of State *Newsletter*, June 1976, pp. 30–34. For further details see the books by Baram and Weil cited in the Bibliography.

2. Nor, according to Assistant Secretary of State Breckinridge Long's *War Diary*, p. 214, did Roosevelt even inform Hull of plans for his 1941 Atlantic Charter meeting with Churchill.

3. Hubert Herring, "The Department of State—A Review with Recommendations to the President," *Harper's Magazine*, February 1937, pp. 225–48.

4. Graham H. Stuart, *American Diplomatic and Consular Practice* (New York: D. Appleton-Century, 1936), p. 95.

5. The Departmental Order issued by Secretary of State Philander C. Knox under date of December 13, 1909, creating the Division of Near Eastern Affairs, is given in Appendix A. It will be noted that in the early days the jurisdiction of the Division extended to a number of countries which we would not consider today to form a part of the Near East, such as Germany, Austria-Hungary, and even Russia. These countries were transferred to other divisions during or shortly after the First World War. See NE divisional memoranda dated October 13, 1926, May 21, 1931, and December 12, 1932, in the Department's archives.

6. *FRUS 1942*, IV, 548, and *FRUS 1945*, VIII, 688; also NE Palestine files for 1943, confidential memorandum, Murray to Secretary of State, November 26, 1943.

7. Humphrey Trevelyan, *Diplomatic Channels* (Boston: Gambit, Inc., 1973), pp. 78–79.

8. See Schechtman (as cited in Bibliography), pp. 412–13.

9. The family of the Sherif of Mecca, Hussein, to whom the British had made their promises of independence during the First World War.

10. Henry L. Feingold, "The Politics of Rescue: A Study of American Diplomacy and Politics Related to the Rescue of Refugees" (Ph.D. dissertation, New York University, 1966), p. 17. (This is also available in book form, as indicated in the Bibliography, but my references throughout are to the dissertation.)

1: THE BILTMORE PROGRAM CALLS FOR A JEWISH STATE

Official sources and archival material: The 1942 *Foreign Relations* volume is vol. IV, *The Near East and Africa*, Department of State Publication 7534 (U.S. Government Printing Office, Washington, 1963), hereafter cited as *FRUS 1942*; pp. 538–58 relate to Palestine.

U.S. Archives: The State Department's Palestine files for the year 1942 (on which the *FRUS* volume is largely based) are found in: Records of the Department of State, Record Group 59, State Department Decimal *Files 867 N.00 and 867 N.01*, National Archives Washington; also *divisional files of the Division of Near Eastern Affairs*, 1942, formerly in the Foreign Affairs Document and Reference Center, Department of State, now transferred to the Archives.

Franklin D. Roosevelt Library, Hyde Park, N.Y.: (1) *Map Room File*: (Roosevelt-Churchill Messages), 1941–45; Boxes 1, 2, 3, 4, 6, 7, 7a, 16, 24, 27, and 165; (2) *President's Secretary's File* (PSF): Box 62, "Palestine"; Boxes 91 and 92, "Cordell Hull"; Box 93, "E. R. Stettinius, Jr."; Box 94, "Sumner Welles"; Box 113-A, "Crimean Conference"; Box 144, "Morris L. Ernst"; Boxes 146 and 149, "Executive Office of the President—Samuel I. Rosenman"; Box 151, "Patrick J. Hurley"; and Box 192, "War Refugee Board"; (3) *President's Personal File* (PPF): File 601, "Zionist Organization of America"; File 7960, "King Ibn Saud"; File 8084, "Chaim Weizmann"; File 7683, "Winston S. Churchill"; File 6533, "Patrick J. Hurley"; File 5575, "Isaiah Bowman"; File 2961, "Sumner Welles"; File 2905, "United Jewish Appeal"; File 357, "Henry Morgenthau, Jr."; and File 2841, "Morris L. Ernst"; (4) *President's Official File* (POF): Boxes 1, 2, 3, and 3186, "Palestine"; File 4847, "David K. Niles"; Boxes 1, 2, 3, and 4 and File 1395, "Political Refugees"; Files 5477 and 5477-A, "War Refugee Board"; (5) *Papers of the War Refugee Board*, Boxes 16, 17, 29, and 46; (6) *Papers of Harry L. Hopkins*; (7) *Papers of Charles W. Taussig*; (8) *Papers of Samuel I. Rosenman*; (9) *Diaries of Henry Morgenthau, Jr.*; and the *Correspondence* (on microfilm) of President Roosevelt with (10) *Justice Felix Frankfurter* and (11) *Rabbi Stephen S. Wise*. This material covers a number of years in addition to 1942.

British Archives, in the Public Record Office, London: Foreign Office *File 371, Eastern, 1942, Palestine and Trans-Jordan*, Files no. 6, 27, and 49. (Covers later years but was open only through 1945 when examined.)

Zionist Archives. (A) In the Central Zionist Archives, Jerusalem: (1) Files of the *Central Offices of the World Zionist Organization and Jewish Agency for Palestine*; *Jewish Agency, American Section*, including the Palestine Office (Washington) of the *Political Department of the Executive of the World Zionist Organization and Jewish Agency for Palestine*, Jerusalem, Tel Aviv, Haifa, and London, 1917–45, including the "Organization Department" of the Jewish Agency Executive. These files, which were open only through 1945 when examined, are of particular interest because they contain many reports from Jewish Agency representatives in Washington giving the Zionist version of the same conversations recorded in the *FRUS* and State Department archives; (B) In the *Zionist Archives, New York*: Miscellaneous records, including copies of the Wise correspondence from the Franklin D. Roosevelt Library (above) and of the Clark Clifford papers from the Harry S. Truman Library (see Notes to Chapter 5); (C) The *Archives* of the *Jerusalem Post*, Jerusalem. All three of these archives cover a number of years.

1. *The Public Papers and Addresses of Franklin D. Roosevelt*, 1942 vol. (New York: Harper & Bros., 1950), p. 38.

2. "Palestine's Role in the Solution of the Jewish Problem," *Foreign Affairs*, vol. 20, no. 2 (January 1942), pp. 324–38.

3. The *Struma* was an overloaded Danube excursion steamer in which nearly 800 Jewish refugees from the Balkans were trying to reach Palestine, via Turkey. When the Turkish authorities refused to allow them to land in the absence of British immigration certificates for Palestine, the ship put to sea from Istanbul and almost immediately sank in the Bosporus from an unknown cause. For details see Parkes, p. 284; Polk, Stammler, and Asfour, p. 181; and Silverberg, pp. 209–10.

4. The Biltmore Conference is described in Halperin, pp. 220–23; Hurewitz, *The Struggle for Palestine*, pp. 156–59; Ilan, pp. 97–101; Laqueur, *A History of Zionism*, pp. 545–52; and Silverberg, pp. 193–95.

5. *FRUS 1942*, p. 552.

6. The demand for the establishment of Palestine as a "Jewish Commonwealth," that is, a Jewish state, represented a landmark for the Zionist movement. Herzl in *The Jewish State* (1896) had called for a Jewish state in "Palestine or Argentina." The 1897 Basle Congress of the Zionist Organization had called merely for a "home" for the Jewish people in Palestine, and the Balfour Declaration also spoke of a "national home" for the Jewish people in Palestine. The Biltmore program was the first public affirmation by the Zionist movement of the goal of a Jewish state in Palestine. See Appendixes C, D, E, and F for texts of all four of these citations.

7. The agitation for a Jewish brigade is described *inter alia* in Laqueur, *History*, and Ilan. See also the Morgenthau Diaries for July 7, 1942, in the Roosevelt Library.

8. The Nazi program is covered in many sources, notably the works of Blum, Burns, Feingold, Goldmann, Ilan, Laqueur, and Wise cited in the Bibliography.

9. This comment appears in many sources. I happen to have extracted it from an article in the *New York Times* for October 20, 1977, p. 46. According to William Stevenson in *A Man Called Intrepid* (New York: Harcourt Brace Jovanovich, 1976), p. 393, Churchill used this phrase at a meeting in the City of London on the final day of the fighting in the North African landings and in a message to Roosevelt at the time.

10. See the British Foreign Office files, Public Record Office, "Minute" by the Head of the Eastern Department, C. W. Baxter, October 16, 1942, reporting a conversation in Washington between Welles and British Minister of State Richard Law; also the Zionist Archives, Jerusalem, report by Nahum Goldmann dated December 4, 1942, of a conversation in Washington between Welles, Weizmann, and himself.

2 : THE UNITED STATES FINDS A POLICY

Official sources and archival material: The 1943 *Foreign Relations* volume covering Palestine is vol. IV, *The Near East and Africa* (1964); hereafter cited as *FRUS 1943*. In preparing this chapter I have also used the following earlier volumes of *FRUS*: for 1936, vol. III, *The Near East and Africa* (1953); for 1937, vol. II, *The British Commonwealth, Europe, the Near East, and Africa* (1954); for 1938, vol. II, same (1955); and for 1939, vol. IV, *The Far East, the Near East and Africa* (1955). I have also gone through the State Department's 1943 Palestine files in the National Archives with the reference numbers given in the Notes to Chapter 1.

See the same Notes for sources at the *Franklin D. Roosevelt Library*, Hyde Park, N.Y., and in the *Zionist Archives* in Jerusalem and New York City.

The pertinent *British Foreign Office archives* at the Public Record Office, London, are identified as: Foreign Office 371, Eastern, 1943, Palestine and Trans-Jordan, File no. 87.

The *Palestine File* in the papers of former Senator *Robert F. Wagner* in the Special Collections Room, Georgetown University Library, Washington, D.C., contains correspondence and other material relating to Palestine and the Zionist movement in Wagner's possession as Senator, as well as a great deal of material relating to his position as chairman of the American Palestine Committee, later the American Christian Palestine Committee.

1. The official record of the first session of the Conference is contained in *The American Jewish Conference, Its Organization, and Proceedings of the First Session, August 29–September 2, 1943*, ed. Alexander S. Kohanski (New York: American Jewish Conference, 1944), in the Zionist Archives, New York. The *Bulletin* of the Conference (which was a continuing body), also on file in the Zionist Archives, for November 19, 1948, states that at the 37th and final meeting of the Interim Committee of the Conference on November 10, 1948, it was decided to wind up the Conference as of December 31, 1948, since its work was considered to have been accomplished with the establishment of the state of Israel.

The best accounts of the Conference are those by Halperin, pp. 219–51, and Silverberg, pp. 225–31. See also Goldmann, pp. 223–24. An article by Emanuel Neumann, a prominent Zionist, entitled "Abba Hillel Silver, History Maker," *American Zionist*, February 5, 1953, covers Rabbi Silver's role at the opening session and later. Additional details about Rabbi Silver can be found in an article by Rabbi Leon I. Feuer, his assistant for some years at The Temple, Cleveland, Ohio, entitled "Abba Hillel Silver, a Personal Memoir," *American Jewish Archives*, vol. 19, no. 2 (November 1967). I was unsuccessful in gaining access to Silver's papers, which are in the custody of his son in Cleveland, Ohio.

2. For a detailed study of the American Zionist Emergency Council and its operations see Doreen Bierbrier, "The American Zionist Emergency Council, an Analysis of a Pressure Group," *American Jewish Historical Quarterly*, vol. 59 no. 1 (September 1970), pp. 82–105. It is from her account that I have taken such details as the Council's budget and total membership in Zionist organizations. The Central Zionist Archives, Jerusalem, contain many circular instructions and reports which are very revealing of the propaganda techniques employed by the AZEC. Other details are to be found in the Wagner papers, cited above.

Among the works cited in the Bibliography, the best accounts of the Zionist campaign are in Lilienthal, Silverberg, Richard Stevens, and Taylor, *Prelude*. See also an unpublished Ph.D. dissertation by Irwin Oder, "The United States and the Palestine Mandate, 1920–1948" (Columbia University, 1956). Senator Wagner's role in the Zionist movement is outlined in J. Joseph Huthmacher, *Senator Robert F. Wagner and the Rise of Urban Liberalism* (New York: Atheneum, 1968), which notwithstanding its title has a good deal to say about Zionism.

3. Letters from Senator Bailey of North Carolina opposing the idea of a Jewish state in Palestine will be found in the National Archives, State Department Palestine file (867 N.01), February 29, 1944, and in Official File 204 (Miscellaneous) in the papers of President Harry S. Truman in the Truman Library, Independence, Missouri

(letter of May 23, 1945, to the President, copy in the National Archives Palestine file for 1945).

4. A summary of Lt. Colonel Hoskins's report was transmitted to the Department of State by the American Minister to Egypt, Alexander Kirk, under date of January 23, 1943; see *FRUS 1943*, pp. 747–51. For additional summaries, prepared by Hoskins in the Department, see ibid., pp. 782–85 and 825–27.

5. For an extract about Palestine from Hurley's report to the President dated May 5, 1943, see ibid., pp. 776–80. Hurley pointed out that the Zionists desired the transfer of the Arab population of Palestine to Iraq. In 1944 Hurley was made Roosevelt's Personal Representative to Chiang Kai-shek. Later he became Ambassador to China, and was very outspoken in his criticism of certain Foreign Service officers on his staff as being "soft on Communism."

6. For the comparatively weak Arab propaganda effort, see the Bierbrier article cited above, also Khouri, p. 32, and Furlonge's biography of Musa Alami, who was the first head of the Arab Information Office network in 1945, esp. p. 140.

7. See *FRUS 1943*, pp. 786–87. See p. 790 for another message from the President, in the form of a letter answering a second message from Ibn Saud, transmitted to the newly appointed American Minister Resident in Saudi Arabia. Many examples of the assurances given to Arab leaders will be found in the *FRUS* Near East volumes for 1944, 1945, 1946, and 1947. See also Appendix G and Appendix K. The significance of the "full consultation" formula is brought out very accurately in Hurewitz, *Struggle for Palestine*, p. 213.

8. For Arab criticisms of the formula see J. Rives Childs, *Foreign Service Farewell: My Years in the Near East* (Charlottesville, Va.: University Press of Virginia, 1969), p. 149 (Childs was Minister, later Ambassador, to Saudi Arabia from 1946 to 1950); and Richard Stevens, p. 150. For Jewish criticism of the formula see Golding p. 92.

9. Such allegations have unfortunately been put forward in a number of quarters, notably by the late Bartley C. Crum in *Behind the Silken Curtain*, chapter entitled "The Secret File in the State Department."

10. The British side of the controversy regarding the issuance of a statement is to be found in the Foreign Office archives referred to above.

11. For accounts of the so-called "Philby Scheme" see H. St. John Philby, *Arabian Jubilee (A Jubilee Biography of Ibn Saud)* (New York: John Day Co., 1953), and Elizabeth Monroe, *Philby of Arabia* (London: Faber & Faber, 1973). For Weizmann's account of the project see his autobiography, *Trial and Error*, II, 432, and also, at greater length, a letter from him to Welles in the Samuel I. Rosenman papers in the Franklin D. Roosevelt Library, Hyde Park, Box 29. See also Hull, *Memoirs*, II, 1533, and Ilan, p. 140–51. Hoskins confirmed to me in June 1974 that he had not known the details of the scheme when he was sent to see Ibn Saud.

12. For these two Departmental papers see *FRUS 1943*, pp. 816–21 (memorandum by Gordon P. Merriam, October 15, 1943), and *FRUS 1944*, p. 594 (memorandum by E. M. Wilson, March 17, 1944, given in Appendix J below); other Departmental papers on the subject will be cited later. Most of these papers were passed through the so-called Inter-Divisional Area Committee on Arab Countries, consisting of Gordon Merriam and myself from the Near East Division and Philip W. Ireland and William Yale from the Division of Territorial Studies. For later plans, see NE memoranda of June 4, 1947, and July 7, 1947, *FRUS 1947*, V, 1096 and 1120.

13. A memorandum of this conversation is given in *FRUS 1943*, pp. 823–24; see also ibid., pp. 827–29, and *FRUS 1944,* p. 560.

14. See Hull, *Memoirs*, II, 1534. The pertinent British record, in the Foreign Office 1943 archives cited above, makes no reference to any such request on Hull's part. The Palestine files of the U.S. State Department for 1943 in the National Archives include Dispatch no. 12278 of November 17, 1943, from the American Embassy at London reporting the Colonial Secretary's announcement in the House of Commons, so the Department was aware of the British decision. Dispatch no. 1186 of May 23, 1944, from the American Consul General at Jerusalem (in the same files for 1944) quotes the Chief Secretary of the government of Palestine as denying a statement by Jewish Agency leader Moshe Shertok to the Inner Zionist General Council to the effect that postponement of the deadline had been as a result of U.S. government pressure. See also Samuel Halperin and Irwin Oder, "The United States in Search of a Policy: Franklin D. Roosevelt and Palestine," *Review of Politics* (Notre Dame), vol. 24, no. 3, (November 1962).

15. Ernst describes his mission to London in his *So Far So Good* (New York: Harper & Bros., 1948). See also Lilienthal, pp. 32–34; Richard Stevens, p. 71; Taylor, *Prelude,* p. 92; and an article by Dr. Harry N. Howard in Taylor and Tetlie's anthology, pp. 217–39, entitled "Conflicts of Interest." The British Foreign Office files, cited above, contain a memorandum dated December 13, 1943, regarding Ernst's conversations with British officials.

Maps 17, 30, and 35 in Gilbert's atlas of the Arab-Israel conflict illustrate the situation of the Jews in Europe and the attempts to find havens for them.

In connection with the Jewish refugee problem generally, I was interested to note a memorandum from Presidential Adviser David K. Niles to President Truman dated May 27, 1946, in the Harry S. Truman Library (President's Official File 204, Miscellaneous) urging him not to bring Jewish displaced persons to the United States.

16. The efforts of the administration to find havens for refugees from Europe are detailed in Blum, pp. 530–33, and Silverberg, pp. 244–46, as well as in the Feingold works cited in the Bibliography. For our immigration quotas see Lilienthal, pp. 34–37, and Hirschmann, *Lifeline,* chap. 17. A very overdrawn and unfair attack on the State Department and its officials will be found in Arthur D. Morse, *While Six Million Died: A Chronicle of American Apathy* (New York: Random House, 1967). See also Burns, pp. 441–42, and William O. Douglas, *Go East, Young Man: The Early Years* (New York: Random House, 1974), pp. 338–413. The State Department's side in the controversy is covered in the *War Diary of Breckinridge Long,* ed. F. L. Israel. Long, an Assistant Secretary of State, was in charge of the Department's refugee activities.

3: PALESTINE BECOMES A POLITICAL ISSUE

Official sources and archival material: The 1944 *Foreign Relations* volume covering Palestine is vol. V, *The Near East, South Asia and Africa, The Far East,* (1965); hereafter cited as *FRUS 1944.* I have also made use of the State Department's 1944 Palestine files at the National Archives, with reference numbers as given in the Notes to Chapter 1. See those Notes also for sources at the Franklin D. Roosevelt Library, Hyde Park, N.Y., and in the Zionist Archives in Jerusalem and New York City.

The pertinent British Foreign Office archives at the Public Record Office, London, are identified as: Foreign Office 371, Eastern, 1944, Palestine and Trans-Jordan, Files 16, 41, 67, 87, 95, 206, and 723.

For the Wagner papers on Palestine, see Notes to Chapter 2.

1. The text of the identical resolutions introduced into the Senate (Wagner-Taft) and House (Wright-Compton) can be found in *FRUS 1944*, p. 560.

2. For the Department's circular telegram of February 16, 1944, see ibid., p. 566.

3. For the letters from Secretary Stimson, dated February 7, and from Secretary Hull, dated February 9, see ibid., p. 563.

4. The subject of the Congressional resolutions has been covered in many writings dealing with that period, notably those of Ilan, pp. 175–85; Laqueur, *History*, pp. 550–54; Silverberg, pp. 237–42; and Richard Stevens, pp. 37–53.

5. Roosevelt's March 9, 1944, note to Rayburn is in the Roosevelt Library, President's Official File No. 700, Box 3. The Zionist Archives in Jerusalem contain a number of reports from Nahum Goldmann, who at the time was representing the Jewish Agency in Washington, about his contacts with the White House and the State and War departments regarding the resolutions, showing how the matter was mishandled by various parties, especially the Zionist leadership. Many of Goldmann's reports are highly critical of Silver. Presidential Counsel Rosenman told Goldmann that Roosevelt was fed up with the entire episode.

6. Silverberg's interpretation of this meeting and the statement that Wise and Silver issued on leaving the White House is particularly astute (pp. 240–41). My version is based largely on a report from the British Embassy, Washington, dated March 21, 1944, giving Rabbi Silver's account of the meeting as told to Isaiah Berlin of the Embassy; Foreign Office File no. 95, 1944, in the Public Record Office, London.

7. *Realities of American-Palestine Relations*, p. 317.

8. See *FRUS 1944*, p. 591, for Stimson's letter and the statement of the House committee.

9. For the statement issued by the State Department on December 11 see ibid., p. 645.

10. For the exchange of telegrams between Roosevelt and Stettinius see ibid., pp. 643–45. It is of interest that when this volume (V, 1944) was published the Department had to obtain the texts from the Roosevelt Library at Hyde Park, as they apparently are not in the Department's files.

11. The insistence of the Zionists, notably Silver, on going ahead with the resolutions regardless of Roosevelt's and Stettinius's advice is recorded in ibid., p. 637, and in Richard Stevens, p. 60.

12. For the text of the 1945 resolution see *FRUS 1945*, III, 841–42.

13. For the Republican and Democratic Palestine planks see *FRUS 1944*, pp. 605, 606.

14. See the Rosenman papers, Roosevelt Library, memorandum of September 16, 1944.

15. Roosevelt's original draft of the message comprised only the first three paragraphs of the text plus the first sentence of the fourth paragraph. The remaining two sentences, which contain the real pledge of support for the state, were added by Wagner, presumably at the request of the Zionists, but revised by Roosevelt in the final version. Wagner had had "undivided" before "Palestine" in the second sentence of the last paragraph, and "I shall do all in my power . . ." where Roosevelt has "if re-elected I shall help . . ."

16. *FRUS 1944*, p. 617.

17. For Henderson's telegram see ibid., pp. 617–19; for Satterthwaite's telegram from Damascus see ibid., p. 621.

18. For Henderson's second telegram see ibid., pp. 626–27.

19. See the memoranda of October 27 and December 13, 1944, ibid., pp. 624–26 and 648–49.

20. The American and British records of the meetings held by Murray and Bowman with Foreign Office officials in April 1944 differ only slightly. See ibid., pp. 600–604, and Foreign Office files no. 95 and no. 16, 1944. The British record does not have Sir Maurice Peterson of the Foreign Office actually stating to the Americans that the Foreign Office would favor a solution based on trusteeship with autonomy for the two communities, but subsequently Eden circulated a paper to the Cabinet endorsing the proposal along these lines that was put forward by Bowman in the talks. Churchill, however, remained an advocate of the Zionist position and on November 4, 1944, in conversation with Dr. Weizmann, told him so (the record of this meeting is in Foreign Office file no. 95). See also Weizmann, *Trial and Error*, II, 436. For Stettinius's report to Roosevelt on returning from London see the President's Secretary's File (PSF), Box 93, Franklin D. Roosevelt Library.

21. The Foreign Office archives contain many of the papers circulated by the Cabinet Committee on Palestine, showing the opposition of the Foreign Office, and of the principal British representatives in the Middle East, to partition. The decision to postpone action until after the war was taken on January 22, 1944.

22. Churchill memorandum to Casey, January 17, 1944, Foreign Office file no. 95, 1944.

23. For discussions of the British plans, as well as Churchill's disclosure of them to Weizmann, see Ilan, pp. 154–67; Hurewitz, *Struggle*, pp. 170–80; and Marlowe, p. 179.

24. Considerable material on the War Refugee Board is to be found at the Roosevelt Library, in the file entitled "War Refugee Board, 1944–1945," Boxes 16, 17, 29, and 46; also in the Diaries of Henry Morgenthau, Jr., at the Library.

25. *Caution to the Winds* and *Lifeline to a Promised Land.*

26. For the activities of the Board, and the general situation with respect to the rescue of refugees during 1944, see the works by Feingold, as well as Blum, pp. 529–33, and Burns, p. 441. As an example of what he considered bureaucratic callousness, Feingold (in his dissertation, chap. 10) recounts how, when Assistant Secretary of War John J. McCloy was asked if the Nazi extermination camp at Auschwitz and the railroad lines leading to it could be bombed from the air, he responded that such an effort would be of doubtful usefulness and "even if practicable, might provoke more vindictive action by the Germans." The obvious comment, that "it is difficult to imagine what more vindictive action than total extermination the Germans could have invented," was made by Stork and Rose, p. 46.

4: ROOSEVELT'S LAST MONTHS

Official sources and archival material: The pertinent *FRUS* citations are the previously cited *FRUS 1944*, vol. V, pp. 655–57; and for 1945, vol. VIII, *The Near East and Africa*, Department of State Publication 8427 (1969), pp. 678–704; hereafter cited as *FRUS 1945*.

The official U.S. record of the Yalta Conference is contained in a special *FRUS* volume, *The Conferences at Malta and Yalta, 1945,* Department of State Publication 6199 (1955). There is no reference to Palestine in this volume.

U.S. Archives: the 1944 and 1945 State Department Palestine files in the National Archives and the 1945 NE divisional files, with the reference numbers given in the Notes to Chapter 1.

The files at the *Franklin D. Roosevelt* Library and at the *Zionist Archives* in Jerusalem and New York City as cited in the Notes to Chapter 1.

British Archives: in the Public Record Office, London, the Foreign Office *File 371, Palestine and Trans-Jordan*, 1944 and 1945, Files no. 16 and 41.

The papers of *Robert F. Wagner* at the Georgetown University Library as previously cited.

1. Churchill's telegram expressing concern for the President's health (dated October 23, 1944) is in the Map Room File at the Roosevelt Library, "Roosevelt-Churchill Messages," Box 7.

2. For Stettinius's memorandum of his December 22 conversation with the President, and our paper for Yalta, which was never used, see *FRUS 1944*, p. 655.

3. Bishop, p. 296.

4. *FRUS 1945*, pp. 681–82.

5. Bishop, p. 248.

6. The correspondence between President Roosevelt and Congressman Celler is in the President's Secretary's File (PSF), Box 62, Roosevelt Library, as is the President's exchange with Senator Wagner.

7. The 1944 Palestine file at the National Archives (876 N.01/11–944) has Stettinius's record of a conversation that he had with Rabbi Wise, Rabbi Silver, and Nahum Goldmann on November 9, when the suggestion was made that the President should take an "expert" on Palestine to his next meeting with Churchill. Our memorandum to Stettinius of November 15, saying it would be "most unfortunate if the Zionists were to have any voice in selecting the advisers to accompany the President," is in the same file.

The correspondence between Roosevelt and Rabbi Wise at the Zionist Archives, New York, and at the Roosevelt Library contains Wise's letter of January 12, 1945, the memorandum that he left with the President at their January 22 meeting, and Wise's follow-up letter of January 24, from which it is possible to reconstruct at least part of their conversation.

8. The meeting at Yalta has been described by a number of eyewitnesses, notably Charles E. ("Chip") Bohlen, who served as Roosevelt's interpreter; James F. Byrnes, then Director of War Mobilization and Reconversion; W. Averell Harriman, at the time Ambassador to Moscow; Harry L. Hopkins (in the Sherwood volume); Fleet Admiral William D. Leahy, the President's Chief of Staff; and Stettinius. According to Harriman (p. 368), Roosevelt suggested Jerusalem as a possible location for the Big Three meeting but Harriman dissuaded him on the grounds that the choice of Jerusalem might involve the participants in the Arab-Jewish controversy. For other accounts see Bishop, pp. 268–433; Burns, p. 578; and Cabell Phillips, *The 1940's*, pp. 222–26. The British side is given in vol. 6, *Triumph and Tragedy*, of Winston Churchill's *History of the Second World War* (Boston: Houghton Mifflin, 1953), pp. 346–89; and in *The Diaries of Sir Alexander Cadogan*, ed. David Dilks (New York: G. P. Putnam's Sons, 1972), pp. 679–709. Cadogan was Permanent Undersecretary of the British Foreign Office.

9. See the accounts of Byrnes, pp. 21–45; Leahy, pp. 295–325; and Stettinius, pp. 278–89.

10. The final dinner discussion of the subject among the Big Three at Yalta is related by Bohlen, Hopkins, Leahy, and Stettinius. After Roosevelt told Churchill and Stalin of his plans to see Ibn Saud, Farouk, and Haile Selassie, Churchill sought Hopkins out and, "greatly disturbed," asked what this was all about. Hopkins, according to a memorandum reproduced in the Sherwood book (p. 872), replied that he had no idea (his private view was that it was "a lot of horseplay"). In an article entitled, "The Conference of Yalta and the Palestine Problem," *Jerusalem Journal of International Relations*, vol. III, no. 1 (Fall 1977), pp. 28–52, Amitzur Ilan, whose thesis I have quoted several times, gives details regarding Yalta and Palestine similar to those I have given here.

11. The official record of the February 14, 1945, conversation between Roosevelt and Ibn Saud is Colonel Eddy's memorandum drawn up immediately afterward; Ibn Saud signed an Arabic text and the President an English text. The latter appears on pp. 2–3 of the 1945 *FRUS*; see also pp. 7–9 for further details of the meeting as reported by Eddy. In *F.D.R. Meets Ibn Saud* (pp. 29–32), Eddy gives an account of the meeting and the President's pledge to the King. He also tells how he was cautioned by Stettinius, Hopkins, and Ambassador to Britain John G. Winant, who was with the President's party aboard the *Quincy*, to safeguard his memorandum most closely "and not entrust it to State Department channels."

For descriptions of Ibn Saud's colorful journey up the Red Sea in the American destroyer *Murphy* see Eddy, pp. 23–28, also an article in the U.S. Naval Institute *Proceedings* (January 1976) by Captain John S. Keating, U.S. Navy (Retired), who commanded the *Murphy*. The day before the meeting with Ibn Saud, the President received Farouk and Haile Selassie aboard the *Quincy*.

The papers of Samuel I. Rosenman at the Harry S. Truman Library (subject file "Palestine") show that in September 1945, Rosenman, who was serving as Special Counsel to President Truman as he had been to President Roosevelt, sent Eddy's memorandum of the conversation, of which he had apparently only just learned, to Admiral Leahy for verification. Leahy (who had been in Roosevelt's party) responded that he had reviewed Eddy's account and found it to be accurate. Memorandum from Rosenman to Truman, September 7, 1945.

While in Egypt, Ibn Saud had a meeting with Churchill at the Fayoum Oasis. The British insisted on sending him home in a British cruiser, which according to Eddy he did not enjoy as much as the American destroyer. His meeting with Churchill, which was not very productive, is covered in Churchill, pp. 397–99, and in the Cadogan *Diaries*, pp. 714–15. See also pp. 689–90 of the 1945 *FRUS*, giving the King's version of the meeting as told to Colonel Eddy.

12. The Wagner papers contain a letter dated August 27, 1945, from Rabbi Silver to Senator Wagner commenting on a report in the *New York Times* for August 24 according to which Azzam Pasha, secretary-general of the Arab League, had revealed to the press the assurances given by the President to Ibn Saud. Silver remarked, rather tartly, "either Azzam's story is manufactured out of whole cloth or else the late President was guilty of a quite incredible piece of deception."

13. Stettinius, p. 289. Among those to whom Roosevelt confided that he considered the meeting to have been a failure were: (1) Churchill: see Bishop, p. 449; (2) Winant: see *The Lyon's Share* by Cecil B. Lyon (New York: Vantage Press, 1973), p. 182; Lyon was serving as First Secretary of the American Legation at Cairo at the time; (3) Bernard Baruch: see Elliott Roosevelt, *As He Saw It* (New York: Duell, Sloan and Pearce, 1945), p. 245; (4) Eleanor Roosevelt: see her *This I Remember* (New

York: Harper & Bros., 1949), p. 342; and (5) Rabbi Wise: see his *Challenging Years,* p. 232. Abba Eban, "Tragedy and Triumph," in Weisgal and Carmichael, eds., p. 276, and Ben Gurion, "Memoirs," extract in *Jewish Observer and Middle East Review,* June 12, 1964, also cite Wise's March 16, 1945, talk with F.D.R. Like Stettinius, Wise was told (p. 232) by Roosevelt that he was planning some new approach to the Palestine problem.

14. See Bishop, p. 479. Bishop says that Rosenman, who drafted the speech, told Mrs. Rosenman afterward that the President had departed from his prepared text forty-nine times and that his extemporaneous reference to the King was "ridiculous." Hopkins's reaction was equally critical. He felt that all Roosevelt could have learned from Ibn Saud was what anyone familiar with the Palestine problem would have known already: "the Arabs don't want any more Jews in Palestine." See Sherwood, p. 872.

15. See *FRUS 1945,* pp. 691–93, for these letters.

16. Although, as noted in Chapter 3, Roosevelt's October 1944 message to Wagner could be interpreted as having been made in a personal capacity, the President told Ibn Saud in their February 14 conversation that he was speaking as Chief Executive of the United States government, and we were careful to repeat this statement (twice) in the letter we drafted.

17. See *FRUS 1945,* pp. 695–96.

18. Both memoranda are in ibid., pp. 694 and 698. For our telegram playing down the significance of the President's meeting with Wise see ibid., p. 696.

19. Blum, pp. 628–30.

20. For the story of Roosevelt's last days at Warm Springs see Bishop, pp. 545–79, Cabell Phillips, *The 1940's,* pp. 246–47, and Bernard Asbell, *When F.D.R. Died* (New York: Signet Books, 1962), esp. p. 36. Asbell has a reproduction of Mme. Shoumatoff's unfinished portrait of the President, which now hangs in the Roosevelt Cottage at Warm Springs. See also Jonathan Daniels, *White House Witness,* (Garden City, N.Y.: Doubleday, 1975), pp. 279–82.

21. For details on the Jewish vote for Roosevelt see Silverberg, p. 158, and Isaacs, chap. 9.

22. Roosevelt's conviction that he would be able to bring the Arabs and Jews together after the war is cited by Hull, II, 1532; Feis, pp. 16–17; and Sumner Welles, *We Need Not Fail* (Boston: Houghton Mifflin, 1948), chap. 2.

23. Frances Perkins, *The Roosevelt I Knew* (New York: Viking Press, 1946), pp. 88–89. Much the same point is made in a letter that I received under date of March 17, 1976, from James Rowe, Jr., recalling a conversation with F.D.R. "when he said that after the war he hoped he could get some TVA projects started in the Mideast." Rowe, who was a White House administrative assistant under Roosevelt, has read this chapter and finds it to be substantially correct.

24. Quoted in Bishop, p. 526.

25. The President's ideas respecting a trusteeship for Palestine are outlined in two conversations with Colonel Hoskins recorded in *FRUS 1943,* pp. 811–14, and *FRUS 1945,* pp. 690–91. Both Silverberg (p. 263) and Taylor, *Prelude,* (p. 85) conclude that the President was thinking of Palestine as a binational state, but he was never explicit. Roosevelt's earlier views about the Arabs are reflected in a conversation he had with Morgenthau on December 3, 1942, when he said he would "put a barbed wire

around Palestine" and move the Arabs out as the Jews moved in (Blum, p. 512). The Zionist Archives in Jerusalem contain a record of a meeting on February 8, 1940, between Roosevelt and Weizmann, at which the President suggested that the Arabs could be taken care of "with a little *bakhsheesh.*"

26. For Roosevelt and Frankfurter, see the correspondence between the two men at the Roosevelt Library, and also *Roosevelt and Frankfurter, Their Correspondence, 1928–1945*, annotated by Max Freedman (Boston: Little, Brown, 1967).

27. See Silverberg, p. 159; Goldmann, p. 204; and Schechtman, p. 117. Emmanuel Neumann, in the article on Rabbi Silver cited earlier (Chap. 2, n.1) says that Roosevelt "had little time and less thought" for the Zionists, while Laqueur in his *History of Zionism* (p. 554) asserts that he "said little and did less" for the Jews. Ben Gurion in his "Memoirs" describes Roosevelt's attitude as "ambiguous." Hull (*Memoirs,* II, 1536) says that the President "at times talked both ways to Zionists and Arabs, besieged as he was by both camps." Hurewitz, *Struggle for Palestine*, p. 226, speculates that Roosevelt and Churchill together might have pulled off a Palestinian settlement after the war; a contrary view is taken by Sykes, *Crossroads to Israel*, chap. 12, and also by Selig Adler, "Franklin D. Roosevelt and Zionism: The Wartime Record," *Judaism,* issue no. 83, vol. 21, no. 3 (Summer 1972).

5: PRESIDENT TRUMAN AND THE 100,000 JEWS

Official sources and archival material: The pertinent *Foreign Relations* volume is *FRUS 1945*, vol. VIII. For citations to the State Department's Palestine files, the British archives, and the Zionist archives, see Notes to Chapter 1.

The Potsdam Conference (July 16–August 2, 1945) is covered in a special issue of the *Foreign Relations of the United States*, entitled *The Conference of Berlin (Potsdam), 1945*, 2 vols., Dept. of State Publications 70153 and 7163 (Washington: U.S. Government Printing Office, 1960).

Materials from the Harry S. Truman Library, Independence, Missouri:

I. *Papers of Harry S. Truman, Official File 204, Miscellaneous Palestine, 1945–1948*

Same, 204 B: Report of the *Anglo-American Committee of Inquiry* (original typed text from Lausanne, April 20, 1946) and other correspondence regarding the committee.

Same, 204 C: Cabinet Committee on Palestine and Related Problems.

Same, 204 D: Jewish State. (File "Jews" gives Truman's correspondence on subject while a Senator, 1941–44.) File 204 D, Miscellaneous, continues through 1953. File *"Endorsements"* relates to persons proposed as Ambassador to Israel. Also *"Mission of U.S. in Israel"* relating to James G. McDonald.

II. *Copies of Papers in Weizmann Archives, Rehovoth, Israel, Relating to Relations Between the United States and Palestine and Israel,* 1946–52 (including many reports from Eliahu Epstein, Jewish Agency representative in Washington).

Copies of Documents in the Weizmann Archives donated by the American Jewish Archives, Cincinnati, Ohio, duplicating many of above.

Documents from the Weizmann Archives relating to President Truman, also duplicating many of above.

III. *Papers of Edward Jacobson,* beginning with World War I. *Boxes 1 and 2: Correspondence with Harry S. Truman,* 1948–52. Microfilm of *Correspondence of Edward Jacobson* from the American Jewish Archives. "Vertical File"—Edward Jacobson (mainly clippings).

IV. *Papers of Samuel I. Rosenman*, Special Counsel to the President, April 12, 1945, to February 1, 1946: containing many original State Department memoranda from NE.

V. *Papers of Clark M. Clifford*, Special Counsel to the President, 1946–53, *Subject File: Palestine*, Miscellaneous, Part 1, Folder 1.
Same, Palestine, State Department: miscellaneous memoranda.
Same, Palestine Correspondence, Miscellaneous, Folders 1, 2, and 3.
Same, Palestine: speeches, miscellaneous.
Same, Palestine: releases and clippings.
Same, Palestine: telegrams and cables.
Same, Palestine: U.S. policy with regard to.
(Xeroxes of many of these Clifford papers are at the Zionist Archives in New York, as explained in the Notes to Chapter 1.)
VI. *File "Foreign Affairs—Palestine"*: mainly clippings.
VII. *Papers of other associates* of President Truman's, including Phileo Nash, Alexander Sachs, Jonathan Daniels, Charles Ross, Frank McNoughton, John W. Snyder, Howard McGrath, Joel D. Wolfsohn, Stanton Griffis, George C. Marshall, and Myron C. Taylor.
VIII. *Microfilm of the Scrapbooks of Edward R. Stettinius, Jr.*, 6 reels, mainly clippings.
IX. *Oral Histories* of the following associates of Truman: Jonathan Daniels, Samuel I. Rosenman, Oscar R. Ewing, A. J. Granoff, and Kenneth M. Birkhead.

Truman—General: Any study of Harry S. Truman must begin with his *Memoirs*, which were published in two volumes in 1955 and 1956. These volumes, though invaluable for the study of his Presidency, give signs of having been prepared in haste and even of occasional inconsistencies. In 1973, twenty years after Truman left the White House, Merle Miller, a writer who had recorded a series of interviews with him for a TV series that was never produced, published *Plain Speaking: An Oral Biography of Harry S. Truman*, which in many ways gives a more balanced portrayal of the Truman Administration and indeed elaborates on some of the statements found in the *Memoirs*.

Also in 1973, Truman's daughter, Margaret Truman Daniel, published a life of her father. This is a highly subjective work, full of sentiment, and regrettably of errors, at least as far as the Palestine question is concerned. Her treatment of the subject will be found on pp. 298–300 and 381–91. In this last section, I have counted no less than nineteen errors of fact, ranging from her summary of the report of the Anglo-American Committee of Inquiry and of Truman's reaction to the report (see Chapter 6, below) to her statement of the purpose of Eddie Jacobson's March 13, 1948, call on the President (see Chapter 9, below). There are also several places where I would differ with her interpretation. I am, for example, not aware of any evidence that would support her assertion (p. 391) that the internationalization of Jerusalem was "a key point" in Truman's policy: indeed, I cannot recall any pronouncements by him on the Jerusalem issue.

Daniels's biography of Truman, *The Man of Independence*, contains much useful information. A brief and unpretentious but also useful biography is *Harry S. Truman*, by Kenneth G. Richards, in the series "People of Destiny" (Chicago: Children's Press, 1968). A recent, well-documented, thoughtful, and comprehensive volume, by a veteran Washington newspaperman, is Robert J. Donovan's *Conflict and Crisis* (1977). This covers only the first Truman Presidency, but a second volume covering 1948 to

1953 is in progress. Besides the accounts in Acheson and Forrestal, a good summary of Truman's early years will be found in Cabell Phillips, *The Truman Presidency*, esp. pp. 251–61. See also Goulden, *The Best Years*, a socio-economic chronicle of the years 1945–50, and McLellan, *Dean Acheson, the State Department Years*.

1. *Memoirs*, II, 132. Truman devotes three chapters (10, 11, and 12) of this volume, as well as a brief passage in vol. I (pp. 68–69), to the Palestine question. Various statements on the issue which he made while a Senator are in a special file at the Truman Library, as noted above. The best known of these, which was made at the time of the Palestine resolutions in Congress in 1944 (see *America and Palestine*, p. 153, also in the file at the Truman Library), urges that the matter be "very circumspectly handled" and adds, "I don't want to throw any bricks to upset the applecart"—hardly an all-out endorsement, though he does affirm his sympathy with the idea of a Jewish homeland.

I know of three studies that have been made dealing specifically with Truman's handling of the Palestine question while President. These are: an unpublished M.A. thesis submitted at the University of Kansas in 1961, entitled "Zionist Pressure Groups and the Palestine Policy of the Truman Administration," by Jean M. Caldwell; an article, "President Truman's Recognition of Israel," by Ian J. Bickerton, *American Jewish Historical Quarterly*, December 1968; and John Snetsinger's book, *Truman, the Jewish Vote, and Israel* (1974). The latter two works were carried out under grants from the Harry S. Truman Institute and both are outgrowths of scholarly dissertations. All three writers made use primarily of papers at the Truman Library, but none of them refers to the official documents in the Archives or to the *FRUS* volumes. None of the three, moreover, shows much familiarity with U.S. government procedures or with the Palestine problem as a whole. Thus, although these accounts contain material that is of some interest, they are essentially superficial examinations of the topic. See my review of the Snetsinger book in the *Middle East Journal*, vol. 28, no. 2 (Summer 1974), in which I made a similar comment and added that Snetsinger did not give sufficient weight to the humanitarian element in Truman's Palestine policy.

2. See Truman, *Memoirs*, II, 133, 163, 164.

3. See a footnote to p. 10 of the 1945 *FRUS* which quotes from an October 19 memorandum from Byrnes to Henderson expressing the opinion that it would be unwise for the President to see them prior to November 6. This was election day in New York City.

4. *F.D.R. Meets Ibn Saud*, pp. 36–37. Truman was hardly accurate when he referred (no doubt offhandedly) to the small number of Arab-Americans in the country (actually some 500,000 at the time), although he may have been thinking instinctively of his own state of Missouri where they probably numbered in the thousands.

5. Emanuel Neumann, "Abba Hillel Silver, History Maker," *American Zionist*, February 5, 1953.

6. The influence exerted by Rosenman and Clifford on U.S. Palestine policy is reflected in the papers of both men at the Truman Library. For Niles, see an unpublished undergraduate honors thesis presented at Harvard University in 1959 by David B. Sachar, entitled "David K. Niles and United States Policy toward Palestine: A Case Study in American Foreign Policy." This thesis is based on a study of Niles's papers, which are in the custody of Dr. Abram Sachar at Brandeis University and to

which I was unable to gain access. His son David Sachar's paper contains many insights, which are of the greatest interest, into Niles's personality and his work at the White House. In December 1975, as will be recounted in Chapter 9, below, I interviewed Clark Clifford and he gave me some interesting details regarding his connection with the work on Palestine.

On December 28, 1976, Mr. Clifford read a paper at a joint session of the American Historical Association and the American Jewish Historical Society, in Washington, D.C. This paper, entitled "Recognizing Israel," was subsequently published in *American Heritage*, vol. 28, no. 3 (April 1977), together with an interview with Mr. Clifford. For more on this see Chapter 9, below.

7. For Jacobson's role, the reader is referred to the Jacobson papers in the Truman Library, including microfilm of his correspondence now at the American Jewish Archives, Cincinnati; also to the extracts from his diary published in the *Washington Post*, May 6, 1973. See also Frank J. Adler's review essay of Margaret Truman's life of her father, in the *American Jewish Historical Quarterly*, and the same author's *Roots in a Moving Stream: The Centennial History of Congregation B'nai Jehuda of Kansas City* (Kansas City: The Temple, Congregation B'nai Jehuda, 1972). Jacobson was a member of this congregation and Adler is its present administrator. He devotes one chapter of his book (Chap. 9) to Truman, Jacobson, and Israel. The statement attributed to Jacobson about his not being a Zionist comes from this book; for a parallel statement to the same effect by Truman see the *Memoirs*, II, 160. When I interviewed Mr. Adler in Kansas City in April 1975, he was kind enough to furnish me with further details regarding the friendship between Truman and Jacobson, which was a very close one. Adler, like myself, is critical of Margaret Truman's book on her father. He considers that Dean Acheson was in error in affirming in his *Present at the Creation* (p. 169) that Jacobson was a "passionate Zionist." I agree with Adler on the basis of the evidence that I have examined.

See also Granoff's "Oral History" at the Truman Library, from which my account of the visits which he and Jacobson used to pay at the White House is taken. Granoff is another source who says Jacobson was not a Zionist. It should be added that not all of Jacobson's contacts with Truman had to do with Palestine: the President continued to get his supply of haberdashery items from his old partner and their correspondence contains many references to such things as hats and shirts.

Silverberg states (p. 386) that it was Maurice Bisgyer, long-time executive vice-president of the Jewish fraternal organization B'nai B'rith, of which Jacobson was a member, who asked Jacobson to try to persuade the President to see Weizmann in the spring of 1948 (see Chapter 9, below).

8. See *FRUS 1945*, p. 748, and *FRUS 1946*, VII, 686. Occasionally Byrnes took an active role in Palestine affairs, as in the fall of 1945 when he conducted the negotiations with the British regarding the Anglo-American Committee of Inquiry.

9. For our memorandum of April 13, just after Truman took office, see the State Department's Palestine file for 1945 at the National Archives. For our two memoranda of April 18 and May 1 for the President, see *FRUS 1945*, pp. 704–6. A third memorandum on the subject under date of May 14 is in ibid., p. 706. Truman's account of his April 20 meeting with Rabbi Wise, including his comment on our advice, is taken from pp. 213–16 of Miller's *Oral Biography*.

10. For the treatment of the Palestine question at San Francisco see Richard Stevens, pp. 95–98, and Golding, pp. 86–88. See also the special volume (no. 1) of the *FRUS* for 1945 devoted to the Conference. Eliahu Elath in his *Zionism at the UN: A*

Diary of the First Days (Philadelphia: Jewish Publication Society of America, 1976) gives details of Zionist activity at San Francisco.

11. See Eban, "Tragedy and Triumph," in Weisgal and Carmichael, eds., p. 278; also Blanche Dugdale's *Diaries*, p. 221.

12. See *FRUS (Potsdam)*, I, 172, also pp. 972–79 for further materials that we supplied on the subject.

13. See ibid., II, 314, for the record of a meeting between Truman, Churchill, and Stalin on July 23 at which Palestine was mentioned tangentially in the course of a discussion of Syria and Lebanon. Churchill remarked that Great Britain was bearing the burden of maintaining order not only in Syria and Lebanon but in Palestine and Iraq as well. He then asked if the United States would like to take Britain's place in all of these areas, to which the President replied firmly: "No, thank you, Mr. Churchill." It will be noted from *FRUS 1945*, pp. 716–17 and 719, that Truman's July 24 memorandum to Churchill during the conference and Attlee's brief acknowledgement of July 31 had to be obtained by the Department from the Truman Library.

For firsthand accounts of the Potsdam meeting see Truman's *Memoirs*, I, 332–412; Churchill's *Triumph and Tragedy*, pp. 649–61; the Cadogan *Diaries*, pp. 761–78; and Harriman's *Special Envoy to Churchill and Stalin*, pp. 483–88; also, for the full story, *Meeting at Potsdam*, by Charles L. Mee, Jr. (London: Andre Deutsch, 1975).

14. *FRUS 1945*, p. 722.

15. Ibid., pp. 722–24, and 736–37.

16. Ibid., pp. 742–43.

17. Memorandum in NE Divisional file, "Palestine and Trans-Jordan," now at the National Archives, dated July 30, 1945.

18. For the full text see Hurewitz, *Diplomacy in the Near and Middle East*, II, 249. The figure of 100,000 Jews, which surfaced in this report and was to attract so much attention in the months to come, originated in a memorandum submitted by the Jewish Agency to the British government in June 1945 (this memorandum is cited by Harrison).

19. Dohse, p. 143.

20. See the NE memoranda of September 21 and 26, in the Palestine files at the National Archives and also in *FRUS 1945*, pp. 745–48. For the exchange of telegrams between Acheson and Byrnes see *FRUS 1945*, pp. 743–44 and 748–49.

21. See the Foreign Office Palestine files for 1945 at the Public Record Office, London, for the record of the decision taken September 6 by a special cabinet committee under the chairmanship of the new foreign secretary, Ernest Bevin, to continue the White Paper quota of 1,500 Jewish immigrants per month pending the consideration of a long-term policy. See also Hurewitz, *Struggle for Palestine*, p. 229, and Marlowe, p. 200.

22. For the correspondence and discussions between the two governments regarding the formation of the Anglo-American Committee of Inquiry, see *FRUS 1945*, pp. 771–819 and 821–40. The President's announcement of November 13 is on pp. 819–20. The negotiations were largely handled by Byrnes and the British Ambassador, one curious detail being that the record of a number of their talks appears in *FRUS* not in the customary memorandum form but as direct dialogue—recalling that Byrnes in his early days had been a court reporter. Further details will be found in the files of the Department and the Foreign Office.

23. Truman, *Memoirs*, II, 143–44.

24. For the Department's statement of October 18, issued along with Roosevelt's April 5 letter to Ibn Saud, see *FRUS 1945*, pp. 770–71; and for the question of releasing additional correspondence, ibid., pp. 783–823 passim. Acheson (p. 171) says that it was his decision that our government should not publish any more of what he terms "these all-too-fulsome documents." The criticism of the "full consultation" formula by the AZEC is on p. 92 of the Golding thesis.

25. *FRUS 1945*, pp. 744–45.

26. Ibid., pp. 749, 750, and 765–66.

27. For details of Jewish immigration into Palestine between 1939 and 1948 see *Statistical Abstract of Israel*, Central Bureau of Statistics of the Government of Israel, 1970.

28. See *FRUS 1945*, pp. 683–87, 698–703, 717–19, 727–33, 734–36, and 745–48.

29. Yale, p. 407. Yale asserts (with considerable truth) that the President's action "jettisoned" our proposal.

30. *Present at the Creation*, p. 170.

31. For the resumption of Jewish terrorist activity and the stepping up of illegal immigration see Begin, Chap. 13. See also Hurewitz, *Struggle*, pp. 233–34, and Silverberg, pp. 290–91. Dohse (pp. 95–96) says that as soon as war broke out in Europe in September 1939, two of the three Jewish underground military organizations in Palestine, the Haganah and the Irgun, suspended all operations. The third, the Stern Gang, did not actually declare a truce, but the net result was that Jewish terrorism was dormant until October 1945. For the mood of the Yishuv, the Jewish community in Palestine, at the time, see Golda Meir's memoirs, Chap. 7, and Weizmann, *Trial and Error*, II, 441–43. Weizmann was opposed to a policy of all-out resistance but was overruled by the more aggressive element in the Jewish Agency personified by Ben Gurion.

32. See Halperin, p. 38. The negative attitude of American Zionists toward the admission of Jewish displaced persons into the United States, and Truman's relatively unenthusiastic pursuit of the matter, are brought out in Lilienthal, pp. 34–37, and Silverberg, pp. 319–20.

6: THE ABORTIVE ATTEMPT AT ANGLO-AMERICAN COOPERATION

Official sources and archival material: For Official correspondence regarding the Anglo-American Committee of Inquiry see the pertinent 1945 and 1946 *FRUS* volumes. The correspondence for 1946 is vol. VII, *The Near East and Africa*, Department of State Publication 8490 (1969), pp. 576–639; hereafter cited as *FRUS 1946*. See also the State Department 1945 and 1946 Palestine files at the National Archives, and the 1945 Foreign Office Palestine file at the Public Record Office, London (I did not gain access to the British archives subsequent to 1945). The files of the committee itself, and of the later Cabinet Committee, including the verbatim transcripts of the hearings, the documentary evidence submitted by various interested parties and considerable administrative correspondence are, as stated in this chapter, stored in a Federal document depository at Suitland, Maryland, from which they can be obtained by request through the State Department.

Three members of the committee have written books about their experiences: Richard H. S. Crossman, Bartley C. Crum, and William Phillips. Crossman later provided considerable background information respecting the committee in his *A Nation Reborn: The Israel of Weizmann, Bevin, and Ben Gurion* (1960), consisting of three lectures given at the Weizmann Institute, Rehovoth, Israel. Of even greater interest are Crossman's Diaries for the period when he served with the Anglo-American Committee; these, along with certain other related materials of his, are now at the Middle East Center, St. Antony's College, Oxford.

I have serious doubts that Crum, who died not long after the committee's mission, wrote *Behind the Silken Curtain* himself. I have long thought that the book was ghostwritten for him by Gerold Frank, a newspaperman of Zionist sympathies who traveled about with the committee and who later was to gain some fame as ghostwriter for such Hollywood personalities as Zsa Zsa Gabor and, more recently, Judy Garland. (Crum pays a glowing tribute to Frank at the outset of the book.) The book seems to have been written in haste, and it contains many inaccuracies. A number of statements are attributed to Loy Henderson and myself that are purely apocryphal. Chapter 2 (pp. 31–44), entitled "The Secret File in the State Department," alleges, quite inaccurately, that the messages in this "secret file," consisting of assurances to Arab leaders that they as well as the Jews would be consulted regarding Palestine (see Chapter 2, above), were sent out by the State Department behind the backs of Presidents Roosevelt and Truman. This is simply not so, but the canard has been picked up by any number of other writers. It is still to be encountered today in books and articles concerning the period; it was repeated as late as 1970, for example (24 years after our mission), in Silverberg's book.

I am indebted to Mrs. Beatrice Phillips Strauss, of Washington, for allowing me to read over the letters which her father, William Phillips, wrote home during the committee's travels and in which I found much background information of interest.

In my book *Jerusalem, Key to Peace*, the reader will find an account of the committee's mission on pp. 63–65 and an appendix (Appendix E) which summarizes the committee's terms of reference and recommendations. See also an article that I wrote on the subject in our house organ, the *American Foreign Service Journal*, vol. 23, no. 7 (July 1946).

Another invaluable primary source is *State in the Making*, the book by David Horowitz of the Jewish Agency who was the Agency's liaison man with the committee (as with the later United Nations Committee).

1. Descriptions of the personalities of the members of the committee will be found variously in Crossman's two books and Diaries and in the accounts of Crum, Phillips, and Horowitz cited. Aydelotte was the only American member who was appointed as a result of a recommendation from NE, although we also suggested O. Max Gardner, former governor of North Carolina, who was on the original list released by the White House but who subsequently declined to serve. This led, interestingly enough, to the naming of Bartley Crum. (Gardner was later appointed Ambassador to Great Britain but he died just after boarding ship in New York en route to England.) A list of the committee's staff appears in the Report.

2. Crossman, Crum, Phillips, and Horowitz all give details of the hearings held in Washington, London, Cairo, and Jerusalem and of its travels. The Jerusalem hearings were reported to the Department by Consul General Lowell C. Pinkerton in a series of messages now at the National Archives.

3. For Prime Minister Ben Gurion's attempt to persuade Einstein to accept the presidency of Israel following Weizmann's death see Moshe Pearlman, *Ben Gurion Looks Back*, chap. 18.

4. This promise is quoted in a variety of sources, including Crossman, *Palestine Mission*, pp. 56–57; Crum, p. 61; and W. Phillips, p. 426; also in my *Jerusalem, Key to Peace*, p. 63. A dispatch from our London Embassy, dated December 18, 1947, giving Bevin's confirmation in the House of Commons that he made this statement, will be found in the Department 1947 Palestine file at the National Archives.

5. From the transcript of the Committee hearings, Record Group 59, Accession no. 71 A 6682, State.

6. Ben Gurion's and Golda Meir's memoirs give descriptions of their appearance before the committee in Jerusalem and other details regarding its activities in Palestine.

7. The most illuminating details regarding the deliberations of the committee while at Lausanne emerge from the Crossman diaries and papers at St. Antony's, Oxford, especially two "notes" dated April 22, 1946, and May 8, 1946, which Crossman prepared for his friend Hector McNeil, then serving as Parliamentary Undersecretary of State for Foreign Affairs. See also Crossman's two books and those by Crum, Phillips, and Horowitz. Phillips's letters to his wife convey very well the atmosphere in which the members worked.

8. Noel Baker's intervention is mentioned in the papers at St. Antony's and was confirmed to me by Beeley during a conversation on October 11, 1974. See also Ilan, p. 236.

9. See Official File 204 at the Truman Library for a copy of an April 16, 1946, memorandum from Administrative Assistant David K. Niles to Appointments Secretary Matthew J. Connelly reporting a telephone conversation with Bartley Crum in Lausanne. The memorandum says that Crum told Niles something of the discussions between the members of the committee, including their agreement on the admission of the 100,000 Jews to Palestine, but declined to discuss any details and warned Niles that the phone was probably being tapped, presumably by agents of the Palestine government CID (Criminal Investigation Department) who we knew had followed us to Lausanne. Loy Henderson, in an interview with me in March 1976, recalled being aware that Niles was in touch with Crum during this period. Sachar's thesis mentions on p. 24 a telephone conversation on April 5 between Nahum Goldmann, in Lausanne, and Meyer W. Weisgal in New York, summarizing for the information of the Jewish Agency the discussions within the committee and attributing different points of view to different members. Blanche Dugdale's diary for April 25, 1946, states that Berl Locker of the Agency actually obtained on that date a copy of the committee's report (completed only on April 20) "in Paris" but she does not give other details. Additional evidence of the way in which the Zionists had penetrated the committee's deliberations is contained in Mrs. Chaim Weizmann's memoir of her husband, *The Impossible Takes Longer*, in which she makes the interesting comment (p. 203) that the committee "had rejected by a majority of eight to four" a proposal to disarm the illegal Jewish armies. She gives no source for these figures. I had been unaware of them.

Ben Gurion in his "Memoirs," *Jewish Observer and Middle East Review*, October 16, 1964, states that during the August 1946 meeting of the Jewish Agency Executive in Paris (see later in this chapter) Goldmann informed his colleagues that he felt he had made a mistake, while in Lausanne at the time the committee was meeting there, in advising certain of the members (presumably Crossman, McDonald, and Crum) to settle for a unanimous report so long as it included provision for the 100,000 Jews rather than pressing for a minority report endorsing partition. From Crossman's papers it appears that partition was a real possibility. Goldmann's comment, incidentally, again reveals the extent of the contacts which the members in question had with the Zionists.

My telegram to the Department (April 18, 1946) urging caution in handling the release of the report is in the 1946 Palestine file at the National Archives.

10. See the 1946 files of the Division of Near Eastern Affairs now in the National Archives.

11. See ibid. Crum (p. 74) dismisses my analysis of our official Palestine policy as "suicidal."

12. For the committee's report, which was published by both governments, see the Bibliography. A limited number of copies was published with six excellent maps prepared by a team of professional geographers on the staff of the committee, under the direction of Dr. E. Christie Willatts of the British Ministry of Housing. In addition to a basic map of Palestine, the report contains maps showing mean annual rainfall, land classification. population, land in Jewish possession, and "Historic Israel and Judah, showing the maximum extent of Hebrew lands at various periods in Biblical times." (The last was mainly the work of William F. Stinespring, professor of biblical history at Duke University, who was a member of our staff.) For what it is worth, the main conclusion to be drawn from this last map is that it was only during the periods when the Jewish kingdom was at its greatest strength, notably at the time of David and Solomon, that the Jews controlled the coastline, although they generally controlled considerable territory east of the Jordan. (In modern Palestine, under the Mandate, the Jews were concentrated in the more fertile plains along the coast.)

Many writers have commented on the committee's report, both favorably and unfavorably. Parkes, generally pro-Zionist, says (p. 293) that the report "showed remarkable insight into the whole problem." Horowitz (p. 92) makes the point that the lack of agreement among the members inevitably resulted in their adopting "a vague formula on a number of cardinal points."

13. For private views of American members of the committee about a binational state, see the 1946 files of the Division of Near Eastern Affairs for my letter dated August 26, 1946, to Philip W. Ireland (then at the American Embassy in Cairo) referring to the talks I had with the committee members after they returned to Washington.

14. See a letter from Consul General Pinkerton in Jerusalem to Gordon Merriam dated August 18, 1945, State Department Palestine file 867 N.00, 1945, National Archives.

15. See the Crossman memoranda for Hector McNeil mentioned above.

16. Truman, *Memoirs*, II, 146. Writing to Bartley Crum on May 15, 1948, Truman said the report of the committee, which he calls the "British-American Commission," was "the correct solution," adding "I think eventually we are going to get it worked out just that way." Truman Library, Official File 204D, Miscellaneous, Box 776. The last remark is hard to explain, since by that time the United States government, under Truman's direction, had backed the UN partition plan and indeed the state of Israel had been proclaimed and recognized by Truman himself the day before.

17. See the excellent article by Kermit Roosevelt, "The Partition of Palestine," *Middle East Journal*, vol. II, no. 1 (January 1948), p. 11.

18. See Christopher Sykes, *Crossroads to Israel*, esp. his comment on p. 297 that the failure to accept the report was the "last occasion when a solution acceptable to the Jewish Agency and ultimately to the Arabs might have been obtained. It was the last crossroads for Britain."

19. As Hurewitz points out, in his *Struggle for Palestine,* p. 246, "any serious attempt to put bi-nationalism into operation in 1946 was foredoomed to failure," largely because of the growth of extremism on both sides. Sir Geoffrey Furlonge comments similarly in his life of Musa Alami (p. 143) that "the report assumed a degree of cooperation which did not exist." For other views see an interview with Elie Eliachar, chief of the Sephardic Jewish Community in Jerusalem and former deputy mayor, a sixteenth-generation Jerusalemite, in the *Jerusalem Post* for September 12, 1975; also Nahum Goldmann, "The Psychology of Middle East Peace," *Foreign Affairs,* October 1975. In the last analysis I am compelled to agree with Marlowe (*The Seat of Pilate,* chap. 12) that the attempt at Anglo-American cooperation in 1946 failed "because nothing could have succeeded except a joint Anglo-American policy which both governments were prepared jointly to impose by force."

20. The appointment of a special Foreign Office committee to review the report, and the conclusions of this group, are mentioned in Sykes's *Crossroads to Israel* and Crossman's *Palestine Mission* and were confirmed to me by Beeley in a conversation on September 4, 1974.

21. See a memorandum by Henderson to Acheson quoted in *FRUS 1946,* p. 587. Richard Stevens (p. 145) cites a State Department survey of U.S. public opinion showing "qualified approval" of the report throughout the country.

22. *FRUS 1946,* pp. 588–89. According to Ilan, p. 253, there is among the Silver papers in Cleveland a "note" by Rabbi Silver stating that it was Niles and Crum who wrote the President's statement.

23. Ibid., pp. 589–90. Crossman in his *Nation Reborn,* chap. 2, says that Attlee insisted on the suppression of Jewish terrorist activities as a condition to the admission of the 100,000 because of the secret evidence presented to the committee by the British military authorities in Palestine and the subsequent advice of the British chiefs of staff. It seems likely that Attlee was also influenced by reports that Jewish displaced persons were receiving military training in the camps in Europe from the Haganah and Irgun—see, for example, a dispatch dated July 1, 1948, from the Office of the U.S. political adviser for Germany at Heidelberg, which though of considerably later date is applicable here (1948 Palestine file, National Archives).

24. For a good summary of the British resentment during this period see Francis Williams, *Twilight of Empire: The Memoirs of Prime Minister Clement Attlee* (New York: A. S. Barnes & Co., 1960), esp. chap. 12.

25. *FRUS 1947,* V, 1020.

26. See Schechtman, pp. 192–93.

27. For Jamali's remarks to Ireland see a telegram dated July 1, 1946, from the U.S. Embassy in Cairo summarizing the Arab reaction to the report, in the National Archives. Ireland saw Jamali while on a tour of the Near East.

28. For the State Department's circular telegram of May 20 see *FRUS 1946,* pp. 610–11.

29. Following the receipt of the report, the Department also asked the views of the Joint Chiefs of Staff regarding the implementation of the committee's recommendations. The Joint Chiefs on June 21 urged in reply that no U.S. armed forces should be used in carrying out the report; see ibid., pp. 622–23, 631–33.

30. In a telegram dated July 23 (ibid., p. 650) the Department stated that the U.S. commitment to consult the Arabs and Jews was considered to have been discharged by the issuance of this invitation to the parties to give their views on the report.

31. Ibid., p. 642. Truman's June 5 telegram to Attlee making this pledge is on pp. 617–18.

32. See ibid., pp. 624–38 passim for messages exchanged on arrangements by the Department and the U.S. Embassy in London.

33. Some of these reports are in the NE divisional files for 1946 and others are in the files of the Cabinet Committee (see below).

34. See the Executive Order of June 11, 1946, ibid., p. 624n. Leslie L. Rood, who had served as senior American secretary to the Anglo-American Committee, was appointed secretary; other staff members from the Anglo-American Committee who also served with the Cabinet Committee were Paul L. Hanna and Frederick V. Loud. Another member of the staff was J. C. Hurewitz, whose book *The Struggle for Palestine* I have found so useful in preparing this study. Hurewitz's firsthand account (pp. 250–62, especially his analysis of the Morrison-Grady Report on pp. 257–58) should therefore be read with particular profit.

35. This is my personal recollection.

36. See a footnote to *FRUS 1946*, p. 644, which reads ". . . approved by President Truman in interview with Grady July 9, 1946"; the original notation in the files on which this item is based is in my handwriting.

37. For the exchange between Attlee and Truman on the arrest of Jewish Agency leaders suspected of terrorist activities see ibid., pp. 639, 641. On July 22, a wing of the King David Hotel in Jerusalem, housing the Palestine Government Secretariat, was blown up by Irgun members disguised as Arabs with extensive loss of life (91 persons were killed). The incident is recounted in some detail in chapter 15 of Menachem Begin's *The Revolt* (Begin was head of the Irgun at the time). This incident, which as Begin concedes was carried out with Haganah concurrence, greatly strained the already fragile relations between the Palestine administration and the Jewish community in Palestine.

38. For discussions in London between the Grady group and the British see *FRUS 1946*, pp. 641–82. The Morrison-Grady plan itself is on pp. 652–67.

39. See ibid., pp. 669–70, and the State Department Palestine file at the National Archives.

40. For leaks in London by members of Grady's staff, see the Palestine files identified above. In a letter to Acheson dated August 12, Grady named three members of his staff as having been involved in passing information regarding his negotiations to the press and to representatives of the Jewish Agency. Under date of July 25 he telegraphed to the Department from London saying that he had just learned that his associate from the Treasury Department, Herbert Gaston, was not in agreement with the plan and had, incredibly, sent a telegram to this effect to the Secretary of the Treasury through commercial channels. The files contain memoranda submitted to Grady while in London from Rood and Hanna (see above) criticizing the plan and urging that firmer assurances be obtained regarding the 100,000 Jews. Schechtman (p. 165) shows that the Zionists were aware of the attitude of Gaston and of some members of Grady's staff, and Crossman in his *Palestine Mission* (p. 196) states that he obtained from American journalists in London details of the discussions that the Grady group was having with the British.

Grady's side of the matter is set forth at length in his draft unpublished autobiography, "Adventures in Diplomacy," a copy of which is at the Truman Library. He considered that he had been let down by disloyal associates and by the President.

41. It was only a coincidence that one of the British members of the Anglo-

American Committee of Inquiry had been Lord Morrison; he had no connection with the so-called Morrison-Grady plan.

42. See Acheson, *Present at the Creation*, p. 175, and William Phillips, p. 474. James G. McDonald, one of the American members, who later became the first American envoy to Israel, mentions the subject in passing in his book *My Mission in Israel*, which is a highly subjective account.

43. Examples of Zionist pressure on Truman to reject the plan can be found in Richard Stevens, p. 152, and Ian Bickerton, "President Truman's Recognition of Israel," *American Jewish Quarterly*, December 1968, p. 194. The Wagner papers contain a speech that Wagner delivered in the Senate on July 30 in which he described the proceedings in London as a "farce."

44. Truman's final rejection of the plan came in spite of a recommendation from Byrnes, then in Paris, that it be accepted. *FRUS 1946*, pp. 671–73. See also the Forrestal *Diaries*, p. 347.

45. See the letter to McDonald in the Truman Library, File 204, Miscellaneous. The letter also says, "It's been a most difficult problem and I have about come to the conclusion that there is no solution, but I will keep trying."

46. For details of the Jewish Agency meeting see Goldmann, *Autobiography*, pp. 232–38, and Ben Gurion, "Memoirs," *Jewish Observer and Middle East Review*, October 16 and 30, and November 13, 1964. See also Horowitz, passim. Maps showing the area in question can be found in Hurewitz, *Struggle*, p. 261, and Sykes, *Crossroads*, and in Martin Gilbert's atlas, map 37. The area was somewhat larger than that proposed for the Jewish province in the provincial autonomy (Morrison-Grady plan). It can be loosely described as "the Peel Commission's plan (1937) plus the Negev." Elizabeth Monroe in her *Britain's Moment in the Middle East* (p. 163) underlines the shift in Zionist thinking away from the goal of a Jewish state in the whole of Palestine, as do other writers. She suggests that this reveals the low point to which Zionist aspirations had fallen by mid-summer of 1946.

47. In connection with the windup of the Cabinet Committee's work, the 1946 Palestine file at the National Archives contains a letter dated October 23 from Grady to Byrnes suggesting the termination of the activities of the committee. Characteristically, Byrnes has endorsed this letter "after November 5" (that is, Election Day).

48. In this conclusion I am obliged to disagree with Dean Acheson, a man whom I greatly admired. On this point, Acheson says on p. 176 of *Present at the Creation* that the plan "had in it the makings of a compromise" and represented a useful precedent for later consideration of the problem. As I have tried to make clear in this chapter, I cannot agree with this interpretation.

7: "BRIDGING THE GAP"

Official sources and archival material: For the official record of the events covered in Chapter 7 see *FRUS 1946*, pp. 683–737, and *FRUS 1947*, vol. V, *The Near East and Africa*, Department of State Publication 8592 (1971), pp. 1000–1050 (hereafter cited as *FRUS 1947*); see also the 1946 and 1947 Palestine files of the Department at the National Archives.

1. The talks held by representatives of the Jewish Agency with British officials are summarized in the memoirs of Ben Gurion and Weizmann, in Goldmann's autobiography, and in the David Sachar Harvard honors thesis, "David K. Niles and

United States Policy toward Palestine." See also Horowitz passim and Hurewitz, *Struggle*, pp. 263-73.

2. The Washington representative of the Jewish Agency, Eliahu Epstein, in a meeting with members of NE on September 5, 1946, stated definitely that partition was now the Agency's preferred solution. See *FRUS 1946*, pp. 692-93.

3. For examples of the Zionist argument that partition should be considered as a "compromise" solution see Ben Gurion, "Memoirs," *Jewish Observer and Middle East Review*, October 30, 1964; and an article by Golda Meir in the *New York Times*, January 14, 1976, p. 33.

By a similar process of rationalization, Menachem Begin's Herut party in 1977 was able to declare that it was a "compromise" for it to renounce the historic claim of the Revisionist party (from which Herut is descended) to Palestine east of the Jordan River (the present Hashemite Kingdom of the Jordan), so that Israel's territorial aspirations in this region would comprise only biblical Judea and Samaria, occupied by Israel in 1967.

4. The deteriorating security situation in Palestine following the deportation to Cyprus is described in Golda Meir's *My Life*, pp. 201-6; Hurewitz, *Struggle*, pp. 259-60; and the Sachar thesis and Blanche Dugdale's *Diaries*, passim. According to a telegram dated November 5, 1946, from the U.S. Embassy in London, the imprisoned Jewish Agency leaders were released at that time in return for a resolution passed by the Jewish Agency condemning terrorism—which can hardly have had much effect. The relations between the Agency and the Mandatory authorities are reflected in Mrs. Meir's characterization (p. 206) of Jerusalem in 1946-47 as "a city occupied by an extremely hostile foreign power." The Zionists and their supporters in the United States often drew a parallel with the Boston Tea Party when praising the exploits of the underground in Palestine. See Silverberg, pp. 318-36, for the American involvement in these activities. See also Monroe, *Britain's Moment in the Middle East*, pp. 163-65, for a description of the atmosphere in Palestine.

5. The name of John G. Winant, former Ambassador to Great Britain, was suggested as observer; see *FRUS 1947*, pp. 1000-1001. Much of the State Department information of the conference came from a series of reports prepared by G. Lewis Jones, First Secretary of the Embassy at London, whose excellent relations with Harold Beeley of the Foreign Office enabled him to keep the Department fully informed regarding the talks.

6. For the NE memorandum of September 12 signed by William Clayton, at that time Acting Secretary of State (sometimes referred to as the "Clayton Memorandum"), see ibid., pp. 693-95. The President's reply does not appear in the Department's files but is quoted in the Sachar thesis, pp. 42-43.

7. For the President's message to Attlee, giving the text of what he proposed to say, and the subsequent exchange with Attlee, see *FRUS 1946*, pp. 701-8. For Truman's rationale, see his *Memoirs*, II, 154, and Acheson's *Present at the Creation*, pp. 176-77. In conversation with the British Ambassador, Acheson was careful to point out that Truman's statement did not actually endorse partition but spoke of "bridging the gap" between the Jewish Agency's plan and the Morrison-Grady plan; *FRUS 1946*, pp. 723-26.

8. Both Richard Stevens (pp. 154-58) and Bickerton quote the Reston column. Representative Celler's letter of October 7 to Truman commending him for the statement is in the Truman papers, File 204, Miscellaneous. Epstein's October 4 report to Jerusalem about his role in drafting the statement is in Box 1 of the

Weizmann papers at the Truman Library. See also the Forrestal *Diaries*, p. 346, and Sachar's thesis, pp. 44–46.

9. The excerpts from Gordon Merriam's memorandum of October 15 are taken, with his permission, from a photostat which he recently sent me. Merriam has also given a photostat to the Truman Library.

10. *FRUS 1946*, p. 708.

11. For Truman's October 25 message to King Ibn Saud see ibid., pp. 714–17, and for Ibn Saud's reply, ibid., pp. 717–20. According to a footnote on p. 714, our Legation at Jidda reported that the King on receiving Truman's message was "extremely vexed" and that he regarded the President's attitude as "hostile"—a curious throwback to President Roosevelt's assurance to Ibn Saud in 1945 that he would make no move "hostile" to the Arab people. Manuel comments (p. 328) on the significance of the President's stressing our interest in the Jewish National Home. For Truman's further message, dated January 24, 1947, see *FRUS 1947*, pp. 1011–14.

12. Wadsworth's call on the President took place on September 26, 1946. For a summary of their conversation see *FRUS 1946*, p. 699. The main topic was the possible consideration of the Palestine problem at the forthcoming General Assembly of the United Nations. Wadsworth reported that the President said that "while there could be no Jewish State, Jews in Palestine could be guaranteed protection under some local autonomy arrangement." As it happened, Palestine was not discussed at the fall 1946 session of the Assembly.

13. For the record of the meetings between the Emir Feisal and the President and between the Emir Saud and the Secretary of State see ibid., pp. 729–31, and *FRUS 1947*, pp. 1007–8. For Acheson's comments see his *Present at the Creation*, pp. 177–78.

14. See *FRUS 1946*, pp. 732–35, for Merriam's memorandum. Henderson's covering memorandum is quoted on p. 732n.

15. This memorandum, dated January 14, 1947, was prepared by Fraser Wilkins, who had just taken over the Palestine desk from me. For the text see *FRUS 1947*, pp. 1004–5.

16. Acheson's memorandum of his conversation with the British Ambassador on January 21 and the curiously entitled "written oral statement" that he handed the Ambassador on the 27th are in ibid., pp. 1008–11 and 1014–15. For Acheson's treatment of the matter, including an account of an earlier meeting with the Ambassador, see pp. 178–80 of his memoirs.

In connection with the use by members of the Near East Division of the terms "entities" or "states," it is worth noting that our September 12 memorandum for the President (the so-called "Clayton Memorandum") had an annex outlining the sort of statement that, as we put it, "represents the most that should be said at this time." This draft statement, which was never used, stressed the need for a settlement, referred to the Anglo-American and Morrison-Grady reports, and pointed out that although the United States had not made any proposals of its own, we would be prepared to support "the eventual establishment of an independent state or independent states in Palestine" provided that this (1) was "in keeping with the basic principles of the Mandate" and (2) offered a reasonable prospect of acceptance by the parties. This last, of course, was an important qualification. Since this draft statement was not accepted by the President, it cannot, in my opinion, be regarded as a statement of policy. As the question of "a state or states" does not seem to have come up again until the end of December, I have thought it preferable to describe the evolution of the Division's thinking in the terms I have used in the text of this chapter.

That by early December the Division was giving serious consideration to the question of partition is shown in a letter that I sent under date of December 3 to Henry S. Villard, Henderson's deputy, who was at the time serving with our General Assembly delegation in New York. With this letter (see the archives) I sent Villard, for his information, a lengthy memorandum prepared by Leslie L. Rood, who as previously explained had been secretary to both the Anglo-American Committee and the Cabinet Committee (the Grady group) and who was then on detail to NE. Rood, who had been an advocate of partition throughout, discussed in his paper the pros and cons of partition and ended up recommending it as the most acceptable alternative.

My comments regarding the attitude of the members of the Near East Division toward partition are based on a lengthy discussion of this subject with Ambassador Loy Henderson in March 1976.

17. Marlowe, p. 218. See also Hurewitz, *Struggle*, p. 278.

18. It happened that John A. Lehrs, an old colleague of Loy Henderson's from their service in the Baltic States, was serving in 1946 at the American Consulate General in Basle. In the fall of 1946, while Lehrs was in Washington on home leave, Henderson and I briefed him about the Palestine question and arranged to have him cover the Zionist Congress for the Department. This turned out to be an excellent arrangement and his reports, a number of which are given in *FRUS 1946*, pp. 727–37, and in the Palestine files at the archives, were very useful to us in NE. The proceedings of the Congress (December 9–24) were summarized in a memorandum prepared by Fraser Wilkins, based on Lehrs's reports and appearing in ibid., p. 735. For Zionist accounts of the meeting see Weizmann, II, 442–43; Goldmann, pp. 239–41; Meir, pp. 199–200; and Blanche Dugdale's *Diaries*, pp. 241–45. See also Richard Stevens, pp. 121–24. The point that the resolution calling for a Jewish Commonwealth did not specify that it had to be in the whole of Palestine is taken from p. 239 of Goldmann's *Autobiography*.

19. For Truman's account of his difficulties with Secretary Byrnes see his *Memoirs*, I, 546–53; for the story of Marshall's mission to China see ibid., II, 66–92.

20. This meeting has been described by two of the participants, Beeley to Lewis Jones of our Embassy (see London's telegram, *FRUS 1947*, p. 1044) and Horowitz in his book *State in the Making*, p. 134.

21. For an outline of the so-called "Bevin Scheme" see a message from Bevin to Secretary Marshall, *FRUS 1947*, pp. 1033–37. In an interview in October 1974, Beeley confirmed to me that he was the author of this plan.

22. "Tragedy and Triumph," in Weisgal and Carmichael, eds., p. 294.

23. For Bevin's announcement about going to the UN and for his criticism of President Truman on February 25 see *FRUS 1947*, pp. 1048 and 1056–57. For the White House statement see ibid., pp. 1057–58.

24. The best interpretation that I have seen of British motivations regarding Palestine is in Monroe's *Britain's Moment in the Middle East*, esp. pp. 157–62. Additional material on this point is to be found on p. 144 of Furlonge's life of Musa Alami. (Furlonge had a long career as a British diplomatic representative in the Middle East.) Feis, p. 80, notes that Sir Stafford Cripps, the Chancellor of the Exchequer in the Attlee government, told the House of Commons on January 20, 1948, that British expenditures in connection with Palestine had amounted to a total of £100,000,000 from January 1945 to December 1947.

25. This decision was reported to the Department in a telegram from the American Consulate General in Jerusalem; see *FRUS 1947*, pp. 1023–24. See also

Jones, p. 61; David Sachar's thesis, p. 50; Dohse, p. 211; and Hurewitz, *Struggle*, p. 281. Begin records in his book *The Revolt* (pp. 319–20) that Bevin's February 18 announcement led to widespread acts of sabotage and terrorism by the underground in Palestine.

26. See Truman, *Memoirs*, II, 96–109, for the story of the inception of the Greek-Turkish aid program.

27. See the Crossman papers at St. Antony's, Oxford. That the British had no intention at that time of giving up the Mandate is confirmed by Hurewitz, *Struggle*, p. 284; Marlowe, p. 230; and Sykes, *Crossroads*, p. 317.

28. Opinions within the British government were divided as to the advisability of taking the Palestine question to the United Nations. Elizabeth Monroe (pp. 165–66) attributes the decision to Attlee personally, and refers to Attlee's parallel decision to get out of India. According to Beeley and Sir John Martin (see Introduction) in interviews I had with them in October 1974, the working level in both the Foreign Office and the Colonial Office was opposed to the decision. As I have already explained, the Colonial Office remained throughout in favor of trying to work things out with the Arabs and Jews by means of some form of partition. The Foreign Office tended to be pro-Arab and hence opposed partition. The views of the Foreign Office working level are reflected in the "Bevin Scheme."

29. Ben Gurion tells the fascinating story of this meeting in his "Memoirs," *Jewish Observer and Middle East Review*, December 25, 1964.

30. See *FRUS 1946*, p. 723.

31. *FRUS 1947*, p. 1048.

8: PALESTINE BEFORE THE UNITED NATIONS

Official sources and archival material: The pertinent Foreign Relations volume is *FRUS 1947*, vol. V. In addition to the State Department Palestine files 867 N.00 and 867 N.01, previously cited, the files in the National Archives also include a new file, beginning with 1947, designated as 501 BB Palestine, which covers the handling of the Palestine question in the United Nations.

Official United Nations documentation includes: *Official Records of the First Special Session of the General Assembly, Verbatim Record, 28 April–15 May, 1947, Lake Success, N.Y.* (United Nations, 1947), and idem, *Second Session of the General Assembly, Plenary Meetings of the General Assembly, Verbatim Record, 16 September–29 November, 1947: vol. I, 80th to 109th Meetings, 16 September–13 November, 1947, vol. II, 110th to 128th Meetings, 13 November, 1947.* See also *Yearbook of the United Nations, 1947–1948*, II, 257ff, (Lake Success, United Nations, Department of Public Information, 1948).

1. The meeting is covered in *FRUS 1947*, pp. 1058–89; for the Secretary of State's report to the President summarizing the session see pp. 1085–86, and for a similar report to the Secretary from Senator Warren Austin, head of the U.S. delegation to the General Assembly, see pp. 1086–88. Of particular interest is the account given both of this session and of the fall session by Trygve Lie, who was serving at the time as the first Secretary-General of the UN, in chapter 10 of his book *In the Cause of Peace*. See also Donovan, pp. 323–31; Hurewitz, *Struggle*, pp. 284–88; and Riggs, pp. 91ff. Donovan, p. 324, says that Truman's attitude toward the Palestine question at the United Nations was greatly influenced by Gromyko's May 14 speech

to the Assembly, as it convinced the President that the U.S. and the U.S.S.R. had now become rivals for Jewish friendship.

2. Loy Henderson told me during an interview in March 1976 that he recalled being struck at the time by the great interest displayed by the Zionists in the nomination of Guatemala. It seems likely that the Zionists had some understanding with Garcia-Granados, such as they evidently had with Bartley Crum and James G. McDonald at the time of the Anglo-American Committee of Inquiry.

3. *FRUS 1947*, pp. 1101–2.

4. For both telegram and letter (characteristically beginning "Dear Austin") see ibid., p. 1103.

5. For the text see ibid., pp. 1120–23.

6. For the background of the Marshall Plan see Truman, *Memoirs*, II, 112–19, and Cabell Phillips, *The 1940's*, pp. 310–15. See also *FRUS 1947*, p. 914.

7. A series of highly informative reports on the visit of the Special Committee to Palestine, prepared by William J. Porter, at the time Vice Consul at Jerusalem and later Ambassador to Korea, Canada, and Saudi Arabia, will be found in *FRUS 1947*, pp. 1107–44. The official Committee version of the visit is contained in the Committee's *Report to the General Assembly*, published in 1947 by the United Nations, Lake Success, in five volumes, as Supplement No. 11 to the *Official Records of the Second Session of the General Assembly*: vol. I comprises the body of the report; vol. II consists of annexes, an appendix, and maps; vols. III and IV contain the oral evidence presented at public and private meetings, respectively; and vol. V is the index.

Since David Horowitz and Aubrey Eban of the Jewish Agency served in a liaison capacity with the committee, their accounts of the committee's mission are of special interest. Horowitz' book *State in the Making* has been previously cited; a nine-page memorandum by Eban, "Impressions of UNSCOP," is among the Crossman papers at St. Antony's College, Oxford. See also Hurewitz, *Struggle*, pp. 288ff, and Lie, p. 158–63.

A great deal of factual information regarding the Palestine Mandate can be found in two pamphlets furnished to the committee by the government of Palestine, *The Political History of Palestine under British Administration* and a *Supplementary Memorandum by the Government of Palestine, Including Notes on Evidence Given to the United Nations' Special Committee on Palestine up to the 12th July, 1947*. Both of these were published by the Government Printer, Jerusalem, in 1947. In October 1974 Harold Beeley told me that he was the author of the *Political History*.

8. See Lilienthal, p. 53. In a letter dated July 21, 1947, to Gordon P. Merriam of the Near East Division, now in the 1947 Palestine files of the Department at the National Archives, Consul General Robert B. Macatee at Jerusalem, commenting on the visit of the committee and the activities of the various members, refers to reports that Jewish women were being procured for Garcia-Granados. Garcia-Granados wrote his own firsthand but very one-sided account of the mission: *The Birth of Israel: The Drama as I Saw It*.

9. The sorry tale of the *Exodus* is related by Feis, pp. 39–40; Lilienthal, pp. 49–51; Hurewitz, *Struggle*, pp. 288–95; and Silverberg, pp. 331–36. See also *FRUS 1947*, pp. 1138–42.

10. The visit to the deserted village is described in an article by the last British High Commissioner for Palestine, Sir Alan Cunningham, entitled "The Last Days of

the Mandate" in the British periodical *International Affairs*, October 4, 1948, pp. 486–87.

11. For the committee's deliberations at Geneva, see the committee's report, chapter 1, also the accounts of Horowitz and Eban. See also Eban "Tragedy and Triumph," in the Weisgal-Carmichael biography of Weizmann. Horowitz tells how he "spent hours going over maps" with the alternate Swedish member of the committee, Paul Mohn, who was serving as *rapporteur* on this subject.

12. For the gist of the report see *FRUS 1947*, p. 1143, also Hurewitz, *Struggle*, pp. 295–98, for a good summary, with map. The committee's report gives the full text of the recommendations and the majority and minority plans.

13. That Ralph Bunche wrote both the majority and minority plans is stated by many sources, and Bunche himself confirmed it to Fraser Wilkins, my successor on the Palestine desk, according to an interview I had with Wilkins in March 1976. From Ambassador Wilkins I also learned of Bunche's account of the last-minute preparation of the maps.

14. The most detailed and thorough criticism that I have seen of the report is contained in a lengthy memorandum dated September 12, 1947, which Dr. Wendell Cleland of the Department's Division of Research for the Near East submitted to Colonel William A. Eddy, formerly Minister to Saudi Arabia, who was then serving as Special Assistant to the Secretary of State for Research and Intelligence. This memorandum is found in the 1947 Palestine files at the National Archives. Many of the comments offered in my text are based on Cleland's analysis. Eddy forwarded the Cleland memorandum to Secretary Marshall, who initialed the copy now at the Archives, and to Henderson. Eddy's covering memorandum contained additional criticism. Shortly afterward, Eddy resigned from the Department in protest over the increasingly pro-Zionist trend of our Palestine policy. Henderson's memorandum of September 22 (see below) should also be read as a reasoned and persuasive critique of the majority plan.

15. Parkes, p. 299. Parkes, although generally sympathetic to the Zionists, discusses the shortcomings of the majority report at some length and calls it a "curious" scheme. Sykes, who leans more to the Arab side in the dispute, goes so far in his *Crossroads to Israel* as to term it "fantastic" (p. 323). On the other hand, Secretary-General Trygve Lie, who clearly was anxious to enhance the effectiveness of the newly created United Nations in solving problems and could thus be expected to view the report in a favorable light, maintains in his book *In the Cause of Peace* (p. 164) that the partition plan was workable and could have been carried out successfully if events had taken a different course.

16. There are two sources in the files for Abdullah's statement. A letter of November 15 to Gordon Merriam of NE from M. Gordon Knox, a Foreign Service officer attached to our delegation in New York, reported a conversation with Omar Dajany, whom he identified as the "agent" of Trans-Jordan at the United Nations, who said Abdullah was "anxious to add the proposed Arab state to his kingdom, and so, unlike other Arabs, is not really opposed to partition." A similar statement is attributed to Abdullah himself in a dispatch dated November 21 from the American Legation in Damascus. According to this report, the Greek chargé d'affaires in Damascus, who was accredited to Trans-Jordan as well as to Syria, had just seen the King, who had "stated frankly that he planned to send the Arab Legion into Palestine and occupy as much as possible of those parts allocated to the Arabs under the

partition plan." According to Lt. General Sir John Bagot Glubb, for many years commander of the Arab Legion, the thinking in Trans-Jordan at the time was that Palestine should be partitioned, with its Arab areas divided among the neighboring Arab states as follows: Galilee to Lebanon, Samaria and Judea to Trans-Jordan, and Gaza and Beersheba to Egypt. See Glubb, p. 57.

17. Bickerton, "President Truman's Recognition of Israel," Appendix to article, pp. 229–40.

18. Forrestal, *Diaries*, pp. 309–23.

19. For the meeting of the General Assembly delegation at which Henderson spoke in opposition to the partition plan of UNSCOP, see *FRUS 1947*, pp. 1147–51, under the heading "Excerpts from the Minutes of the Sixth meeting of the United States Delegation to the Second Session of the General Assembly, September 15, 1947, 10 a.m." In an interview in March 1976, Ambassador Henderson told me that these "minutes" do not square exactly with his recollection of the meeting. He suggested that his September 22 memorandum on the subject should be consulted for a more accurate statement of his views. Henderson explained to me that at the time he had just returned from a trip to Greece and had been asked by Under Secretary Lovett to go to New York on short notice to brief Secretary Marshall, who was there as head of our Assembly delegation. To his surprise, he was immediately taken by Marshall into the full delegation meeting, and asked to comment on the UNSCOP report. Henderson also paraphrased for me (see text) what he said at the September 15 meeting and what Mrs. Roosevelt said to him, and also gave me a written summary.

20. See the Sachar thesis already cited, p. 85. In a tribute to General Hilldring published in *Near East Report*, a Washington newsletter favorable to Israel, on the occasion of the General's death in January 1974, a former associate of his in the Department, Herbert Fierst, gave a similar explanation for Hilldring's being placed on the delegation.

21. For instances of Hilldring's being in direct touch by telephone with the White House during the Assembly session see *FRUS 1947*, pp. 1179, 1271. The first of these instances involved Niles and the second the President. There were undoubtedly many other instances, since Niles and Hilldring were known to be close.

22. The official UN record of the session has already been cited. Both Horowitz and Hurewitz, *Struggle*, treat the proceedings at some length. The coverage of the Assembly in the 1947 *FRUS* begins on p. 1151, with Secretary Marshall's September 17 statement to the Assembly, and runs through p. 1294.

23. The text given is from the National Archives. The paper also appears in *FRUS 1947*, pp. 1154–58.

24. The British decision to give up the Mandate was made known to Secretary Marshall by the British Ambassador and Creech-Jones the day before the latter made his statement in the Assembly (ibid., p. 1164). Beeley told me in London in 1974 that the Cabinet had not reached a decision in the matter by the time the British delegation sailed for New York, and that he flew over a few days later with a copy of the decision in his pocket.

I have already referred the reader to Elizabeth Monroe's *Britain's Moment in the Middle East* for what I consider to be the best explanation of the reasons for the British withdrawal from Palestine (see pp. 161–70). She considers the last straw to have been a particularly revolting incident which occurred in late July 1947, when the bodies of two British sergeants who had been kidnapped by the Jewish underground in Palestine were found garroted and booby-trapped.

25. For the conversation between Wadsworth and the Arab delegates on October 3 see *FRUS 1947*, pp. 1171–73, and for Henderson's October 6 memorandum to Lovett, ibid., p. 1175.

26. Truman, *Memoirs*, II, 156–58. On October 1, 1947, in a letter to Senator Wagner on the same subject, President Truman commented that he had encountered "no pressure . . . except from the Jews"—which seems to imply that there was no pressure on the part of either the Arabs or the oil companies. Wagner papers, Georgetown University, "File of Presidential Letters."

27. For the Arab reaction to our announcement that we were supporting partition see *FRUS 1947*, pp. 1179–1281, passim, also the 1947 Palestine files at the National Archives. Ibn Saud's October 30 message is on p. 1212 of the *FRUS* volume, and Truman's November 21 reply is on p. 1277.

28. The reasoning behind the Soviet attitude is well expressed by Hurewitz, *Struggle*, p. 306.

29. *FRUS 1947*, pp. 1198–99. The problems encountered by the Near East Division in trying to follow what was going on at the United Nations can be seen in a number of documents in ibid., notably on pp. 1215 and 1229.

30. According to Bickerton (p. 209) it was Eddie Jacobson who was instrumental in getting the President to receive Weizmann in November 1947, as he was in March 1948 (see Chapter 9). The President's phone call to Hilldring is on p. 1271 of the *FRUS* volume. For Weizmann's account see his *Trial and Error*, II, 457–59. The importance of the Negev to the Jews is explained in Eliahu Elath's *Israel and Elath: The Political Struggle for the Inclusion of Elath in the Jewish State* (London: Weidenfeld and Nicolson, 1966, for the Jewish Historical Society of England), passim. Eliahu Epstein, who was serving as representative of the Jewish Agency in Washington at the time of Israel's independence and who later was to have a distinguished career as Israeli ambassador to Washington and to London and as president of the Hebrew University in Jerusalem, adopted the name Elath after independence from this port on the Red Sea, a biblical site mentioned in Deut. 2:8 and in I Kings 9:26. I owe to him many of the insights into Zionist policy that are reflected in this book.

31. *FRUS 1947*, pp. 1281–82.

32. The various stages by which the partition plan moved through the subcommittees of the Ad Hoc Committee to the floor of the Assembly are detailed not only in ibid. but also in Golding, pp. 193–241; Hurewitz, *Struggle*, pp. 301–9; Khouri, pp. 48–58; and Lilienthal, pp. 53–73. See also Horowitz, passim, and the one-sided account in the previously cited book by Garcia-Granados, chaps. 23 and 24.

33. For details regarding pressure on Haiti, Liberia, and the Philippines see Lilienthal, pp. 60–70; Richard Stevens, pp. 176–85; Golding, pp. 227–30; and Kermit Roosevelt, "The Partition of Palestine," *Middle East Journal*, January 1948, pp. 14–15. See also two memoranda in the 1947 Palestine files at the Archives, one by Henry S. Villard (deputy to Henderson) dated November 28 and one by Paul H. Alling (then attached to our delegation) dated November 29.

34. See a memorandum in the Palestine files dated January 18, 1948.

35. Richard Stevens, p. 178, gives examples of the Zionists' cultivation of the Latin Americans. The Zionist offer to make the Cuban ambassador President of Cuba comes from a memorandum prepared by Gordon Merriam under date of November 23, in the Palestine files at the Archives.

36. See the files of the Policy Planning Staff at the National Archives, in Tab A to Policy Planning Staff Memorandum no. 19 of January 19, 1948.

37. Truman, *Memoirs*, II, 158.

38. *FRUS 1947*, p. 1309.

39. Goldmann, p. 245; Horowitz, p. 201.

40. Daniels, p. 317.

41. Jacobson, "Diary," *Washington Post*, May 6, 1973.

42. Sumner Welles, *We Need Not Fail*, p. 63.

43. Feis, p. 43.

44. *FRUS 1947*, pp. 1283–84.

45. Official File 204, Miscellaneous, Truman Library. Both Schechtman (p. 247) and Silverberg (p. 361) pinpoint to Thanksgiving Day the issuance of instructions by Truman to step up efforts by the U.S. to bring about partition.

46. Quoted in Golding, p. 238.

47. Miller, p. 216.

48. See the Forrestal *Diaries*, p. 346; also Donovan, passim.

49. See Golding, p. 235, and Christina Jones, *The Untempered Wind*, p. 70. Mrs. Jones throughout this period lived at the Friends School in Ramallah, just outside Jerusalem.

50. For descriptions of the reaction in New York and in Palestine see Golding, Laqueur, *History*, Lie, Schechtman, Silverberg, and Collins-Lapierre. The Collins-Lapierre book, *O Jerusalem!*, an ambitious work based largely on interviews with individual Jews and Arabs who participated in the events of 1947–48, contains many fascinating details, though it is clearly pro-Zionist in approach; see my review in the *Middle East Journal*, vol. 27, no. 1 (Winter 1973), pp. 91–92. The files of the *Jerusalem Post*, the leading English-language newspaper in Israel, then known as the *Palestine Post*, provided me with many items of information regarding this period.

51. These are in the Truman Library, Official File 204, Miscellaneous Box 773.

52. For the criticism of King Farouk see telegram no. 21 to the Department from Ambassador S. Pinkney Tuck at Cairo dated January 7, 1948, in the 1948 Palestine files at the Archives. Nuri Said's similar criticism of both the President and Mrs. Eleanor Roosevelt was reported by the Embassy at Baghdad in its telegram no. 797 of December 30, 1947, also at the Archives.

53. The text of the partition resolution, no. 181 (II) of November 29, 1947, can be found in the *Official Records* of the General Assembly and in many other places, for example, in a convenient compilation of *United Nations Resolutions on Palestine, 1947–1965*, issued by the Institute of Palestine Studies, Beirut (n.d.).

54. Hurewitz, *Struggle*, p. 302, gives details of the territorial changes in the partition resolution as compared with the UNSCOP report. Since the total area of Palestine is 10,429 sq. mi., the proposed Jewish state of 5,500 sq. mi. would be about 53 percent of the total; for the area see *Palestine, Problem and Promise*, by Robert R. Nathan, Oscar Gass, and Daniel Creamer (Washington, D.C.: Public Affairs Press, 1946), p. 101.

ๆ. THE STATE OF ISRAEL IS BORN

Official sources and archival material: For 1947 events, see the 1947 *Foreign Relations* volume, Departmental files at the National Archives, and United Nations documents, already cited.

The 1948 *FRUS* series for the Near East, South Asia, and Africa, volume V, was issued in two parts, one relating to Palestine and Israel and one relating to other areas. The one with which we are concerned is Part 2, Department of State Publication 8840 (Washington: U.S. Government Printing Office, 1976). It runs to 1,730 pages (plus appendixes), and is subtitled "Israel: Interest of the United States in the Arab-Israel controversy over the future of Palestine; the issue at the United Nations; creation of the state of Israel; entry of Arab forces into Palestine" (hereafter cited as *FRUS 1948*). A feature of this volume, unique among others in the series as far as I am aware, is the inclusion of certain maps. This compilation of documents is a masterly one, as I can testify from my own examination of the documents in the National Archives and elsewhere on which it is based. Particularly useful is a series of "Editorial Notes" which are scattered through the text. My only criticism of this volume would be that, no doubt for good and sufficient reasons, the published papers do not contain as many examples as I should have liked of the series of outstanding reports received during this period from our Consulate General in Jerusalem.

The State Department Palestine files at the National Archives and the papers at the Truman Library bear the reference numbers already cited. For the United Nations, see the *Official Records* of the Security Council and General Assembly for 1948 (and as previously cited for 1947); also *United States Participation in the United Nations* (Report by the President to the Congress for the year 1948), Department of State Publication 3437, International Organizations and Conferences Series, III. 29, released April 1949; also a United Nations publication *The Palestine Question* (n.d.), issued by the UN Department of Public Information, Press and Publication Division.

1. The British decision to withdraw from Palestine by May 15 was actually conveyed by Foreign Secretary Bevin to Secretary Marshall, who was then in London, on November 28, the day *before* the General Assembly passed the partition resolution: see *FRUS 1947*, p. 1289, also pp. 1298 and 1301. For the official announcement by Colonial Secretary Creech-Jones in the House of Commons, see dispatch no. 2929 of December 18 from the Embassy at London, in the 1947 Palestine files at the National Archives.

2. See *FRUS 1947*, p. 1295 (Farouk), p. 1318 (Abdullah), and p. 1292 (attacks on Legations at Damascus and Baghdad); also telegram no. 567 of December 3 from the Consul General at Jerusalem, regarding outbreaks of violence in Palestine.

3. See Begin, *The Revolt*, Chap. 26.

4. Copies of Truman's letters of December 2 to Morgenthau and December 12 to Weizmann are at the Truman Library, the former in Official File 204, Miscellaneous, and the latter among the papers from the Weizmann Archives.

5. Telegram no. 1695 of December 26 to Cairo, in *FRUS 1947*, pp. 1319–21. A similar message to Jidda for King Ibn Saud, dated January 13, 1948, is in the 1948 files at the Archives. Both messages express the hope that the Arabs will acquiesce in the partition decision, and both were personally initialed by the President as well as by the appropriate Departmental officers. Note that the Department used the word "decision" although as explained previously the General Assembly's resolution was merely a recommendation.

6. *FRUS 1947*, pp. 1322–28.

7. Azcárate, *Mission in Palestine*, pp. 4–5. Azcárate, who had formerly served with the League of Nations and as Ambassador of the Spanish Republic to London, was technically Assistant Principal Secretary to the commission under Ralph Bunche but seems to have done the day-to-day work. His firsthand account is indispensable.

Later on, Azcarate became secretary to the Consular Truce Commission in Jerusalem and from 1949 to 1952 he served in a similar capacity with the UN Palestine Conciliation Commission. Chapter 10 of Trygve Lie's *In the Cause of Peace* is a more sympathetic account of the commission. Sir Henry Gurney, the last Chief Secretary of the Government of Palestine, whose diary of the final days of the Mandate, entitled "Palestine Postscript" is now at St. Antony's College, Oxford, says, like Azcarate, that the members were a poor lot. Both Azcarate and Gurney express the opinion that the members would probably have been assassinated if they had set foot in Palestine. The 1948 Palestine files of the Department, now at the National Archives, contain the key messages from our United Nations Mission at New York regarding the commission as well as the texts of its reports to the Security Council. These and many other documents will also be found in *FRUS 1948*.

8. On January 26 Under Secretary of State Robert A. Lovett sent for the British Ambassador and expressed concern regarding the fact that the British were continuing to supply arms to the Arabs whereas we had declared an embargo on arms shipments to both Arabs and Jews. On January 29, the Ambassador returned to explain to Lovett, on instructions from London, that the United Kingdom had treaties with certain of the Arab states under which it was bound to supply arms. The UK, however, was prepared to consider a moratorium on shipments for six months; Lovett told him this was not satisfactory.

Elizabeth Monroe points out that three different Cabinet departments (the Colonial Office, the War Office, and the Foreign Office) were sharing responsibility for Palestine at this time. Her wry comment is that the only thing the British did well was the actual evacuation of troops from Palestine. A quotation she gives from Bevin's March 23 statement in the House of Commons, that "the fundamental point of British policy" was "to get out of Palestine," can be matched by a message of February 9 from our Consulate General at Jerusalem. See Monroe, p. 169.

9. See the 1948 Palestine files, under date of February 6. Hurewitz, *Struggle*, p. 309, gives a full account of the Arab reaction to the partition resolution.

10. This study, entitled "Possible Developments in Palestine" (ORE 7–48), dated February 28, 1948, was previously classified "Secret" but was made available to me by the Agency under the provisions of the Freedom of Information Act. It is an extremely well done analysis of the situation and of the alternatives for U.S. policy. For the text see *FRUS 1948*, pp. 666–75.

11. The 1948 Palestine files contain many reports from Jerusalem and neighboring Foreign Service posts regarding military operations. The figures for dead and wounded are from consular reports. See also Christina Jones.

12. See Meir, pp. 214ff, for the story of this mission to the United States to raise funds and for Ben Gurion's tribute. See also Teddy Kollek's autobiography, pp. 66–89.

13. Pearlman, pp. 138–39.

14. The text of this report and associated correspondence, including the comments of our Mission to the UN, are in the Mission's reports in the 1948 Palestine files. For extracts from the report see *FRUS 1948*, pp. 630–31. The Jewish Agency agreed with the commission that an international force would be needed to implement partition: see Moshe Shertok's letter of February 22 to Acting Secretary of State Lovett, in ibid., pp. 645–48, and also in the Palestine files.

15. Discussion of the advisability of supporting partition first appears on pp. 1283 and 1313 of the 1947 *FRUS*. The 1948 Palestine files contain memoranda by Samuel

K. C. Kopper of the Near East Division (January 27) and Loy Henderson (February 6), recommending a change in policy. I am indebted to Ambassador Henry S. Villard, formerly Deputy to Henderson but by 1948 a member of the State Department's Policy Planning Staff, for the background of the paper which he drafted under date of January 19 and which was forwarded to the Secretary by the Chief of the Policy Planning Staff, George F. Kennan, with the latter's endorsement. For the Kopper, Henderson, Rusk (see below), and Villard papers see *FRUS 1948*, pp. 563–66, 600–603, 587–89, and 545–54. A second Policy Planning Staff paper, along similar lines, is on pp. 619–25.

16. See Manuel, p. 341, for Forrestal's appearance before the Special Subcommittee of the House Armed Services Committee, January 19, 1948.

17. The February 12 National Security Council meeting is reported in the Forrestal *Diaries*, pp. 370–74, and in a memorandum dated February 13 from Robert McClintock of Rusk's staff, in the 1948 Palestine files and in *FRUS 1948*, pp. 627–28.

18. Khouri, p. 60, says that the Pentagon estimated at the time that as many as 160,000 American troops would be required to implement partition.

19. For Austin's statement and the subsequent discussion in the Council see *Official Records of the Security Council*, pp. 264–67, as well as *United States Participation in the United Nations*, p. 39ff; also the UN document *The Palestine Question*, and *FRUS 1948*, pp. 651–54.

20. The meetings of the permanent members of the Security Council are covered in a series of reports by our UN Mission appearing in *FRUS 1948*, pp. 707–36 passim.

21. The Zionist and Arab reactions are covered in many papers in the 1948 Palestine files. The figure of $35 million for the UJA is taken from Golding, p. 281.

22. For the text of Clay's telegram see the Forrestal *Diaries*, p. 387. The message is also mentioned in Feis and in Richard Stevens.

23. Clifford's memoranda of February 17, March 6, and March 8, urging Truman not to abandon partition, are in the Clifford papers at the Truman Library. In a letter dated February 23, 1948, Judge Joseph M. Proskauer, president of the American Jewish Committee, told Lovett that President Truman had just told him that the United States was not about to abandon partition; see the Palestine files.

24. See Truman, *Memoirs*, II, 160–61, also a letter from Jacobson to Dr. Josef Cohn dated March 30, 1952, in the Zionist Archives in New York and in the Truman Library. For Weizmann's account see his *Trial and Error*, II, 472. The editors of the 1948 *Foreign Relations* volume on Palestine state (p. 737) that they have been unable to find an official record of the conversation between the President and Weizmann.

25. For the text see the three UN documents cited above. Extracts are in *FRUS 1948*, pp. 742–44.

26. See the records of the U.S. Senate at the National Archives, Record Group 46. Lie calls Austin's statement a "blow" to the United Nations. In an interview in February 1976 Ambassador Robert McClintock (since deceased) told me that he was one of the principal authors of the trusteeship proposal.

27. See Truman, *Memoirs*, II, 161–63; the quotation given is on p. 163. Margaret Truman Daniel in her life of her father (pp. 387–89) also suggests that trusteeship was a State Department idea to which Truman never agreed.

28. See Chapter 5, n. 6 above. The paper was later published in *American Heritage*, April 1977, along with an interview with Clifford on the subject. In a footnote to this article Mr. Clifford expresses appreciation to Harold P. Luks (a

graduate student at George Washington University) for assistance in preparing the paper, which I understand Luks actually wrote. Incidentally, it contains a number of inaccuracies.

29. Marshall's and Lovett's memoranda, both dated March 22, in the 1948 Palestine files, seem to me sufficient proof that Truman had seen the Austin statement in advance and approved it, although he probably was not aware of the timing. Philip C. Jessup, at that time a member of our UN Mission under Austin, says the same thing on p. 265 of his book *The Birth of Nations*. That the President knew of the proposal in advance was also confirmed to me by Ambassador Henderson and by Mr. Lovett in interviews in March 1976 and May 1976, respectively. The editors of the *Foreign Relations* volume have an "Editorial Note" on pp. 744-46 which bears out this interpretation, as does Donovan on p. 379 of his recent book on Truman.

30. Mrs. Roosevelt's letter to Marshall of March 22 offering to resign from the Human Rights Commission, and Marshall's reply of March 24, are in the 1948 Palestine files. See also Lash, p. 130. This book has much interesting material about Mrs. Roosevelt and the Palestine question.

31. A memorandum of conversation in the Palestine files reports a meeting which Marshall and Lovett held with Shertok and Epstein of the Jewish Agency on March 26, at which the Zionist representatives made clear their opposition to the truce-with-trusteeship plan; see also *FRUS 1948*, pp. 761-64.

32. Weizmann, *Trial and Error*, II, 476, and *FRUS 1948*, pp. 807-9.

33. For Niles's proposal that Hilldring should take over the Department's work on Palestine in place of Henderson see the Sachar thesis, p. 85. This action was also suggested in a letter of March 23 to Clifford from William Batt of the Democratic National Committee, in the Clifford papers at the Truman Library.

34. For the text see *FRUS 1948*, pp. 759-60. A footnote on p. 760 states: "A copy of the President's statement in the Elsey papers contains a marginal notation in the handwriting of Mr. Elsey that the statement was drafted on March 24-25 by Messrs. Clifford, Bohlen, and Rusk, with the advice and counsel of Senator McGrath and Messrs. Ewing and Niles."

35. The truce-with-trusteeship proposal led to the submission of a number of "think pieces" by members of NE. On March 24, Henderson pointed out to the Secretary that our government was assuming a heavy responsibility in making this proposal. On the 28th he pointed out to Lovett that redoubled efforts would undoubtedly be made by the Jews to circumvent the embargo and that our law enforcement agencies should guard against this. Under date of April 22 he recommended that the Palestine situation be "tackled dramatically" in an all-out effort to keep the peace and concentrate on an eventual settlement. Meanwhile, Merriam was warning as of April 14 that we had managed to avoid "plunging into a deep abyss" but there was still heavy going ahead. All these papers, as well as Henderson's conversation with the Saudi minister, are in the 1948 Palestine files: Henderson's two memoranda and the record of his conversation with the Saudi are also in the 1948 *FRUS*, pp. 756-57, 840-42, and 859-60, respectively. Meanwhile, the White House was coming under heavy fire from the Zionists and their supporters with respect to the embargo. The Clifford papers, which contain considerable correspondence on the subject, show that on March 24 the President met with Marshall, Henderson, and others from the Department and Clifford, Niles, and others from the White House to discuss the question of lifting the embargo. It was decided to wait a couple of weeks (in point of fact the embargo was retained).

36. The developments at the United Nations are covered in the UN documents

already identified and in the books by Lie and Azcarate. For the Consular Truce Commission, see *FRUS 1948*, pp. 857–58, 880. Syria, too, had a career consular official stationed in Jerusalem, in addition to Belgium, France, and the United States, but Syria refused to be included.

37. The 1948 Palestine files contain the text of messages sent on March 31 by the Palestine Commission to the Arab Higher Committee and the Jewish Agency stating that because of the lack of cooperation which the commission was encountering, particularly from the Mandatory power, it would not be possible to set up Arab and Jewish provisional councils on April 1 as provided in the partition resolution. The files contain several urgent appeals by the commission to the British government for cooperation.

38. This paper, prepared by Fraser Wilkins of NE, is in *FRUS 1948*, pp. 813–17, also in the Truman papers and the Niles papers.

39. Quoted in Lie, p. 172. McClintock reported to Lovett in a memorandum of April 22 that there was little if any enthusiasm at the United Nations for our truce-with-trusteeship proposal (*FRUS 1948*, pp. 845–46) and Feis says the same in his book, pp. 58–59. See also an essay by George T. Mazuzan, "United States Policy toward Palestine at the United Nations, 1947–1948," in *Prologue*, the journal of the National Archives, vol. VII, no. 3 (Fall 1975), pp. 163–76.

40. For the worsening situation in Palestine, see the daily situation reports sent in by our Consulate General at Jerusalem, in the 1948 Palestine files; also Azcarate, pp. 16–48, Gurney's diary at St. Antony's, Furlonge's life of Musa Alami, pp. 151–55, and Jones, pp. 78–83. See also Jacques de Reynier, *1948 à Jerusalem*. De Reynier was in Jerusalem with the International Red Cross and his firsthand observations are of the greatest interest. Also of particular interest is Dov Joseph's *The Faithful City*. Joseph, a Canadian Jew, was Military Governor of Jerusalem. A typical consular comment is in a telegram dated April 26 saying that the authority of the Mandatory government is "crumbling away."

41. See the accounts of Nils Lund, an executive of Gulf Oil, and Heinrich Kappes, a German Quaker, to be found under date of May 11 and May 14 in the 1948 Palestine files, also the diary of R. M. Graves, the last British chairman of the Jerusalem Municipal Council, published as *Experiment in Anarchy*.

42. I am indebted for many details of the last days of the British regime to four Foreign Service colleagues, Robert B. Houghton, William J. Porter, Stuart W. Rockwell, and Wells Stabler, who were serving in our Consulate General during this period, and to Fraser Wilkins, my successor on the Palestine desk. Collins and Lapierre's *O Jerusalem!* covers most of the events that I describe but the authors' access to a remarkable number of primary sources has to be balanced against the fact that their treatment borders on the sensational.

43. Jewish Agency announcements regarding the setting up of a provisional government upon the British departure are in the consular reports, in two telegrams dated March 26 and April 24. Details regarding the extent of the Jewish community's organization can be found in Horowitz, *State in the Making*, passim, and in Laqueur, *History*, chap. 11. The contrasting Arab attitude of complacency is well brought out in Furlonge's work, p. 93ff.

44. Azcarate, p. 21.

45. See Jones, p. 89, and McDonald, p. 176.

46. See Davis, p. 58, and Erskine Childers, "The Other Exodus," *The Spectator* (London), May 12, 1961. See also Martin Gilbert's atlas, maps 49 and 56.

47. The classic account of Plan Dalet is to be found in an article bearing that title by Walid Khalidi in *Middle East Forum*, the journal of the Alumni Association of the American University in Beirut, for November 1961. Khalidi quotes extensively from Hebrew sources, notably Yigal Allon, later Foreign Minister of Israel, at the time head of the *Palmach*, which was the striking force of the Haganah. See also an essay by the British journalist Erskine Childers, "The Wordless Wish: From Citizens to Refugees," in I. Abu-Lughod, ed., *The Transformation of Palestine* (Evanston, Ill.: Northwestern University Press, 1971). (This essay may also be found as an appendix, pp. 230–67, to *Hearings before the Special Subcommittee on Investigations*, Committee on International Relations, U.S. House of Representatives, September 30–November 12, 1975.) Childers became well known for his article "The Other Exodus" (see n. 46 above) in which he detailed the results of an examination of transcripts of broadcasts in Arabic during this period. He reported that, contrary to frequently voiced allegations from Jewish sources, there was no evidence of any appeals broadcast by Arab leaders to the Arabs of Palestine to flee from their homes. For more on this subject see Hadawi, pp. 102–8; an extract from the official *History of the War of Independence*, prepared by the History Section of the Israeli General Staff (Tel Aviv: Maarakhot, 1968), quoted on p. 39 of the *Journal of Palestine Studies* (Beirut), issue no. 26, vol. VII, no. 2 (Winter 1978): and an article by Musa Goldenberg in the same journal (issue no. 27), vol. VII, no. 3 (Spring 1978), p. 14.

Further background on the exodus of Arab refugees may be found in Hurewitz, *Struggle*, pp. 313ff, and in the pamphlet *A Palestine Entity?* (1970) by Peretz, Wood, and myself (republished in 1977 as *The Palestine State*).

48. The growth of the Arab military preparations is detailed in many reports from our posts in the Arab world, in the 1948 Palestine files.

49. According to Schechtman, p. 293, this was Dean Rusk's idea; but see also *FRUS 1948*, pp. 891–92.

50. The meeting on May 8 between Marshall and Shertok, when Shertok insisted that the Zionists had to go ahead with their plans to set up a state, is in the 1948 Palestine files and is also referred to by Ben Gurion in Pearlman's book, *Ben Gurion Looks Back*, pp. 10–11. As early as April 29 Shertok had written a letter to Marshall stating the Jewish Agency's opposition to any delay in setting up the state.

51. See Goldmann, pp. 246–47, and also an interview with him by Rouleau of *Le Monde* reprinted in the *Manchester Guardian Weekly* for January 9, 1975.

52. For the account of her meeting with Abdullah on May 11 see Meir, pp. 216–20; for their earlier meeting in November 1947, see pp. 214–15. The May 12 meeting in Tel Aviv is described on p. 221.

53. For a detailed discussion of the story of Esther, now generally considered to be apocryphal, see Carey Moore, "Archeology and the Book of Esther," *Biblical Archeologist*, vol. 38, nos. 3 and 4 (September–December 1975).

54. Memorandum dated May 9. Copies of most of the Clifford memoranda are also in the Zionist Archives in New York City. In an interview in December 1975 when I quoted from some of these memoranda, Mr. Clifford readily conceded that it was possible to interpret them as having been motivated primarily by domestic political considerations, but he laid great stress on the President's precarious situation at the time in terms of the 1948 election.

55. In late 1975 and early 1976 I had the opportunity to talk to all of the then living participants in this meeting—Lovett, Clifford, McClintock (before his untimely death in the fall of 1976), and Wilkins. (Truman, Marshall, Niles, and Connelly were

by then dead.) I also discussed the meeting again with Wilkins in 1977. My account is based on what they told me and on McClintock's memorandum, prepared at the time, which appears in the 1948 Palestine files and in *FRUS 1948*, pp. 972–76. The *FRUS* volume also has an "Editorial Note" on the meeting, as well as the text of a proposed statement to be made by the President, which Clifford read aloud at the meeting. The Clifford paper read at the 1976 meeting of historians in Washington, giving his recollections of the meeting in 1948, follows much the same lines as his conversation with me in December 1975. In the 1976 paper Clifford stressed, as he did in talking to me, that Lovett had been instrumental, following the meeting, in persuading General Marshall to come around to a position of agreeing with the President on the matter of recognition, and that Truman would never have agreed to recognition unless the Secretary of State had also agreed. Lovett in talking to me made the point that General Marshall's attitude was based primarily on the conviction that the President, as Chief Executive, was in charge of our foreign policy. Therefore I think it is safe to conclude with Clifford that in the time between the May 12 meeting and the May 14 announcement by Truman that he was recognizing the new Jewish state forthwith, General Marshall did indeed come round to support recognition, and that Lovett played an important role in this process.

56. This account is based mainly on consular reports in the Palestine files, and on Azcarate, Gurney, Jones, and Collins-Lapierre. See also the books by Zeev Sharef, who was secretary to the Provisional Government of Israel at the time, and Bernard Postal and Henry W. Levy. A telegram from the Embassy at London dated May 6 explained that the British had determined that the Mandate would end one minute after midnight, May 14/15, but were anxious for security reasons not to have this known. The authorities in Palestine told Consul General Wasson the same thing; see *FRUS 1948*, pp. 945–46.

57. For a description of the divided Jerusalem of the years 1948–67 see my book *Jerusalem, Key to Peace.*

58. See Meir, esp. pp. 223–25; also Collins-Lapierre, pp. 354ff, and Laqueur, *History of Zionism*, chap. 11. The text of the proclamation (Appendix L) may be found in Moore's documents and in Gervasi's *The Case for Israel*, where it appears as Appendix 10, pp. 204–8.

59. This is pointed out by Goichon, I, 247.

60. The following paragraphs are based largely on my interviews with several of those involved: Epstein (now Elath) in September 1974, Clifford (December 1975), Henderson (March 1976), and Lovett (May 1976). A lengthy memorandum by Lovett, dated May 17, in which he details these events is in the 1948 Palestine files and in *FRUS 1948*, pp. 1005–7. Elath particularly emphasized Clifford's role in the decision to recognize Israel immediately.

61. See Epstein's telegram of May 14 to Jerusalem explaining that he took the responsibility for writing the letter requesting recognition; Weizmann Archive papers, Truman Library.

62. See a notation in the Palestine files showing that the Department's circular telegram warning our posts in the Middle East that we were about to extend recognition arrived too late to be of any use. *FRUS 1948*, pp. 990–91.

63. Ibid., p. 992. In a memorandum dated May 16 (ibid., pp. 1001–2) Henderson cautioned Lovett that the Secretary's letter dated May 14 (which was actually handed to Epstein on May 17) should be drafted most carefully, as we were not certain as to the extent of Epstein's authority to speak for the new government and should avoid

the implication that we were recognizing a particular set of borders for the state. By intent, the letter was addressed to Epstein at his street address only. President Truman does not appear to have sent a written reply. Several accounts of these events, e.g. Eban, "Tragedy and Triumph," p. 311, quote Truman (referring to Weizmann) as declaring after recognition was announced, "The old Doctor will believe me now."

64. My account is based mainly on Jessup's version in his *The Birth of Nations*, chap. 7. Jessup says that our mission urged the Department to provide it with instructions as to how it was to proceed if the U.S. should recognize the new government, as was being widely predicted, but no instructions were received. For the text of the telegram, dated May 4, see *FRUS 1948*, p. 897. The pertinent UN documents will be found in the UN sources previously cited.

65. For the first choice of Van Zeeland for Mediator see Lie, p. 185. Azcarate comments (p. 93) that the resolution of May 14 setting up the position of Mediator (originally called Commissioner—final text on pp. 994–95, *FRUS*) made hardly any mention of his role with respect to truce negotiations, which was to become so vital a part of his functions. This was in fact the origin of the UN truce-keeping function carried over to this day in UNTSO (The United Nations Truce Supervision Organization), which after the 1949 Armistice agreements was given the task of supervising the armistices and maintaining the truce and which is still in existence. Dean Rusk, at the time Director of the Office of United Nations Affairs, wrote a letter on June 13, 1974, to the Director of the Historical Office of the Department giving his recollection of the events of May 14, 1948 (*FRUS 1948*, p. 993), which confirms essentially the account given here.

66. See Garcia-Granados, chap. 26.

67. The Soviet Union's recognition had far-flung consequences. A telegram dated May 23 from our Embassy at Karachi reported a raid by tribesmen from the Northwest Frontier Province who crossed Afghanistan into Soviet territory in protest against the Soviet action. The Arab reaction to Truman's recognition is reported in many messages from our posts in the Arab world. For example, our Minister in Jidda reported on May 15 that the Saudi Arabian government was "profoundly shocked" and might break relations with the United States (this did not occur).

68. Marshall's exchange with Mrs. Roosevelt, and his account of his talks with the President about the events of May 14, are in the 1948 Palestine files. This exchange is also quoted in *FRUS 1948*, p. 1015.

69. Two studies of the 1948 Palestine War are Edgar O'Ballance, *The Arab-Israel War, 1948*, and Dan Kurzman, *Genesis, 1948: The First Israeli-Arab War*. Hurewitz and Khouri also cover the hostilities admirably. See Furlonge, pp. 148–63, for the Arab debacle.

70. The Clifford papers contain much correspondence regarding the 1948 election and the importance of gaining the support of American Jews. More on this will be said in the Epilogue.

71. See Donovan, p. 25. In this evaluation of Truman I have drawn on many sources, including the Donovan, Forrestal, Goldmann, Jessup, and Snetsinger books as well as conversations as noted here and there.

EPILOGUE

1. Stork and Rose, p. 50.
2. H. St. John Philby, *Arabian Jubilee*, pp. 218–19.

3. Golding, pp. 26, 85, 264.

4. See the previously cited article by Samuel Halperin and Irwin Oder, "The United States in Search of a Policy," *Review of Politics*, July 1962.

5. Doreen Bierbrier, "The American Zionist Emergency Council," *American Jewish Historical Quarterly*, vol. 59, no. 1 (September 1970), p. 100.

6. See, for example, Feingold, *The Politics of Rescue*, and Schechtman. On this general subject see also Robert H. Trice, Jr., "Domestic Political Interests and American Policy in the Middle East," unpublished Ph.D. dissertation, University of Wisconsin, 1974.

7. For details on the voting record of American Jews see Isaacs, *Jews and American Politics*.

8. Jimmy Breslin, *How the Good Guys Finally Won* (New York: Viking Press, 1975), p. 33. The reference is of course to Hobbes's *Leviathan*.

9. *FRUS 1945*, p. 722.

10. See, for example, an interview with Elie Eliachar, chief of the Sephardic Jewish Community in Jerusalem and former deputy mayor, a sixteenth-generation Jerusalemite, in the *Jerusalem Post* for September 12, 1975; also an article by Nahum Goldmann, "The Psychology of Middle East Peace," *Foreign Affairs*, October 1975.

11. "Tragedy and Triumph," in the biography of Weizmann edited by Weisgal and Carmichael, p. 280.

12. For example, Richard Crossman, in his *Palestine Mission* (1947) predicts this on p. 204. I would have made the same comment at the time. In his *A Nation Reborn* (1960) Crossman says (chap. 3) that this assumption has been "falsified" by subsequent developments, mainly the Arab exodus.

13. The only person who predicted the Arab exodus, so far as I have been able to ascertain, was Camille Chamoun, later President of Lebanon; see Airgram A-200 from the Legation at Beirut dated May 11, 1948, in the 1948 Palestine files of the Department at the National Archives. Chamoun, a member of the Lebanese cabinet at the time, made the prediction in a press interview just after returning from the United Nations.

Bibliography

The literature on the Palestine problem is so voluminous that it is obviously impossible to prepare an all-inclusive bibliography. I have attempted here merely to list those sources that I have found to be of the greatest use in preparing the present study. Most of them are mentioned in the Notes and are commented on there. I have annotated others where appropriate in the alphabetical list that follows.

The Notes contain specific citations to official sources such as the *Foreign Relations of the United States* (the published U.S. diplomatic correspondence of the United States Government) for the years covered in this study (1942–48); the State Department's Palestine files at the National Archives, Washington, D.C.; the British Foreign Office archives at the Public Record Office, London; the Zionist Archives in New York City and Jerusalem; the files at the Franklin D. Roosevelt Library, Hyde Park, New York, and the Harry S. Truman Library, Independence, Missouri; and the relevant United Nations documents.

Among official reports the reader is especially recommended to the Peel Report, *Palestine, Royal Commission Report* (London: H.M. Stationery Office, 1937, Cmd. 5479), and the *Report of the Anglo-American Committee of Inquiry*, 1946, issued in this country as State Department Publication 2536, Near East Series 2, U.S. Government Printing Office, and in England as Cmd. 6808, H.M. Stationery Office. These are both masterly treatments of the basic issues. Three publications of the Government of Palestine which are indispensable are *A Survey of Palestine*, prepared for the Anglo-American Committee of Inquiry (Jerusalem: The Government Printer, 1946), and *The Political History of Palestine under British Administration*, prepared for the United Nations Special Committee on Palestine (Jerusalem: The Government Printer, 1947), and a *Supplementary Memorandum* to the latter.

Documents relating to various aspects of the Palestine question appear in a number of the works cited in the Bibliography, but I should call special attention to the following: J. C. Hurewitz, *Diplomacy in the Near and Middle East* (reissued as *The Middle East and North Africa in World Politics: A Documentary Record*); Walter Z. Laqueur, *The Israel-Arab Reader*; Ralph H. Magnus, ed., *Documents on the Middle East*; and John Norton Moore, ed., *The Arab-Israel Conflict*.

Acheson, Dean. *Present at the Creation: My Years in the State Department.* New York: W. W. Norton, 1969.

Antonius, George. *The Arab Awakening.* London: Hamish Hamilton, 1938. A definitive treatment of the Arab national movement.

Arakie, Margaret. *The Broken Sword of Justice: America, Israel, and the Palestine Tragedy.* London: Quartet Books, 1973.

Azcarate, Pablo de. *Mission in Palestine, 1948–1952.* Washington, D.C.: Middle East Institute, 1966.

Badeau, John S. *The American Approach to the Arab World.* New York: Harper & Row, 1968. Published for the Council on Foreign Relations.

Baram, Philip. *The Department of State in the Middle East, 1919–1945.* Philadelphia: University of Pennsylvania Press, 1978.

Barbour, Neville. *Palestine, Star or Crescent?* New York: Odyssey Press, 1947. (Published in England as *Nisi Dominus*; reprinted 1968, under that title, by the Institute of Palestine Studies, Beirut.)

Begin, Menachem. *The Revolt: The Story of the Irgun.* New York: Henry Schuman, Inc., 1951. Republished in abridged form by Nash, New York, in 1977.

Bell, J. Bowyer. *Terror Out of Zion.* New York: St. Martin's Press, 1977. Gives an account of "Plan Dalet."

Ben Gurion, David. "Memoirs," *Jewish Observer and Middle East Review* (London), 1963–65, in 40 installments. Extracts published in book form by the World Publishing Co., Cleveland, 1970.

Ben Gurion Looks Back. See under Pearlman, Moshe.

Bentwich, Norman, and Bentwich, Helen. *Mandate Memories.* London: Hogarth Press, 1965.
Norman Bentwich, a British Jew, was appointed Attorney General of Palestine in 1920.

Bickerton, Ian. "President Truman's Recognition of Israel," *American Jewish Quarterly,* December 1968.

Bishop, Jim. *FDR's Last Year, April 1944–April 1945.* New York: Morrow, 1974.

Blum, John Morton. *Roosevelt and Morgenthau.* Boston: Houghton Mifflin, 1970. Based on the Morgenthau diaries.

Bohlen, Charles E. *Witness to History.* New York: W. W. Norton, 1973.

Burns, James McGregor. *Roosevelt: The Soldier of Freedom, 1940–1945.* New York: Harcourt Brace Jovanovich, Inc., 1970.

Bryson, Thomas A. *American Diplomatic Relations with the Middle East.* Metuchen, N.J.: Scarecrow Press, 1977.

Byrnes, James F. *Speaking Frankly.* New York: Harper & Bros., 1947.

Caldwell, Jean M. "Zionist Pressure Groups and the Palestine Policy of the Truman Administration." Unpublished Master's thesis, University of Kansas, 1961.

Cohen, Naomi W. *American Jews and the Zionist Idea.* New York: KTAV Publishing House, 1975.

Collins, Larry, and Lapierre, Dominique. *O Jerusalem!* New York: Simon and Schuster, 1974.

Crossman, Richard H. S. *A Nation Reborn: The Israel of Weizmann, Bevin, and Ben Gurion.* London: Hamish Hamilton, 1960.
Three lectures given at the Weizmann Institute, Rehovoth, Israel, 1959.

——. *Palestine Mission: A Personal Record.* New York: Harper & Bros., 1947.

Crum, Bartley C. *Behind the Silken Curtain.* New York: Simon and Schuster, 1947.

Daniel, Margaret Truman. *Harry S. Truman.* New York: Morrow, 1973.

Daniels, Jonathan. *The Man of Independence.* Philadelphia and New York: J. B. Lippincott Co., 1950.

Davis, John H. *The Evasive Peace.* London: John Murray, 1968. Reissued 1976 with a new preface and postscript by the author and a foreword by Eugene Black, by Dillon-Leiderbach, Lakewood, Ohio.

DeNovo, John A. *American Interests and Policies in the Middle East.* Minneapolis: University of Minnesota Press, 1963.

Dohse, Michael. "American Periodicals and the Palestine Triangle, April, 1936, to February, 1947." Unpublished Ph.D. dissertation, Mississippi State University, 1966. Available through University Microfilms, Ann Arbor, Michigan.

Donovan, Robert J. *Conflict and Crisis: The Presidency of Harry S. Truman, 1945–1948.* New York: W. W. Norton, 1977.

Drinan, Robert F. *Honor the Promise.* Garden City, N.Y.: Doubleday, 1977.

Dugdale, Blanche. *See* Rose, N. A., ed.

Eban, Abba. *An Autobiography.* New York: Random House, 1977.

——. *My People: The Story of the Jews.* New York: Behrman House and Random House, 1968.

Eddy, William A. *F.D.R. Meets Ibn Saud.* New York: American Friends of the Middle East, 1954.

Feingold, Henry L. *The Politics of Rescue; The Roosevelt Administration and the Holocaust, 1938–1945.* New Brunswick, N.J.: Rutgers University Press, 1970. (Also a Ph.D. dissertation with the same title, submitted at New York University in 1966.)

——. "The Roosevelt Administration and the Efforts to Save the Jews of Hungary," in *Hungarian Jewish Studies,* ed. Randolph L. Braham (New York: World Federation of Hungarian Jews, 1969).

Feis, Herbert. *The Birth of Israel: The Tousled Diplomatic Bed.* New York: W. W. Norton, 1969.

Fink, Reuben, ed. *America and Palestine.* New York: American Zionist Emergency Council, 1944.
A collection of documents, statements, and resolutions in favor of the Zionist position.

Fisher, Sidney M. *The Middle East, a History.* New York: Alfred A. Knopf, 1969.

Forrestal, James G. *Diaries.* Edited by Walter Millis. New York: Viking Press, 1951.

Frischwasser-Ra'anan, H. F. *Frontier of a Nation.* London: Batchworth, 1955.

Furlonge, Sir Geoffrey. *Palestine Is My Country: The Story of Musa Alami.* New York: Praeger, 1969.

Garcia-Granados, Jorge. *The Birth of Israel: The Drama as I Saw It.* New York: Alfred A. Knopf, 1948.
A completely pro-Zionist work.

Gervasi, Frank. *The Case for Israel.* New York: Viking Press, 1967.

Gilbert, Martin. *The Arab-Israel Conflict—Its History in Maps.* London: Weidenfeld and Nicolson, 1974.

Glubb, Sir John Bagot. *A Soldier with the Arabs.* New York: Harper & Bros., 1957.

Goichon, A.-M. *Jordanie Réele.* 2 vols. Paris: G. P. Maisonneuve et Larose, 1967, 1972.

Golding, David. "United States Foreign Policy in Palestine and Israel." Unpublished Ph.D. dissertation, New York University, 1961. Available through University Microfilms, Ann Arbor, Michigan.

Goldmann, Nahum. *Autobiography*. New York: Holt, Rinehart and Winston, 1969.

Goulden, Joseph C. *The Best Years, 1945–1950*. New York: Atheneum, 1976.

Graves, R. M. *Experiment in Anarchy*. London: Gollancz, 1949.

Hadawi, Sami. *Bitter Harvest*. New York: New World Press, 1967.

Halperin, Samuel. *The Political World of American Zionism*. Detroit: Wayne State University Press, 1961.

Halpern, Ben. *The Idea of the Jewish State*. Cambridge: Harvard University Press, 1961. Reprinted 1969.

Harriman, W. Averell. *Special Envoy to Churchill and Stalin, 1941–1946*. Written with Elie Abel. New York: Random House, 1975.

Hertzberg, Arthur, ed. *The Zionist Idea*. Garden City, N.Y.: Doubleday, 1959. Contains contributions by twenty Zionist writers and a 100-page essay by the editor.

Herzl, Theodor. *The Jewish State*. Translated from the German; first published 1896. New York: American Zionist Emergency Council, 1946.

Hirschmann, Ira. C. *Caution to the Winds*. New York: David McKay, 1962.

——. *Lifeline to a Promised Land*. New York: Vanguard Press, 1946.

Hirst, David. *The Gun and the Olive Branch: The Roots of Violence in the Middle East*. London: Faber & Faber, 1977.

Horowitz, David. *State in the Making*. Translated from the Hebrew. New York: Alfred A. Knopf, 1953.

Howard, Harry N. *The King-Crane Commission*. Beirut: Khayats, 1963.

Hull, Cordell. *Memoirs*. With the assistance of Andrew Berding. 2 vols. New York: Macmillan, 1948.

Hurewitz, J. C. *Diplomacy in the Near and Middle East: A Documentary Record*. 2 vols. Princeton, N.J.: Van Nostrand, 1956.

——. *The Middle East and North Africa in World Politics: A Documentary Record*. 2 vols. New Haven and London: Yale University Press, 1975, 1979. [This is a revised edition of the 1956 volumes.]

——. *The Struggle for Palestine*. New York: W. W. Norton, 1950. Paperback ed., Schocken Books, 1976, with a new introduction by the author.

Ilan, Amitzur. "The Origins and Development of American Intervention in British Palestine Policy." Unpublished Ph.D. dissertation, Oxford University, 1974.

Ingram, Doreen. *Palestine Papers, 1917–1922*. New York: George Braziller, Inc., 1973.

Isaacs, Stephen J. *Jews and American Politics*. Garden City, N.Y.: Doubleday, 1974.

Israel, F. L., ed. *The War Diary of Breckinridge Long; Selections from the Years 1939–1944*. Lincoln: University of Nebraska Press, 1966.

Jansen, Mrs. Michael E. *The United States and the Palestinian People*. Beirut: Institute for Palestine Studies, 1970.

Jeffries, J. M. N. *Palestine, the Reality*. London: Longmans Green & Co., 1939.

Jessup, Philip C. *The Birth of Nations*. New York: Columbia University Press, 1974.

Jones, Christina. *The Untempered Wind: Forty Years in Palestine*. London: Longmans Green & Co., 1975.

Joseph, Dov. *The Faithful City*. New York: Simon and Schuster, 1960.

Khadduri, Majdia D. *The Arab-Israel Impasse*. Washington, D.C.: Robert B. Luce, Inc., 1968.

Khalidi, Walid. *From Haven to Conquest.* Beirut: Institute for Palestine Studies, 1971.

Khouri, Fred J. *The Arab-Israel Dilemma.* Syracuse: The University Press, 1968. Reissued in paperback, 1976.
Contains numerous appendixes and an impressive bibliography.

Koestler, Arthur. *The Thirteenth Tribe.* New York: Random House, 1976.
An account of the Khazar tribe from the Russian steppes who embraced Judaism in the Middle Ages.

Kollek, Teddy. *For Jerusalem: A Life.* With his son, Amos Kollek. New York: Random House, 1978.
The biography of the colorful mayor of Jerusalem, which *inter alia* gives details of his procuring of arms for the fledgling state of Israel in 1948.

Kurzman, Dan. *Genesis 1948: The First Israeli-Arab War.* Cleveland: World Publishing Co., 1970.

Laqueur, Walter Z. *A History of Zionism.* New York: Holt, Rinehart and Winston, 1972.

——. *The Israel-Arab Reader.* New York: Citadel Press, 1968.

Lash, Joseph P. *Eleanor: The Years Alone.* New York: W. W. Norton, 1972.

Lawrence, T. E. *Seven Pillars of Wisdom.* London: Jonathan Cape, 1926.

Leahy, William D. *I Was There.* New York: Whittlesey House, 1950.

Lie, Trygve. *In the Cause of Peace.* New York: Macmillan, 1954.

Lilienthal, Alfred. *What Price Israel?* Chicago: Henry Regnery Company, 1953.

——. *The Zionist Connection.* New York: Dodd, Mead & Co., 1978.

Lord, John. *Duty, Honor, Empire: The Life and Times of Col. Richard Meinertzhagen.* New York: Random House, 1970.
Meinertzhagen (not a Jew) was one of the early British Zionist sympathizers and a confidant of Weizmann.

McDonald, James G. *My Mission in Israel.* New York: Simon and Schuster, 1951.

McLellan, David S. *Dean Acheson, the State Department Years.* New York: Dodd, Mead & Co., 1976.

Magnetti, Donald, with Sigler, Mary Ann. *An Introduction to the Middle East.* Huntington, Ind.: Our Sunday Visitor, Inc., 1973.

Magnus, Ralph H., ed. *Documents on the Middle East.* Washington, D.C.: American Enterprise Institute, 1969.

Manuel, Frank. *The Realities of American Palestine Relations.* Washington, D.C.: Public Affairs Press, 1949.

Marlowe, John [pseud.]. *The Seat of Pilate.* London: Cresset Press, 1959.

Meir, Golda. *My Life.* New York: G. P. Putnam's Sons, 1975.

Miller, Merle. *Plain Speaking: An Oral Biography of Harry S. Truman.* New York: Barkley-Putnam, 1973.

Monroe, Elizabeth. *Britain's Moment in the Middle East, 1914-1956.* London: Chatto & Windus, 1963.

Moore, John Norton, ed. *The Arab-Israel Conflict.* 3 vols. Princeton: Princeton University Press, 1974.

O' Ballance, Edgar. *The Arab-Israel War, 1948.* New York: Praeger, 1957.

Parkes, James. *Whose Land? A History of the Peoples of Palestine.* New York: Taplinger Pub. Co., Inc., 1971. (Revised ed. of a 1949 work.)

Pearlman, Moshe. *Ben Gurion Looks Back in Talks with Moshe Pearlman.* New York: Simon and Schuster, 1965.

Peretz, Don C.; Ward, Richard J.; and Wilson, Evan M. *A Palestine Entity?* Washington, D.C.: Middle East Institute, 1970. Reissued as *The Palestine State*, 1977, Kennikat Press, Port Washington, N.Y.

Phillips, Cabell. *The 1940's, Decade of Triumph and Trouble.* New York: Macmillan, 1975.

———. *The Truman Presidency: The History of a Triumphant Succession.* New York: Macmillan, 1966.

Phillips, William. *Ventures in Diplomacy.* Boston: Beacon Press, 1952.

Polk, William R. *The United States and the Arab World.* Cambridge: Harvard University Press, 1965.

Polk, William R.; Stamler, David M.; and Asfour, Edmund. *Backdrop to Tragedy.* Boston: Beacon Press, 1957.

Postal, Bernard, and Levy, Henry W. *And the Hills Shouted for Joy, the Day Israel Was Born.* New York: David McKay, 1973.

Pounds, Norman J., with Maps by Robert J. Kingsbury. *An Atlas of Middle Eastern Affairs.* New York: Praeger, 1963.

Rand McNally's Historical Atlas of the Holy Land. Edited by Emil J. Kaeling. New York: Rand McNally, 1959.

Reynier, Jacques de. *1948 à Jerusalem.* Neuchâtel: Éditions de la Baconniere, 1969.

Riggs, Robert E. "The Policy of the U.S. with Respect to Political Questions in the General Assembly of the United Nations." Unpublished Ph.D. dissertation, University of Illinois, 1955. Available through University Microfilms, Ann Arbor, Michigan.

Robinson, Donald. *Under Fire—Israel's 20-Year Struggle for Survival.* New York: W. W. Norton, 1968.

Roosevelt, Kermit. "The Partition of Palestine," *Middle East Journal*, January 1948.

Rose, N. A., ed. *Baffy: The Diaries of Blanche Dugdale, 1936–1947.* London: Valentine, Mitchell, 1973.
    Blanche Dugdale was Balfour's niece.

Sachar, David B. "David K. Niles and United States Policy toward Palestine: A Case Study in American Foreign Policy." Unpublished undergraduate honors thesis, Harvard University, 1959.

Sachar, Howard M. *Europe Leaves the Middle East, 1936–1954.* New York: Alfred A. Knopf, 1972.

Safran, Nadav. *The United States and Israel.* Cambridge: Harvard University Press, 1963. Reissued in greatly expanded form as *Israel, The Embattled Ally*, 1978.

Schechtman, Joseph B. *The United States and the Jewish State Movement: The Crucial Decade, 1939–1949.* New York: Herzl Press, 1966.

Sharef, Zeev. *Three Days: An Account of the Last Days of the British Mandate and the Birth of Israel.* Translated from the Hebrew. London: W. H. Allen, 1962.

Sherwood, Robert E., ed. *Roosevelt and Hopkins.* New York: Harper & Bros., 1949.

Silverberg, Robert. *If I Forget Thee, O Jerusalem: American Jews and the State of Israel.* New York: Morrow, 1970.

Snetsinger, John. *Truman, the Jewish Vote, and Israel.* Stanford: Hoover Institution Press, 1974.

Stein, Leonard. *The Balfour Declaration.* New York: Simon and Schuster, 1961.

Stettinius, Edward R., Jr. *Roosevelt and the Russians: The Yalta Conference.* Garden City, N.Y.: Doubleday, 1949.

Stevens, Georgiana G., ed. *The United States and the Middle East.* Englewood Cliffs, N.J.: Prentice Hall, 1964.

Stevens, Richard. *American Zionism and U.S. Foreign Policy, 1942–1947.* New York: Pageant Press, 1962. Reprinted by the Institute for Palestine Studies, Beirut, 1970.

Stork, Joe, and Rose, Sharon. "Zionism and American Jewry," *Journal of Palestine Studies* (Beirut), vol. III, no. 3 (Spring 1974).

Storrs, Sir Ronald. *Memoirs.* New York: G. P. Putnam's Sons, 1937. (Published in England under the title *Orientations.*)
Storrs was the first Military Governor of Jerusalem.

Sutton, Phyllis M. *And This Is How It Was.* Beirut: n.p., n.d.

Sykes, Christopher. *Crossroads to Israel.* London: Collins, 1965.

——. *Two Studies in Virtue.* London: Collins, 1953.
The essay "The Prosperity of His Servant" is a study of the Balfour Declaration.

Taylor, Alan R. *Prelude to Israel: An Analysis of Zionist Diplomacy, 1897–1947.* New York: Philosophical Library, 1959.

——. *The Zionist Mind.* Beirut: Institute for Palestine Studies, 1974.

Taylor, Alan R., and Tetlie, Richard J. *Palestine, A Search for Truth.* Washington, D.C.: Public Affairs Press, 1970.

Truman, Harry S. *Memoirs.* vol. I, *Year of Decisions*; vol. II, *Years of Trial and Hope.* Garden City, N.Y.: Doubleday, 1955, 1956.

Tuchman, Barbara. *Bible and Sword.* New York: New York University Press, 1956. This covers the British Palestine connection up to the establishment of the Mandate.

Vester, Bertha Spafford. *Our Jerusalem.* Garden City, N.Y.: Doubleday, 1955. Mrs. Vester was for years the guiding spirit of the American Colony, a part eleemosynary, part commercial venture in the Holy City.

Weil, Martin. *A Pretty Good Club: The Founding Fathers of the U.S. Foreign Service.* New York: W. W. Norton, 1978.

Weisgal, Meyer W., and Carmichael, Joel, eds. *Chaim Weizmann: A Biography by Several Hands.* New York: Atheneum, 1963. With a preface by David Ben Gurion.
Among the contributors are Weisgal, Isaiah Berlin, Israel Sieff, Ritchie Calder, Louis Lipsky, Abba Eban, Jon Kimche, and Richard H. S. Crossman.

Weizmann, Chaim. *Trial and Error.* 2 vols. Philadelphia: Jewish Publication Society, 1949.

Weizmann, Vera. *The Impossible Takes Longer—the Memoirs of Vera Weizmann as Told to David Tutaev.* New York: Harper & Row, 1967.

Wilson, Evan M. "The American Interest in the Palestine Question and the Establishment of Israel," *American Academy of Political and Social Science Annals* (Philadelphia), May 1972, pp. 64–73.

——. *Jerusalem, Key to Peace.* Washington, D.C.: Middle East Institute, 1970.

——. "The Palestine Papers, 1943–1947," *Journal of Palestine Studies,* (Beirut), vol. II, no. 4 (Summer 1973), pp. 33–54.

An analysis of the correspondence relating to Palestine in the *FRUS* volumes for the years indicated.

Wise, Stephen S. *Challenging Years.* New York: G. P. Putnam's Sons, 1949.

Yale, William. *The Near East.* Ann Arbor: University of Michigan Press, 1958.

Zeine, Zeine N. *Anglo-Turkish Relations and the Emergence of Arab Nationalism.* Beirut: Khayats, 1958.

Index

Abd al-Aziz Ibn Saud, King of Saudi
Arabia, *see* Ibn Saud
Abd al-Hadi, Awni, 75–76
Abdul Ilah, Emir, 51f
Abdullah, Emir of Trans-Jordan (later
King of Jordan), 14, 42, 51, 65, 115,
130, 141
Acheson, Dean G., 1f, 98, 106, 199,
207f; described, 3; as Under
Secretary, 59, 63–66 passim, 69, 91,
100ff
Ad Hoc Committee, *see under* United
Nations
Adler, Frank J., 199
Akzin, Benjamin, 152
Allen, George V., 4
Alling, Paul H., 4, 8, 41
American Council for Judaism, 27, 41,
90, 94, 115
American Emergency Committee for
Zionist Affairs, 24, 31. *See also*
American Zionist Emergency
Council
American Jewish Committee, 17, 30f,
60, 115
American Jewish community: prewar
attitudes of, 16–18, 27; Biltmore
Conference, 24–25; political apathy
of, 29; supports Jewish state, 67;
sends arms to Palestine, 134. *See also*
Zionists
American Jewish Conference, 30–31, 60
American Jewish Congress, 17, 26
American Palestine Committee, 45
American University of Beirut (AUB),
18

American Zionist Emergency Council
(AZEC), 31f, 35, 40, 44, 64
Amery, Leopold S., 72
Anglo-American Committee of
Inquiry: proposed by Attlee, 64, 200;
preparations for, 68–69; in
Washington, 69–72; members, 70–71,
202; London hearings, 72–73; Cairo
hearings, 73–74; Jerusalem hearings,
74–76; in Lausanne, 77–78, 203–4;
Wilson memorandum for, 79–87;
report of, 87–88, 204; reactions to
report, 89–91; Cabinet Committee to
implement, 92–95
Anglo-American talks (London, April
1944), 46–47
Anti-Zionists, *see* American Council for
Judaism
Arab Higher Committee, 14, 90, 107,
116, 132, 137; boycotts UNSCOP
hearings, 110
Arab League, 90, 130, 132
Arab Legion, 141
Arab state, proposed, 72, 107, 111
Arab states: prewar status of, 14–15;
reactions of, to Zionist agitation in
U.S., 32–33, 42, 51f; reactions to
Congressional hearings (1944), 41–
42; to U.S. campaign endorsements,
45; letters to Roosevelt (1945), 51–52;
protest Truman's post-Potsdam
remarks, 61–62; reactions to
proposed U.S.-British inquiry, 64;
testify at Washington and London
hearings of joint committee, 72–73;
reactions to committee report, 90–91;